From Childhood to Chivalry

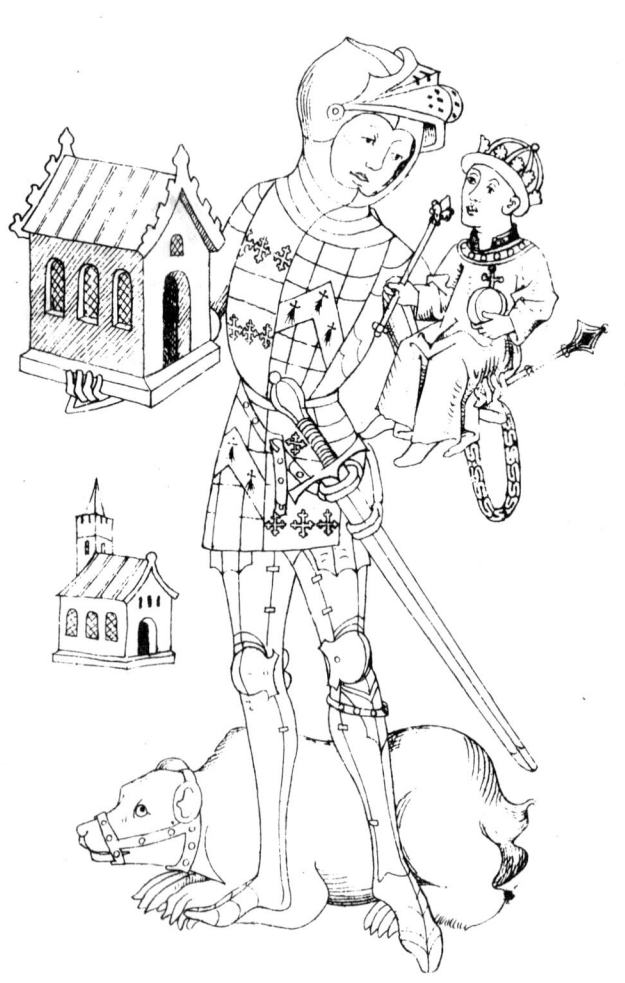

From Childhood to Chivalry

*The education of the English kings
and aristocracy 1066–1530*

Nicholas Orme

METHUEN   LONDON & NEW YORK

For Rona
Ps. cxi, v.7

First published in 1984 by
Methuen & Co. Ltd
11 New Fetter Lane, London EC4P 4EE

Published in the USA by
Methuen & Co.
in association with Methuen, Inc.
733 Third Avenue, New York, NY 10017

© *1984 Nicholas Orme*

Typeset by Servis Filmsetting Ltd, Manchester
Printed in Great Britain at the
University Press, Cambridge

British Library Cataloguing in Publication Data

Orme, Nicholas
From childhood to chivalry.
1. Upper classes—Education—England—History
I. Title
371.96'2'0942   LC4945.G7

ISBN 0-416-74830-9

Library of Congress Cataloging in Publication Data

Orme, Nicholas.
From childhood to chivalry.
Bibliography: p.
Includes index.
1. Education of princes—England—History.
2. Education of princesses—England—History.
3. Upper classes—Education—England—History.
4. Education, Medieval.
5. Great Britain—History—1066–1687. I. Title.
LC4945.G7076 1984   371.96'2'0942   84-6668

ISBN 0-416-74830-9

Contents

Illustrations

(between pages 68 and 69)

(The illustration facing the title page shows the young Henry VI being held by his knightly master, Richard Beauchamp, earl of Warwick (BL, Cotton MS Julius E iv/6, folio 23).)

Preface

The story of how the English kings and aristocracy grew up and were educated in the 'age of chivalry' between the Conquest and the Reformation is an important and a rewarding subject, with many sources of information. Important, because these were the leaders of society in politics, war and government, the patrons of culture and a powerful section of those who ruled the Church. Rewarding, because aristocratic education at its best was a sophisticated and far-reaching process. Royal and noble children were trained by many kinds of people, in a variety of places and in a wide range of knowledge and skills. They learnt to speak, to read and to write; to worship God and behave correctly; to dance, make music and work with textiles; and to play games, hunt and fight. To study their training is not to retire into a narrow field of history, but to wander freely through the world of adult ideas and activities. The history of aristocratic education is also a survey of aristocratic culture.

The following study is concerned with all those who were born into the aristocracy, both boys and girls, from birth until about the age of 21. It does not include those who were born lower down in society and who rose to aristocratic status in later life. With this exception, it embraces everyone from the royal family through the peerage nobility and the knights down to those who came, by the fifteenth century, to be called esquires and gentlemen. The word 'aristocracy' and the adjectives 'noble' and 'gentle' are used to mean all the members of this group collectively. Sometimes, of course, it is necessary to distinguish between different grades within the aristocracy, and this has been done when required. The study begins with the home life into which noble children were born, and with the people who brought them up: their parents and nurses, masters and mistresses, servants and young companions. The second chapter describes how they left home to be trained in great households, religious houses, universities, schools and the inns of court. The third examines the treatment of noble education in literature, both fictional and serious, and this is followed by a survey of the knowledge and techniques which children learnt. Chapter four deals with the basic accomplishments of speech, religious belief and good behaviour; Chapter five with what are nowadays called 'the arts' of reading and writing, music, dancing and applied art; and Chapter six with physical education and training for war. The final chapter considers the type of person whom the system produced, and then extends its view beyond the aristocracy across the wider history of education in medieval England. It looks at the developments which took place between the twelfth century and the fifteenth, and ends by discussing how medieval education compared with, and contributed towards, the education of Renaissance England in the sixteenth century.

When we attempt to judge the medieval contribution to the history of education, we usually give the chief credit to the Church and the clergy. They developed literary studies, which are still often assumed to be the essence of education, and they invented the modern school and university which we still find indispensable. The contribution of the aristocracy is less well known, but we owe them something too. Their infiltration of the clerical schools and universities, with secular careers in mind, helped to transform these places from professional training centres into the liberal institutions of today. Their wealth and importance helped to stimulate the writing of the first modern studies of child-rearing and educational policy, initially aimed at the nobility alone but subsequently extended to the rest of society. Their passion for music, dancing, arms-training, hunting and archery, helped to promote the teaching of non-literary subjects, the writing of treatises about them, and the admission of them into the formal curriculum. The education of the clergy in the middle ages rose like a church spire, reaching an unequalled height at the level of a doctor of divinity, but with a narrow base. It only took certain children for its purpose, largely confined them to literary studies, and sought to make them into specialists, so that it was, in many respects, the forerunner of modern professional training. Aristocratic education, on the other hand, spread like the roofs and gables of a manor house: less lofty, but facing in several directions. It included all its children from their birth, taught them a wide range of subjects and skills besides the intellectual, and prepared them for careers both leisured and active, secular and clerical, male and female. In its scope and ambitions it came nearer to education as it touches us all today.

I would like to conclude by thanking the University of Exeter, which very considerately granted me study-leave to write this book, and my colleagues in the Department of History and Archaeology who kindly covered for me in my absence. The generosity of the warden and fellows of Merton College, Oxford, who elected me to a visiting fellowship in 1982, gave me excellent facilities for working during a long period. My wife's support and encouragement have been, throughout, my strength and inspiration.

Nicholas Orme,
University of Exeter,
September 1983.

Abbreviations

BIHR	*Bulletin of the Institute of Historical Research*
BJRL	*Bulletin of the John Rylands Library*
BL	British Library, London
BRUC	A.B. Emden, *A Biographical Register of the University of Cambridge to AD 1500*
BRUO, i–iii	A.B. Emden, *A Biographical Register of the University of Oxford to AD 1500*
BRUO, iv	A.B. Emden, *A Biographical Register of the University of Oxford, AD 1501–1540*
CCR	*Calendar of Close Rolls*
CPR	*Calendar of Patent Rolls*
EETS, os, es, ss	Early English Text Society, original series, extra series, supplementary series
EHR	*English Historical Review*
HMC	*Royal Commission on Historical Manuscripts*
LPFD, Henry VIII	*Letters and Papers, Foreign and Domestic, Henry VIII*, ed. J.S. Brewer and others
OED	*Oxford English Dictionary*, ed. J.A.H. Murray and others
PRO	Public Record Office, London
RS	Rolls Series
TRHS	*Transactions of the Royal Historical Society*
VCH	*The Victoria History of the Counties of England*, ed. W. Page and others

One Growing up at home

BIRTH AND DEATH

On 15 July 1273, St Edith's Day, the wife of Nicholas, baron of Stafford, gave birth to a son in their home at Madeley in Staffordshire.[1] Her joyful husband wrote at once to ask Roger de Pywelisdon, who lived at a distance, to come to Madeley to be the boy's godfather and lift him from the font. Next day he sent his servants to announce the birth to another friend, Hugh de Wrottesle of Wootton. The news reached Stafford town, and the prior of St Thomas's subsequently recalled that many rejoiced to hear it. Later the happy father rode in person to others of his knightly neighbours to tell them of his good fortune. The baby was taken to Madeley church to be baptized within a few days of its birth, in case it should die before it was christened, and it was given the name of Edmund. In accordance with the medieval rite of baptism, salt was put into its mouth, its ears and nostrils were wetted with saliva, oil was smeared on its breast and back, and it was totally immersed in the font three times: once on the right side, once on the left and once face downwards. We do not know who lifted the baby from the font, but

[1] *Calendar of Inquisitions Post Mortem*, vol iii, London, 1912, pp. 128–9; see also Cockayne, *Complete Peerage*, xii part i, 172–3.

it was not Roger de Pywelisdon, for although he made all haste to reach the church, the christening was over before he arrived. Edmund's father died when he was 14, and the boy became a ward of the Crown. When he was 21 and eligible to take over control of his father's lands, he had to prove his age before the escheator of Staffordshire. He called the surviving witnesses to testify to the date that he was born, and they did so. It is from their testimony that we learn of the time and circumstances in which the birth took place.

A number of similar proofs of age, chiefly of men and women of the lesser aristocracy, survive from the late thirteenth century onwards. Their details are not always wholly accurate, since they were meant primarily to help a young man gain his lands, not to enlighten historians in search of the facts of his birth.[2] But many of them speak, and no doubt truthfully, of the bustle and importance surrounding the birth of a noble child. Friends and relations were summoned to the christening, and rewarded the servants who brought them the news with money, a robe or a golden ring. Sometimes the news arrived at a feast, causing general rejoicing, and (as we enter the era of written records) the fact might be inscribed in the service books of the local church. The higher the rank of the parents, the greater the pomp and the circumstance. King Edward III and his wife Queen Philippa were staying at Woodstock on 16 June 1330 when Philippa gave birth to her first child, the Black Prince. Edward was so delighted that he gave the yeoman who told him about it a pension of forty marks a year for life for bringing the welcome news.[3] To the man who brought him the news of the birth of his second surviving son, Lionel of Antwerp, he gave £100,[4] and to three ladies who told him of the safe arrival of his third son, John of Gaunt, £200.[5] Outside the palace, the birth of a prince could set off popular celebrations just as it does today. When Edward I was born at Westminster in 1239, the citizens of London took the place of his birth as a special compliment to them, and there was public dancing to the music of drums and tambourines. When night came,

[2] On these records, see R.L. Hunnisett, 'The reliability of inquisitions as historical evidence', *The Study of Medieval Records*, ed. D.A. Bullough and R.L. Storey, Oxford, 1971, pp. 206–7, and Sue S. Walker in *Mediaeval Studies*, xxxv (1973), pp. 306–23.
[3] *CPR 1330–4*, p. 74.
[4] *CCR 1339–41*, p.7.
[5] ibid., *1341–3*, p. 467.

the streets were illuminated with large lanterns.[6]

Such joy was often short-lived. Too many medieval children died in infancy or through the epidemics and accidents of childhood, even in the households of the aristocracy with their better standards of housing, food and care. One estimate for medieval populations as a whole has suggested an infant mortality rate of 15–20 per cent in the first year of life and 30 per cent by the age of 20.[7] A large number of noble children failed to reach maturity, even if this is brought forward to the age of puberty: 12 for girls and 14 for boys. Of the children of Henry III, two boys and two girls grew up successfully, but five at least died during infancy or childhood.[8] Edward I's large family included fourteen children by two wives, but only eight of these reached adulthood: three boys and five girls. Edward II, his father's successor, was in fact the fourth son. Much the same was true of the twelve children of Edward III and Philippa. Two boys and one girl died in infancy, and three more girls were buried in their teens, leaving five boys and two girls to grow up and live full adult lives. It might be thought that the deaths of so many children would render parents callous or indifferent to the fate of their offspring, but there is no great evidence of this. They certainly bore in mind the possibility that their children might die. A Somerset father could leave money to Cannington Priory to support his daughter *if* she lived to be 10,[9] and the practice we shall encounter of sending noble sons to university in pairs seems to reflect the fear of one of them dying too soon.[10] But the wish to beget a line of descendants is a basic one, and must have been strong in medieval times. The fashion for being depicted on a funeral monument surrounded by one's children begins in England in the early fifteenth century, but the emotions it represents are probably much older.[11]

The likelihood is that most aristocratic parents took trouble to safeguard the lives of their sons and daughters, not the reverse.

[6] Matthew Paris, *Chronica Majora*, ed. Luard, iii, 539.

[7] J.C. Russell, 'Population in Europe, 500–1500', *The Middle Ages*, ed. C. Cipolla, Brighton and New York, 1976, pp. 45–7.

[8] For this and all royal family data, see Powicke and Fryde, *Handbook of British Chronology*, pp. 34–9.

[9] *Somerset Medieval Wills, 1383–1500*, ed. F.W. Weaver, Somerset Record Soc., xvi (1901), p. 28.

[10] Below, p. 67.

[11] Muriel Clayton, *Victoria and Albert Museum: Catalogue of Rubbings of Brasses*, London, 1968, pp. 37–120.

When children fell ill, money was freely spent on doctors and the medicines they prescribed. Henry son of Edward I had borage, sandalwood, barley-sugar, candy and pears bought to cure him and tempt his appetite in 1274.[12] The countess of Suffolk, whose youngest son Alexander de la Pole fell ill at school at Ipswich in 1416–17, paid for the barber of Ipswich to give him medicine and shave his head.[13] Edward IV in 1473, when making arrangements for the bringing up of his eldest son, the prince of Wales, along with other noble youths, ordered a physician and a surgeon to be permanently present in their household.[14] The poet Langland believed that the plagues of the mid-fourteenth century had made parents too careful of their offspring. 'Do not please them out of reason', he urged, 'for any power of the pestilence.'[15] Sir Thomas Elyot thought the same in 1530; parents were so protective of their children that they refused to send them away from home to be educated, for fear of death.[16] When all their efforts failed and children died, noble parents may have grieved as much as parents grieve today. 'A great while after my brother died', says a schoolboy in a set of school exercises from Oxford of about 1500, 'my mother was wont to sit weeping every day. I trow that there is nobody which would not be sorry if he had seen her weeping.'[17] Some late-medieval fathers and mothers provided permanent memorials of their dead children in the form of monumental effigies in churches. The brass of Thomas Heron, son of the treasurer of the king's chamber, who died at 14 in 1518, still survives at Little Ilford in Essex. It shows him wearing his boy's robe and his penner and inkhorn for use in school: the image of an early-Tudor schoolboy, destined never to grow up.[18]

[12] Johnstone in *BJRL*, vii (1922–3), pp. 397–9, 414.
[13] BL, Egerton Roll, 8776 m 5.
[14] Orme in *BIHR*, lvii (1984).
[15] *Piers Plowman*, B text, v, 34–6.
[16] *The Governor*, book i, chapter 13.
[17] *A Fifteenth Century School Book*, ed. Nelson, p. 17.
[18] M. Christy and W.W. Porteous, 'Some interesting Essex brasses', *Transactions of the Essex Archaeological Soc.*, new series, viii (1901), pp. 264–5; compare *VCH Hampshire*, ii, 275 and plate. The Grey Friars' church, London, of which we possess a complete list of monuments, had one to a specified boy, Thomas Scales, and several others which may have been of children (C.L. Kingsford, *The Grey Friars of London*, Aberdeen, 1915, p. 92, cf. pp. 93, 104, etc.).

CONCEPTS OF CHILDHOOD

How was childhood defined in medieval England, and who were thought of as children? As in our own day, there was no simple definition of the matter, either academic or legal, but a variety of co-existing ideas and practices. Since ancient times, poets and philosophers had been accustomed to think of life as falling into a series of distinct stages or divisions: 'the ages of man'.[19] Writers differed about the number of ages, and schemes of three, four, five, six, seven, ten and twelve were propounded at one time or another in classical Greece and Rome or in the Middle Ages. It was possible, if you believed in three ages, to ignore childhood altogether. The fourteenth-century English poem *The Parlement of the Three Ages* is a debate between a young man of 30, a middle-aged man of 60, and an old man of 100.[20] Most proponents of three or four ages of man, however, regarded childhood as the first age, consisting of a single undivided period from birth until about 20.[21] A single concept of childhood was also present in the English common law, which came to regard every young person as an 'infant', and believed that he or she only achieved full legal status at the age of 21.[22] It was also reflected in English speech. Until about the middle of the fifteenth century the English words for children had general rather than specialized meanings, covering the whole of childhood. 'Baby' could be used of older boys as well as infants, and a 'child' could be anything from a baby to a young knight riding out on adventures in his late teens.[23] Chaucer calls his knightly hero Sir Thopas a 'child', and the references to Child Roland and Childe Harold in Shakespeare and Byron belong to the same tradition.

The other commonest schemes of the ages of man in medieval England were those of 6 or 7. These differed in postulating divisions of childhood, rather than a unity. Thus Isidore of Seville, the

---

[19] On what follows, I am indebted to the excellent article of Beryl Rowland in *Poetica*, iii (1975), pp. 17–29. An older work by J.W. Jones in *Archaeologia*, xxxv (1853), pp. 167–89, is still useful.

[20] *The Parlement of the Thre Ages*, ed. Offord, p. 4.

[21] See Owst, *Literature and Pulpit*, p. 534; *The English Works of Sir Thomas More*, ed. W.E. Campbell and others, 2 vols, London and New York, 1931, vol i, f ciii; and for the age of 20, *Songs, Carols and other Miscellaneous Poems*, ed. R. Dyboski, EETS, es, ci (1908), p. 93.

[22] Holdsworth, *History of English Law*, iii, 510–20.

[23] *Middle English Dictionary*, ed. Kurath and Kuhn, sub 'babe', 'child'.

seventh-century scholar widely read in medieval Europe, stated in his work on *The Etymologies of Words* that human life consists of six parts, beginning with *infantia* from birth to 7, *pueritia* from 7 to 14, and *adolescentia* from 14 to 28.[24] In his *Book of Numbers* he adopted a seven-fold division of life, without specifying all the age divisions, and identified a separate period within *infantia*: the first seven months when the infant has no teeth.[25] Isidore's schemes were combined and restated by Bartholomew Glanville, the English Franciscan scholar whose work *On the Properties of Things* (c.1250) was the encyclopaedia chiefly read in England between the thirteenth and the sixteenth centuries. In Bartholomew's plan *infantia* lasts from birth to 7 (of which the first seven months are toothless), and *pueritia* from 7 to 14. *Adolescentia* begins at 14 and ends at 21, 28 or (in the opinion of some physicians) 30 or 35.[26] The educational writers of most influence in medieval England – Aristotle and Giles of Rome – held similar, though not identical, views. Aristotle, thinking primarily of boys, said that children should remain at home for the first years of their lives, being reared and excused study or labour. At 5 they should become onlookers at study and exercise, and full participants at 7. Education was to last from 7 till 21, with a division taking place not at 14 but at puberty, which Aristotle realized occurred in boys at different ages.[27] Giles of Rome, who wrote his work *On the Rule of Princes* in about the 1270s, followed Aristotle closely, including the concern with boys alone when he wrote 'children'. He also saw the first period of life as lasting from birth to 7, and marked by feeding, growth and movement, not formal studies. The next stage lasted from 7 to 14, but because children differed, the age of 14 should be regarded flexibly since some are stronger at 12 than others at 16 or 18. This period was to be a time of study and moderate exercise. Finally, from 14 (or thereabouts) noble boys were to learn to ride and fight and how to cope with adult institutions such as marriage. Giles was also tolerant about when education should end, and thought that this could happen at 21, 23 or 27.[28]

---

[24] *Isidori Hispalensis Episcopi Etymologiarum*, ed. W.M. Lindsay, 2 vols, Oxford, 1911, ii, book xi, chapter 2.

[25] *Patrologia Latina*, ed. Migne, vol lxxxiii, Paris, 1862, col 188.

[26] *De Proprietatibus Rerum*, book vi, chapter 1 (ed. Seymour, i, 291–2).

[27] *Politics*, book vii, chapter 17.

[28] Giles of Rome, *De Regimine Principum*, book ii, part ii, chapters 15–17 (ed. Molenaer, pp. 216–23).

So much for the theorists. What impact had their theories on society? As has been noted, the English language for long lacked words for dividing childhood into separate parts. It was not until the fifteenth century that the Latin terms used by Isidore and Bartholomew began to pass into English as 'infancy', 'puerice' and 'adolescency', thus making it possible to talk in the vernacular about these more sophisticated divisions of childhood.[29] The evidence of English life as opposed to English thought shows that the divisions of 7, 14 and 21 had a certain degree of importance, but were by no means paramount. When children were baptized, their godparents were ordered to keep them from fire and water until they were 7 and, presumably, able to fend for themselves.[30] Seven, or the seventh year, seems to have been a traditional point for noble children to pass from the care of women to tuition by males, but this was frequently disregarded and we shall encounter examples of aristocratic boys who had male tutors and schoolmasters from as early as the age of one.[31] Seven was held by the Church to be the minimum age of marriage, and under 7 marriages were technically impossible, but this too was ignored in practice and noble parents planned and executed marriages for their children at all ages from birth onwards.[32] At the age of 9 a child bride who lost her husband was eligible to receive a dower (one third of his property, for life), and a child marriage could be dissolved up to the age of 12 for a girl and 14 for a boy. These were considered to be the ages of puberty, at which marriages could become consummated and hence indissoluble. Fourteen was the age by the late thirteenth century at which noble girls came out of wardship and could inherit property; it was also the point at which, in the poll-taxes of 1377–81, children became adults and subject to be charged.[33] Sixteen was the age at which a girl who had previously been in wardship could marry. At 17 a boy could be ordained as a subdeacon, and at 19 he could take a vow to become a

---

[29] *Middle English Dictionary*, ed. Kurath and Kuhn, sub 'adolescence, -i', 'infanci(e)', and *OED* sub 'puerice'.

[30] *Manuale ad Vsum Sarisburiensis*, ed. Collins, pp. 32, 37–8. Confirmation was not tied to a specific age, and could be given at any time after baptism (below, p. 129).

[31] Below, pp. 18, 144–5.

[32] On marriage, see Pollock and Maitland, *History of English Law*, ii, 389–92, and below, pp. 36–7.

[33] On wardship and inheritance, see Pollock and Maitland, *History of English Law*, i, 319–20; ii, 436–47, and Holdsworth, *History of English Law*, iii, 510–20.

monk, involving a lifelong commitment to celibacy in either case.[34] Noble boys came out of wardship when they were 21, and this was also the age of majority for all other legal purposes. Clerics, however, could not be ordained priests until they were 24, and since most clergy waited till then to take the orders of subdeacon and deacon as well, entry into a fully committed and celibate clerical life generally took place in the mid-twenties. In short, the variety of theories about the divisions of childhood was matched by differences of practice. Medieval children grew up at different rates for different purposes, and 7, 14 and 21 were not the only years that counted. There have been many changes of detail since the Middle Ages, but modern society has inherited the same complexity of rules and ideas.

THE NURSERY

The English knight Sir Walter of Bibbesworth, who wrote about the bringing up of children for a noblewoman in the middle of the thirteenth century, says simply that a woman approaching the time of her delivery provides herself with a midwife.[35] No doubt he took it for granted that, in an aristocratic household, the woman's lady companions and female servants would prepare the bedroom for the lying-in, the necessary utensils and the cradle in which to lay the new-born child. Bartholomew Glanville describes the midwife's duties. She comforts the mother, anoints the entrance of the womb to assist the delivery, and helps the child to emerge at the birth. She knots its navel-string at the length of four inches, washes the child, rubs it with a balm of salt and honey, and swathes the child in cloths.[36] The pictorial life of Richard Beauchamp, earl of Warwick, who was born in 1382 shows his mother, the countess, in bed in a room with a fireplace, just after her delivery. A lady in a head-dress holds the baby, and three serving women wait in attendance: one stirring a pot on the fire, one bringing a bowl and spoon to the countess, and one inspecting an open box in which may lie the

[34] *Corpus Juris Canonici*, ed. E. Friedberg, 2 vols, Leipzig, 1879–81, ii, col 1140; Knowles, *Religious Orders in England*, i, 285.
[35] Bibbesworth, *Traité*, ed. Owen, p. 44, lines 1–4.
[36] *De Proprietatibus Rerum*, book vi, chapter 10 (ed. Seymour, i, 305).

birthday gifts.[37] In the royal household the lying-in of a queen was accompanied by formal ceremonies which were written down in 1493 to establish a rule for future occasions.[38] The chamber for the lying-in was to be richly furnished with a canopied bed, carpets, and hangings of arras upon the walls and ceilings. The dominant hues were the rich royal colours of gold and crimson. The windows too save one were covered with hangings, so that the queen might lie in light or darkness as she pleased. When the birth was expected, the queen went to a nearby chapel to be 'houselled' or receive communion, like a pilgrim departing abroad or a knight going off to the wars – all three of whom might suffer sudden death. When she went back to her chamber, all the men of the household were shut out. The birth of a royal child, like that of all medieval children apparently, took place in the presence of women alone, while the father, his friends and male servants awaited the outcome elsewhere.[39]

When children are born today, attention is largely concentrated upon the act of birth, the new-born baby and the health and achievement of the mother. In medieval times much of this interest was diverted towards a second process: the spiritual birth of the child by means of its baptism. All babies were baptized and the ceremony was carried out in close association with birth, sometimes as early as the delivery itself (the midwife being directed to christen the child herself if it seemed in danger of death) and not later than eight days afterwards.[40] At baptism the child received a name and, more importantly, was made a Christian, thus giving it the chance of salvation to which without baptism it possessed no right. As Langland expressed it in the 1370s,

> a barn that born is of wombe,
> Til it be christned in Cristes name and confermed of the
> bisshop,

---

[37] BL, Cotton MS Julius E.iv/6, f. 1; *Pageant of the Birth, Life and Death of Richard Beauchamp, Earl of Warwick*, ed. Viscount Dillon and W.H. St J. Hope, London, 1914, pp. 1–2. Scenes of birth are quite common in medieval manuscripts: see, e.g., those of Alexander the Great in Bodleian Library, MS Bodley 264, f.2ᵛ; and St Edmund of Bury in BL, Harley MS 2278, f. 13ᵛ.

[38] *A Collection of Ordinances*, pp. 125–7.

[39] On this and the next paragraph, see P. Niles in *Medieval Prosopography*, iii (1982), pp. 95–107.

[40] ibid.

It is hethene as to heveneward and helplees to the soule.[41]

Like physical birth, baptism had its parents: the godparents or 'gossips' fixed at a minimum of three by the Council of York in 1195, two men and a woman for a boy and vice versa for a girl.[42] They were chosen by the child's parents, or at least by the father. When the baptism took place, in a nearby private chapel or parish church, the senior godparent of the same sex as the baby named the child and lifted it out of the font. The name might be a family one: that of a parent or grandparent. The four eldest sons of Edward I were called John, Henry and Edward after their father and his ancestors, and Alfonso after the father of the queen. At other times a saint's name was preferred. Mary de Mohun (born 1282) was named because she was born on the eve of the feast of the Virgin Mary's Conception,[43] and Thomas of Brotherton (born 1300), the fifth son of Edward I, because his mother prayed successfully to St Thomas Becket to be eased of the pain of her labours.[44] Very commonly, however, the name-giver conferred his or her own name upon the child, emphasizing the close relationship, social as well as spiritual, which baptism was considered to create between godparents and their children. Godparents had long-term spiritual and temporal duties, besides the initial ceremonial ones. 'More belongs to a small child', warned Langland, 'than the taking of a name and him never the wiser.' Godparents who saw their children in trouble or need and did not relieve them, he threatened, would do penance in purgatory.[45] Priests at baptisms told godparents to help the natural parents care for the child while it was helpless, see it taught the Paternoster, Ave Maria and Creed, and have it brought to be confirmed by the bishop as soon as he came within seven miles of the place.[46] Aristocratic godparents had the power to forward their children's careers, and doubtless often did so. Queen Philippa got the pope to confer a benefice on her godson and namesake, Philip de Beauchamp, in 1345 when he was only 5: a good foundation for

---

[41] *Piers Plowman*, B. xv, 448–50.
[42] *Councils and Synods, I, 871–1204*, ed. Dorothy Whitelock and others, 2 vols, Oxford, 1982, ii, 1048–9.
[43] *Calendar of Inquisitions Post Mortem*, iii, 327.
[44] *Willelmi Rishanger Chronica*, ed. H.T. Riley, RS, 1865, pp. 438–9.
[45] *Piers Plowman*, B, ix, 74–8.
[46] *Manuale ad Vsum Sarisburiensis*, ed. Collins, pp. 32, 37–8.

what, until his early death, promised to be a successful career in the Church.[47]

In the early days of life, of course, it was food and care that mattered more than advancement. Not every noble mother deputed the feeding of her baby to a nurse, as is often supposed. Some evidently suckled their children themselves, though it is not yet possible to say how many. Walter of Bibbesworth makes no mention of a nurse in his account of birth and childhood, and Giles of Rome leaves the matter open: if the child is not to take milk from his mother, a nurse should be chosen who shares her physical characteristics.[48] The Bible offered the examples of Sarah, Hannah and the Virgin Mary as women who nursed their own children,[49] and there are stories of noble ladies feeding babies in one or two of the medieval romances.[50] The employment of nurses, however, was evidently very common among the aristocracy, though the record of the fact in individual cases is rather elusive. References abound to nurses in medieval records, but then as now they applied to nurses who offered care as well as those who fed, and it is usually difficult to know which is meant. The terms 'wet-nurse' and 'dry-nurse' are not found until the end of the Middle Ages. We know that Richard I was fed at the breast of Hodierna Neckham of St Albans, along with her son Alexander who subsequently had a distinguished career as a scholar and ended his life as abbot of Cirencester.[51] Margaret of France, the second wife of Edward I, certainly hired wet-nurses for her son Thomas of Brotherton, for we are told that when he was put to the breast of a French nurse he began to cry and to vomit milk till all despaired of his life. When an English nurse was provided instead, the little nationalist grew better and recovered.[52] The royal

[47] *BRUO*, i, 136–7.
[48] *De Regimine Principum*, book ii, part ii, chapter 15 (ed. Molenaer, pp. 216–18).
[49] Later urged as a powerful argument by Elizabeth Clinton, countess of Lincoln in *The Countess of Lincoln's Nurserie*, Oxford, 1622.
[50] E.g. Sir Ector's wife apparently intends to suckle her own son Kay but is required to feed Arthur instead and to send her own son to another woman (Malory, *Works*, ed. Vinaver, i, 10–11). Prince Blanchardyn is also breast-fed by his mother (*Caxton's Blanchardyn and Eglantine*, ed. L. Kellner, EETS, es, lviii (1890), pp. 12–16).
[51] London, College of Arms, MS Arundel 6, f. 135ᵛ (a reference kindly communicated by Dr Margaret Gibson); *Rotuli Litterarum Clausarum*, ed. T.D. Hardy, vol i, London, Record Commission, 1833, p. 416.
[52] *Willelmi Rishanger Chronica*, ed. Riley, pp. 438–9.

ordinances of 1493 imply that Elizabeth of York deputed her children to a wet-nurse too, and that this was thought to be desirable for the future.[53] A great many names of the nurses of the royal children have survived from Hodierna onwards, through the appearance of payments and rewards to them in the records of the medieval Crown. The coming to the throne of members of the peerage in the fifteenth century – Henry IV, Edward IV and Henry VII – has led to the preservation of their nurses' names as well. Many of the women are specifically mentioned as being married, strengthening the probability that they were nursing mothers who fed their noble charges at the breast. Their social rank is suggested by the fact that Richard II's nurse, a Frenchwoman, married his tailor, and Edward VI's dry-nurse was the wife of a barber surgeon.[54] They were probably women of good free status, not from the lowest orders of society. The royal nurses were well rewarded for their services with pensions for life. Henry VII gave his nurse £13 6s 8d, Edward IV his £20, and Richard II his £30.[55] Joan Astley, the nurse of Henry VI, beat them all with £40 a year for life in 1424.[56]

The royal or noble baby had other attendants besides its mother and nurse. Sometimes, perhaps, a wet-nurse was kept on to give services of other kinds after the child was weaned. Walter of Bibbesworth advised mothers to provide themselves with a 'rocker', a woman to rock the cradle, and there are several later references to such rockers or 'rocksters' as they were also called.[57] The nursery establishment of the earl of Northumberland in 1512 maintained two rockers and a child servant, and that of the royal household was bigger still.[58] The ordinances of 1493 enumerate five female servants for a new-born baby: the nurse and four rockers.[59] Earlier in the century, the 3-year-old Henry VI had six in 1424: a principal nurse, a day-nurse, a chamberwoman, a laundress and two others unspecified.[60] This made up a small department of its own within

[53] For sixteenth-century examples of the practice, see *Child Marriages*, ed. Furnivall, pp. 40, 50.

[54] *CPR 1377–81*, pp. 120, 609; Nichols, *Edward the Sixth*, i, p. xxxiii.

[55] *CPR 1485–94*, p. 95; *CPR 1467–77*, p. 439; *CPR 1377–81*, p. 120.

[56] *CPR 1422–9*, pp. 84, 179.

[57] Bibbesworth, *Traité*, ed. Owen, p. 45; Johnstone in *BJRL*, vii (1922–3), p. 390; *OED* sub 'rocker', 'rockster'.

[58] *Regulations of the Household of Henry Algernon Percy*, ed. Percy, p. 253.

[59] *A Collection of Ordinances*, pp. 125–7.

[60] Wolffe, *Henry VI*, p. 36.

the royal household, needing someone to take charge of it, and for this purpose there developed by the thirteenth century the duty of 'lady mistress of the nursery'. The lady mistress, unlike the nurse, was an aristocratic lady, usually of mature age, who looked after the royal nursery and the successive babies who were brought up in it, over a number of years. Marie de Valoynes, who figures as keeper of the children of Edward I in 1269–70, was probably an early functionary of this kind.[61] Elizabeth of St Omer, wife of a household knight of Edward III, is styled 'mistress of the king's children' in 1334, and Isabella de la Mote, a lady of France, likewise in 1341.[62] The nursery of Henry VI was in the charge of Elizabeth Ryman, one of his mother's ladies, in 1424, and it is possible that Lady Alice Butler, who was appointed to teach him in that same year, held a similar role.[63] The mistress of the king's nursery under Edward IV was Lady Elizabeth Darcy, who helped bring up the young Edward V.[64] Her reputation survived the violent events of the 1480s, and when a nursery was established by Henry VII for Prince Arthur in 1486, she was appointed to run it.[65] At least a few of the great lay magnates employed similar ladies to supervise the bringing up of their own children. In the household of Henry earl of Derby, later Henry IV, Mary Hervy occurs as the 'mistress' of the 6-year-old Henry (afterwards Henry V) and his younger brother in 1393–6,[66] and Margaret Hexstall, gentlewoman, who was appointed to look after the young children of the duke of Buckingham in 1502, was probably another lady of the same kind.[67]

Men too became involved in the care of noble babies at an early age. By the late fifteenth century the attendance of a physician on the royal children was a matter of course. The ordinances of 1493 required him to accompany the nurse at every meal and supervise the meat and drink that she gave to the baby; later on he was available to give medicine to the children as they grew up. Young boys and girls must have come into contact with the squires and grooms of their parents' households at an early age, and in the

[61] *Calendar of Liberate Rolls*, vol vi, *1267–72*, pp. 103, 108, 116.
[62] Tout, *Chapters*, v, 319–20; PRO, E 101/389/11.
[63] Wolffe, *Henry VI*, pp. 28, 35–6.
[64] *CPR 1476–85*, p. 241.
[65] *Materials for the Reign of Henry VII*, ed. Campbell, ii, 349.
[66] PRO, DL 28/1/4; DL 41/10, 43/10, &c.
[67] *A Relation of England*, ed. Sneyd, pp. 75–6.

greatest families of all, the departure of fathers and mothers on the endless journeys of aristocratic life often involved the leaving behind of the children in a small household of their own with male officers to look after it. Separate households for the royal children are already apparent by the middle of the thirteenth century.[68] A knight or royal clerk would act as head of the household and 'keeper' or 'master' of the royal children. Apart from the ladies attending the youngest children, there would be chaplains, menial household servants, minstrels and sometimes other noble children being reared alongside those of the king.[69] The heir to the throne, as he grew up, would acquire his own household, and this grew large in size by the end of the Middle Ages. The household of the one-year-old Prince Edward, son of Henry VI, was cut down to thirty-eight staff in 1454, and that of the young Edward V was fixed at fifty in 1471–3.[70] These independent or semi-independent households probably spread to a few great noble families too, when the father and mother both wished to move about frequently. Margaret Hexstall's appointment in 1502 was to help run a household of seventeen servants looking after the duke of Buckingham's children at Bletchingley in Surrey. The household had at its head, apparently, one of the duke's councillors. Margaret was to attend on the children, presumably to look after them, and not to take them away without the councillor's advice. She was to supervise the provision of food for the household, and to see that the children were served with four or five dishes of flesh and fish each day.[71] Clearly, such children learnt to live in a noble style from a very early age.

By the thirteenth century there were books, not yet wholly devoted to the bringing up of young children but offering advice on the matter among their other concerns. Aristotle himself, a chief classical author studied in medieval universities, alluded to babies and their care in the seventh book of the *Politics*. Their diet should be based on milky food, not wine which leads to disease. Crying and screaming should be tolerated, since they strengthen the body, and not impeded as Plato recommended in the *Laws*. Older children

[68] Tout (*Chapters*, i, 256) suggests that the first was that of the future Edward I in *c*.1254.
[69] Below, pp. 28–9.
[70] *Proceedings of the Privy Council*, ed. Nicolas, vi, 233; Myers, *Household of Edward IV*, p. 94.
[71] *A Relation of England*, ed. Sneyd, pp. 75–6.

should be allowed to move freely, kept amused and accustomed to the cold from their earliest years to harden them for war. Giles of Rome repeated these precepts in about the 1270s, but he misunderstood Aristotle's opinion on crying and quoted him as saying that it should be discouraged because it weakened the spirits.[72] The fullest account of baby-care which circulated in medieval England was that of Bartholomew Glanville in his encyclopaedia. Bartholomew gives a whole chapter to the care of the infant and another to the duties of the nurse, both evidently reflecting what was done as well as advising what ought to be.[73] The nurse baths the baby, and should do so frequently. She anoints it with oil of myrtles or roses. She feeds it first from the breast and later with food, chewed in her mouth and pushed with her fingers into the mouth of the baby. She swathes the child in sheets and cloths, with the limbs stretched out and tied with cradle bonds, lest they should grow deformed. She dances the child up and down and rocks it in the cradle. She talks to it and lisps her words in baby-talk. She lulls the child with cradle-songs and, says Bartholomew, should put it to sleep in a dark place lest its eyes be dazzled with bright lights. Sleep is important for children, because it concentrates their warmth in their inner parts and helps them to digest. Walter of Bibbesworth adds to this some observations on children as they grow older.[74] They start to crawl as soon as they can use their feet. Directly this happens they cover themselves with dirt, and a boy or girl should be assigned to follow them round and see that they do not stumble or fall. A dribbling mouth should be wiped with a cloth, called in English a 'slavering clout'. When a child stretches out its hand in the morning for bread, it should be given a lump or a slice. At dinner time it is good to open an egg, taking off the shell and the white and giving the child the yolk, or to cut up an apple and give it the flesh after paring the core and the peel. Later on it should be encouraged to dress itself and learn how to do up its buttons. Neither Bartholomew nor Walter had much space to give to nursery life, but they both perceived its interest and importance, and recorded many little details for which we are grateful now. For this they have an honourable place in the history of childcare.

[72] *De Regimine Principum*, book ii, part ii, chapter 15 (ed. Molenaer, p. 218).
[73] *De Proprietatibus Rerum*, book vi, chapters 4, 9 (ed. Seymour, i, 299–300, 304).
[74] Bibbesworth, *Traité*, ed. Owen, pp. 45–6, 61–5.

MASTERS AND MISTRESSES

As noble children grew older it became necessary to find new officers to care for them and teach them. Nurses and rockers gave way to masters and mistresses. Aristocratic parents appointed others to see to the day-to-day bringing up of their older children, as they did in the nursery, because they were absent or busy or wished to have the services of specially qualified people. The employment of deputies does not mean, however, that parents took no active part in the rearing of their children; far from it. Theirs was the duty of organizing their sons' and daughters' education, of choosing masters and mistresses, and of planning marriages and careers. Often, even at the highest social levels, they must have influenced and intervened in the educational process. Asser records how the young King Alfred, though he had a master, was impelled to learn to read through the encouragement of his mother, the queen.[75] Gerald of Wales tells how his father, an Anglo-Norman baron of the mid twelfth century, noticed the interest of his son in clerical matters and decided that he should be trained for clerical life.[76] Bartholomew Glanville describes fathers teaching their sons in youth 'with speech and with words',[77] and though these sounds have long since died upon the air, the sentiments survive in many letters from the fourteenth and fifteenth centuries, in which parents mingle pleas to work hard and behave well with threats of displeasure if the contrary is done.[78] The further down the social scale we pass into the ranks of the lesser knightly and gentle families, where parents were more often at home and closer to their children, the more likely it is that they involved themselves directly with their children's education. Walter of Bibbesworth's treatise was prepared for Denise de Mountchesney, a noble lady, with the initial purpose of helping her to teach her children French,[79] and a poem of about 1300, derived from Walter's work, includes among a list of female occupations the statement that 'woman teacheth child on book'.[80] Other treatises of

[75] Asser, *Life of King Alfred*, ed. Stevenson, p. 20.
[76] Gerald of Wales, *Autobiography*, trans. Butler, p. 35.
[77] *De Proprietatibus Rerum*, book vi, chapter 14 (ed. Seymour, i, 310).
[78] See for example, Richardson in *Formularies which bear on the History of Oxford*, ed. Salter and others, ii, 360–419 passim; *Paston Letters*, ed. Davis, i, 27, 42; *The Paston Letters*, ed. J. Gairdner, vol i, Edinburgh, 1910, pp. 121–2.
[79] Bibbesworth, *Traité*, ed. Owen, pp. 43–4.
[80] W.W. Skeat, 'Nominale sive Verbale', *Transactions of the Philological Soc.*, 1903–6, p. 7*.

the later Middle Ages include one by a knight to instruct his son in the management of his estates, a second by an esquire whose son desired to learn the use of the astrolabe, a third in which a lady tells her son the terms he needs to know when hunting, and a fourth in which another knight explains to his son the English system of land tenure.[81] Later still, Roger Ascham has left us a portrait of his early patron, Sir Humphrey Wingfield, going personally into the fields with the children of his household in about 1530, with bows and arrows to see them learn to shoot.[82] Unlike the teaching of masters and mistresses, that of fathers and mothers has left little trace in records. It existed, none the less, and we must be careful not to underestimate the impact that it may have had.

The age at which noble children passed from the informal education of the nursery to formal studies under a master or mistress is difficult to fix precisely and probably varied a good deal. In the case of girls, who stayed in the care of women throughout their childhoods and whose education was less formally organized than that of boys, the transition from informal to formal learning was not very obvious anyway. Even for boys, who experienced a definite change from petticoat government to formal education under men, there seems to have been no general agreement on when the change should occur. Aristotle suggested that boys should become on-lookers at formal study when 5 and students when 7. Bartholomew seems undecided whether to begin *pueritia* – the age at which boys are placed under tutors – at the age when they are weaned (in other words at about 2) or at 7. Giles of Rome implies the latter age.[83] Henry VI was six and a half when he passed from the care of Dame Alice Butler to that of the earl of Warwick in 1428,[84] and so was his son Edward in 1460, his lady mistress being discharged from attending him then on the grounds that he was old enough to be committed to the care of men.[85] Edward VI in the following century noted in his autobiography that he too was brought up among

[81] *Walter of Henley*, ed. Oschinsky, pp. 308–9; Chaucer, *Works*, ed. Robinson, pp. 545–61; Hands, *English Hawking and Hunting*, pp. xxxii–xliv; Sir Thomas Littleton, *Tenores Novelli*, London, 1482 etc., last page.

[82] Ascham, *English Works*, ed. Wright, p. 97.

[83] *Politics*, book vii, chapter 17; *De Proprietatibus Rerum*, book vi, chapter 5 (ed. Seymour, i, 300–1); *De Regimine Principum*, book ii, part ii, chapters 16–17 (ed. Molenaer, pp. 216–20).

[84] *Proceedings of the Privy Council*, ed. Nicholas, iii, 143, 294, 296–8.

[85] *CPR 1452–61*, p. 567.

women until he was 6.[86] The age of 6 or 7 seems therefore to have been one approved time to take a boy out of the nursery and give him to male tutors, but the two regimes might also overlap. Henry the Young King, the eldest son of Henry II, had a master called Mainard in 1156 when he was one, and Mainard remained in his service for at least three years.[87] Henry II's grandson William, the son of his daughter Matilda and Henry the Lion of Saxony, had a similar master in England in 1184–5, from about the time of his birth until he was one.[88] At the end of the Middle Ages Edward V was given a male governor when he was 3 and a grammar master three years later, the latter of whom is said to have taught Edward's brother Richard as well when Richard was only 2.[89] The children of Henry VII: Arthur and Henry VIII, also had schoolmasters at the age of 4 or 5.[90] So the division between a female-dominated infancy and a male-ruled childhood must often have been apparent rather than real, and some male figures (doctors, servants and sometimes masters) may have swum into the consciousness of their charges at a very early stage.

The best recorded arrangements for providing boys with tutors in the Middle Ages relate to the eldest son of the king. From at least the eleventh century it was usual to entrust the care of the eldest son to a knight with the general duty of protecting him and teaching him. William the Conqueror himself spent his early years before the age of 10 in the charge of Turold or Turketil, seigneur of Neuf-Marché-en-Lions (d. 1036),[91] and William's eldest son Robert Curthose had a 'pedagogue' (probably a knight) called Hilger when he was 12 in 1066.[92] The practice continued within the Norman dynasty and its

[86] Nichols, *Edward the Sixth*, ii, 209.
[87] *The Great Rolls of the Pipe, 2, 3 and 4 Henry II*, ed. J.S. Hunter, London, 1844, pp. 66, 101, 180; *The Great Roll of the Pipe, 5 Henry II*, London, Pipe Roll Soc., i (1884), p. 58.
[88] *The Great Roll of the Pipe, 32 Henry II*, ibid., xxxvi (1914), p. 49.
[89] *CPR 1467–77*, pp. 401, 417, 592.
[90] For Arthur's first known schoolmaster, John Rede, see *BRUO*, iii, 1555. A book was bought for Henry in 1495 (Bentley, *Excerpta Historica*, p. 105).
[91] Thompson, *Literacy of the Laity*, pp. 167, 184 n 14.
[92] *Regesta Regum Anglo-Normannorum*, ed. H.W.C. Davis, vol i, Oxford, 1913, p. 1; David, *Robert Curthose*, p. 6. I interpret 'pedagogue' as a knightly master by analogy with the examples in the next note.

successors in England down to the end of the fifteenth century.[93] The earliest royal tutors, like that of Robert, were called by writers *pedagogus*, from the Latin word for the slave in classical Rome who guarded noble boys and accompanied them to school. During the twelfth century, however, the word was largely replaced by *magister* in Latin, *me[i]stre* in French and eventually 'master' in English which meant both a guardian and a teacher. The master might be assigned to his charge at a very early age, as Mainard was, and remain with him until his late teens. Henry I's ill-starred son William was still in the care of his master when he died at the age of 16 in 1119. Masters might die, retire or be replaced, and Richard II was brought up by three in succession. Sometimes the master may have governed the prince's household too, since in the case of Edward the Black Prince we only hear of masters of his household, and the governor of Edward V, Lord Rivers, certainly held household responsibilities in the 1470s. The details of the system of tuition are obscure. Although it was traditional to appoint a knight as master and there were recognized terms to describe him, the mastership seems to have been a duty rather than an office. No appointments to it are recorded until the fifteenth century, and the names of masters only survive as stray references in chronicles or financial accounts. Consequently we know little about the relationship of the masters with their pupils, but there are signs that it was sometimes a close one lasting even until death. Othuer, the illegitimate son of Hugh, earl of Chester, and *pedagogus* of Henry I's son William, was with him in the White Ship when it went down in the Channel in 1119, and is reported to have thrown his arms round

---

[93] Othuer was *tutor . . . et pedagogus* of Prince William (d. 1120) (Orderic, *Ecclesiastical History*, ed. Chibnall, vi, 304–5); Mainard *magister* of Henry the Young King (above, note 87); Philip d'Aubigny *magister* of Henry III (Roger of Wendover, *The Flowers of History*, ed. H.G. Hewlett, vol ii, RS, 1887, p. 262); Hugh Giffard *pedagogus* of Edward I (Paris, *Chronica Majora*, ed. Luard, iv, 553); Guy Ferre *magister* of Edward II (Johnstone, *Edward of Caernarvon*, pp. 15–17); and Sir Nicholas de la Beche and Sir Bartholomew Burghersh 'masters of the household' of Edward the Black Prince (an analogous office?) (Tout, *Chapters*, v, 319–20). Richard II had three *magistri* in turn: Sir Richard Abberbury (*CPR 1377–81*, p. 155), Sir Guihard d'Angle (*Chronicon Angliae, 1328–1388*, ed. E.M. Thompson, RS, 1874, p. 162) and Sir Simon Burley (*The Anonimalle Chronicle, 1333 to 1381*, ed. V.H. Galbraith, Manchester, 1927, p. 123). The fifteenth-century masters are discussed below.

the prince and to have perished with him in the water.[94] Sir Simon Burley, who carried the young Richard II on his shoulder to his coronation in 1377, was afterwards one of his pupil's most loyal partisans and died at the hands of Richard's enemies in 1388. Richard tried hard to save his life, and the queen, Anne of Bohemia, went on her knees to plead for him before the duke of Gloucester, but to no avail. The murder of Gloucester nine years later was in part the vengeance of Richard for his tutor's death.[95]

A prince's knightly tutor probably supervised most aspects of his growing up and education. No doubt he advised him what to wear, how to behave in chapel and at table, to speak properly and deal correctly with other people. He could have taught the prince dancing, singing and playing on musical instruments, since these were general noble accomplishments, as also were riding, hunting and jousting. What the master did not know himself there were plenty of experts to help with: chaplains, minstrels, huntsmen, and men who could teach reading and grammar. Medieval Englishmen were familiar with the classical practice by which young kings and princes were taught to read and study by academic tutors. It was well known that Aristotle had tutored Alexander the Great and that Nero had been schooled by Seneca. In the twelfth century one royal grammar master, Matthew, who taught the young Henry II to read Latin in the 1140s, appears to have held a position with identity and status, since he attested Henry's early charters as 'teacher of the duke' (*doctor ducis*) and was remembered for his work in later years.[96] Subsequent princes were certainly taught to read and to understand Latin, but an office of prince's grammar master failed to develop until the fifteenth century, and records before that time hardly ever mention the names of those who did the task. It is unlikely that they were famous scholars of the day. True, a medieval writer reports that Richard de Bury, the well-known bishop and bibliophile, instructed the young Edward III in about the early 1320s, but the report, if accurate, relates to a time when Bury (who had studied at Oxford but not graduated) was still only an administrative clerk in the royal service.[97] The statement that

[94] Orderic, *Ecclesiastical History*, ed. Chibnall, vi, 305–5.
[95] *Chronique de la Traison et Mort de Richart Deux Roy Dengleterre*, ed. B. Williams, London, 1846, pp. 9–10, 133.
[96] Richardson in *EHR*, lxxiv (1959), pp. 193–7.
[97] *Historia Dunelmensis Scriptores Tres*, ed. J. Raine, Durham, Surtees Soc., ix (1839), p. 127; *BRUO*, i, 324.

Walter Burley, another famous scholar, taught the Black Prince in the 1330s comes only from the late sixteenth century, and may be mere conjecture.[98] Nor is there any evidence that the teachers were professional schoolmasters, a title and office restricted until the fifteenth century to those who taught in public schools. They were probably simply literate clerks or chaplains from the prince's household, seconded for a time to teach him and then re-assigned to other duties. Bury (if the evidence about him is reliable) was of this kind, and so was John Paynel, who is definitely known to have been a teacher of letters to Edward III and later became chamberlain of Chester and rector of Rostherne in Cheshire.[99] The situation is probably reflected accurately in the middle-English poem *Ipomedon*: the king's son is given into the care and teaching of a knight (who is named), and the knight appoints 'a clerk' (unnamed) to teach the boy to read.[100] As far as can be seen, the prince's knightly tutor was the only person sufficiently prominent to be called his 'master', and the teacher of reading and grammar, like minstrels and huntsmen, fell into the category of ordinary house-hold servants who simply helped with the prince's training as part of their general work.

In the fifteenth century changes took place in the traditional system of educating the king's eldest son, introducing more elaborate and formal arrangements. Appointments of masters began to be recorded. In 1422 Henry V assigned his uncle Thomas Beaufort, duke of Exeter, to have the governance of his son and heir, Henry VI, and the choosing of his servants.[101] Beaufort died at the end of 1426, and eighteen months later Richard Beauchamp, earl of Warwick was formally appointed instead to look after the young king and to teach him.[102] Edward IV made a similar formal appointment of his brother-in-law, Lord Rivers, in 1473 to look after his son the young Edward V, and gave him the new titles of 'governor and ruler' in what was now consciously thought of as an

[98] Ibid., p. 313; there is nothing, however, against boys of different ages being educated together.

[99] *CCR 1327–30*, p. 573; Tout, *Chapters*, iii, 25.

[100] Hue de Rotelande, *Ipomedon*, ed. Kölbing, p. 258.

[101] Wolffe, *Henry VI*, p. 29.

[102] 1 June 1428 (*Proceedings of the Privy Council*, ed. Nicolas, iii, 296–8). But Warwick was already styled *magister regis* on the previous 8 May (ibid., p. 294).

'office'.[103] The drafting of peers to be masters, rather than simple knights, was another new development, investing the mastership with greater status and importance. The appointment of Rivers was accompanied moreover by the issue of formal ordinances, the first of their kind to survive, prescribing the daily regime which the prince was to follow, timed by the clock, with directions for the conduct of his household.[104] The fifteenth century also provides us with the first clear cases of professional schoolmasters being employed to teach the prince his grammar. John Somerset, who was rewarded in 1432 for teaching the young Henry VI as well as for ministering to his health, was a former master of the grammar school of Bury St Edmunds.[105] John Giles, who was grammar master to Edward V and his brother Richard from 1475 till 1483, is not known to have been a public schoolmaster, but he had taught the young duke of Buckingham in the household of the queen from 1465 to 1467 and was evidently a 'career' teacher rather than a temporary one.[106] Somerset and Giles mark the beginning of an upgrading of the function of teaching reading and grammar to the prince, and the appointment for the purpose of professional men as specialized and self-conscious as the masters of public schools in the world outside.

The education of Edward V ended in tragedy. Edward IV made arrangements of unprecedented elaboration for his son's upbringing, but he also allowed him to fall too far beneath the control of one unpopular group of courtiers. When the prince's education was first planned in 1473, he was given a large council of twenty-five members to administer his affairs, with a wide and varied membership including the queen, the archbishop of Canterbury and the king's brothers Clarence and Gloucester.[107] By 1483, when Edward IV died, effective control of the prince had become

---

[103] PRO, C 66/532 m 15; *CPR 1467–77*, p. 417. The new titles may have been necessary because 'master' was now coming to mean 'schoolmaster'. They were not thought of as breaking with tradition, since Rivers was given the powers that other men had held in past times.

[104] Discussed below, pp. 115–17.

[105] *BRUO*, iii, 1727–8; *CPR 1429–36*, p. 241.

[106] A.R. Myers, 'The Household of Queen Elizabeth Woodville, 1466–7', *BJRL*, l (1967–8), pp. 491–2; *CPR 1467–77*, p. 592; *CPR 1476–85*, pp. 241, 373, 481. He was probably a layman, in view of the rewarding of him with annuities rather than benefices.

[107] *CPR 1467–77*, p. 366.

concentrated in the hands of the queen's family, the Wydevilles. Not only was Anthony Wydeville Lord Rivers the prince's governor, but the queen's son Sir Richard Grey was a powerful member of the prince's household, and her cousin Richard Haut was its executive controller.[108] The unpopularity of this group stimulated and enabled its enemies, Gloucester and Buckingham, to seize the household officers as they brought the new young king to London, and to send Rivers, Grey and Haut to imprisonment. Edward was probably so close to the victims emotionally (as Richard II had been to Burley) that Richard could never feel safe until he had eliminated the boy as well, and did so. Henry VII, after he ascended the throne in 1485, seems to have made a deliberate change of policy by not appointing noble masters for his own sons, lest the political fortunes of the masters should compromise the future of the children. He followed recent tradition to the extent of appointing Sir Richard Pole, his own cousin and a relative by marriage of the Yorkist royal family, as chamberlain of the household of his eldest son, Prince Arthur.[109] But no one appears to have held the ancient title of 'master' or the more recent one of 'governor' on behalf of either Arthur or his younger brother Henry. When Henry VIII made plans for the education of his own sons, Henry Fitzroy, duke of Richmond in the 1520s and Edward VI in the 1530s, he likewise provided them with officers to supervise their households, rather than noble masters on the previous model.[110] Instead, the educations of the early-Tudor heirs to the throne were marked by a further rise in the status of the grammar master. Arthur was taught reading and grammar by four or five masters in succession, of whom one, John Rede, formerly headmaster of Winchester College, was a career schoolmaster, while two others, Bernard André and Thomas Linacre, were men of letters.[111] Henry VIII had also a series of

---

[108] BL, Sloane MS 3479, f. 53ᵛ.

[109] *CPR 1485–94*, p. 434; *CPR 1494–1509*, p. 29.

[110] *LPFD, Henry VIII*, iv part iii no 5807 (p. 2595); Nichols, *Edward the Sixth*, i, p. xxvii.

[111] Arthur learnt the first elements of letters 'very quickly' (*Memorials of King Henry VII*, ed. Gairdner, p. 43); was then taught 'higher studies' by John Rede, *c*.1491 (ibid.; *BRUO*, iii, 1555); then by Bernard André, *c*.1496–*c*.1499 (ref. as above; *BRUO*, i, 33); then by Thomas Linacre, *c*.1499 (*BRUO*, ii, 1148); finally by an un-named Scot to 1502 (*Privy Purse Expenses of Elizabeth of York*, ed. Nicolas, p. 28).

masters, beginning with the poet John Skelton and continuing with John Holt who had previously taught in three schools, including Magdalen College School, Oxford, and Chichester. Henry's third master, William Hone, had also once been master of Chichester School.[112] The rise of the schoolmaster as against the knightly master chimes with the growing emphasis in the Renaissance on the study of Latin grammar. But the non-academic accomplishments continued to be learnt, and Henry VIII in particular grew up to be expert at music, dancing and a wide range of athletic pursuits.

Masters were also employed from the twelfth century onwards to look after and teach the younger sons of the royal family and the sons of the rest of the aristocracy. Ralph the *magister* of the children of Aubrey de Vere, earl of Oxford, attested a charter not later than 1187,[113] and the master of Henry II's grandson, William of Saxony, at about the same time has already been mentioned. In the households of the king and of at least a few of the great lay magnates, the master could be a knight like that of the heir to the throne. Sir Roger of Acaster filled such a role for Richard earl of Cornwall, the younger son of King John, in 1217–23,[114] and Sir Hugh Giffard, who dropped dead suddenly in 1246 of an apoplexy, probably did the same for Edmund earl of Lancaster, the younger son of Henry III.[115] Henry IV in 1377, when he was still only son and heir of the duke of Lancaster, had a knight as his master too: the Frenchman Guillaume de Mountendre.[116] In other cases the master may have been of lower rank than a knight, like Thomas of Aldon, master to Edward de Bohun (a younger son of the earl of Hereford) in 1326; Aldon was a king's yeoman, a man of property, and a political associate of the Hereford family.[117] The same general tradition

---

[112]   Henry was taught to spell by John Skelton, *c.*1499 (*BRUO*, iii, 1705–6); then by John Holt, *c.*1502–4 (*BRUO*, ii, 953–4), and by William Hone *c.*1504 (*Grace Book Γ, containing the Records of the University of Cambridge 1501–1542*, ed. W.G. Searle, Cambridge, 1908, p. 37; *BRUO*, ii, 956).

   Arthur and Henry also had the first known professional French master in England: Giles D'Ewes (*Dictionary of National Biography*).

[113]   Dugdale, *Monasticon*, ed. Caley, vi part i, 309.

[114]   *Rotuli Litterarum Clausarum*, ed. Hardy, i, 325, 481, 495, 576.

[115]   Paris, *Chronica Majora*, ed. Luard, iv, 553, where he is called master of the *sons* of Henry III.

[116]   PRO, DL 28/3/1; *CPR 1374–7*, p. 471.

[117]   PRO, E 101/381/11 no 89; he had previously been an associate of Hereford's ally Bartholomew Badlesmere in 1321 (*CCR 1323–7*, p. 8).

probably shaped the development in the royal household by 1471–3 of an office of 'master of the henchmen' held by a knight or squire responsible for teaching the noble youths of the household how to sing, dance, ride and behave themselves – in fact all the subjects they learnt except for grammar.[118] The names and status of noble masters, however, are often unidentifiable, and the further down the aristocracy we go in the scale of wealth and importance, the less probable it is that household knights and squires were available to be used as masters. The more likely it is that the task was done by others.

Clerics were obvious alternatives to knights as tutors, since they were always to be found in noble households but were cheaper to employ. Thomas of Woodstock, Edward III's youngest son, was in the custody of Robert of Holm, a royal financial clerk, at the age of 11 in 1366.[119] Robert Lord Hungerford and John Lord Tiptoft each sent their eldest sons to study at Oxford in the 1430s and 1440s in the charge of graduate clergy.[120] Henry VI at the same period is said to have given the care of his half-brothers Edmund and Jasper Tudor to 'virtuous and worthy priests, both for teaching and for right living and conversation'.[121] Clerics were equal with knights in the potential range of their teaching. They too could give instruction in behaviour, both in church and in hall; they knew about horses and how to ride them, and some of them were learned in matters of chivalry. One of the chief English textbooks of heraldry and the art of war in the fifteenth century was written by Nicholas Upton, precentor of Salisbury Cathedral,[122] and in the 1450s Vegetius's classical treatise on war was translated into English verse by a parson of Calais.[123] In any case, assistance in matters such as music, riding or hunting would probably have been forthcoming from other members of the household. The clerical tutor may have taught reading and grammar himself or, like Robert of Holm, have paid someone else to do so. Like those of the heirs to the throne, the early teachers of grammar to noble boys were probably clerics who taught part-time, who were not primarily schoolmasters and consequently

[118] Myers, *Household of Edward IV*, pp. 126–7.
[119] Devon, *Issues of the Exchequer*, p. 189.
[120] Discussed below, p. 71.
[121] *Henry the Sixth*, ed. James, pp. 8–9, 30–1.
[122] *BRUO*, iii, 1933–4.
[123] Vegetius, *Knyghthode and Bataile*, ed. Dyboski and Arend.

not recorded as such. William Lord Roos (d. 1413) provided for one of his domestic chaplains to teach grammar to his sons, and Thomas Howes, a Norfolk rector, was at least peripherally involved with education in the Paston family in 1461.[124] Gradually, however, the employment of professional masters spread to the households of the nobility as it did to that of the heir to the throne, and by the early sixteenth century such men were becoming quite common.[125]

Just as boys had masters, so aristocratic girls (or at least the most important of them) had mistresses: noble ladies similar to the mistresses of nurseries, but charged with the bringing up of girls in later childhood and adolescence. One of the earliest ladies whom we hear of with the title of mistress was Cecilia of Sandford, the wife and mother of knights, who acted in this role to Eleanor (born 1215), the youngest daughter of King John, and afterwards to Joan, one of the scions of the baronial Mountchesney family. Cecilia had a reputation for learning and eloquence, and when she died in 1251 the chronicler Matthew Paris paid her the tribute that her birth was noble but her morals nobler still.[126] Several other mistresses are recorded in the royal family and its cadet branches during the later Middle Ages.[127] They were generally the wives or widows of household knights or courtiers, and are found in attendance on girls from infancy to early adulthood. Isabella the queen of Edward II and her namesake the wife of Edmund earl of Cambridge both had mistresses in England from their own countries, France and Castile,

[124] *The Register of Henry Chichele*, vol ii, ed. E.F. Jacob and H.C. Johnson, Oxford, Canterbury and York Soc., xlii (1937), pp. 23–4; *Paston Letters*, ed. Davis, ii, 258.

[125] Below, p. 57–8.

[126] Paris, *Chronica Majora*, ed. Luard, v, 235–6.

[127] Ladies with the title *magistra, magistrix* or *maitresse*, or with analogous functions, include Joan or Janet Jermy[n], sister of Alice countess of Norfolk, in charge of Edward II's daughters Eleanor and Joan in 1326 (PRO, E 101/381/11 no 109); Isabella de la Mote of Edward III's daughters Philippa and Elizabeth in 1340–1 (PRO, E 101/389/11); Katherine Waterton of Henry IV's daughter Philippa in 1402–3 (PRO, E 361/5 m 14); Margaret Lady Berners of Edward IV's daughter Elizabeth of York in 1468 (PRO, E 403/41 sub 1 Dec) and Joan Lady Dacre of Edward IV's daughter Mary in 1482 (London, College of Arms, MS I.11, f 21). Mary I, daughter of Henry VIII, had at least three mistresses in turn: Margaret Bryan in 1516 (*LPFD, Henry VIII*, ii part i, p. 874); Elizabeth Denton in 1517 (ibid., part ii, p. 1191); and Margaret countess of Salisbury in 1520 (ibid., iii part i, p. 323).

when they were married and in their early twenties.[128] The best known of all medieval English mistresses is Katherine Swynford, the wife of one of John of Gaunt's knightly retainers, who became the mistress of Gaunt himself in about 1371, when she was just turned 20 and before she was widowed in the following year. She stayed on in Gaunt's service during the 1370s, bearing his children while acting nominally as mistress to the daughters of his first marriage, Philippa and Elizabeth.[129] Her devotion was duly recognized in 1396 when Gaunt made her his third wife.

Mistresses were sufficiently common in noble households by the end of the fourteenth century to prompt Chaucer to break off his description of Virginia, the noble heroine of 'The Physician's Tale', to offer general advice to 'maistresses . . . that lordes doghtres han in governaunce'.[130] He characterizes them as ladies of mature years, in their 'olde lyf', and asserts that they are chosen for their offices either because they have always followed a virtuous way of life or, quite the reverse, because they have given way to temptation 'and knowen wel ynough the olde daunce' but have forsaken such ways for ever. Of whatever kind they are, he concludes, they should not slacken, for Christ's sake, in teaching virtue to their pupils. If Chaucer's wife were the sister of Katherine Swynford, as is possible, his encounters with a mistress well known for her frailty were close ones and give interest to his writing. Like the boy's master, the mistress is likely to have provided general teaching on dress, behaviour, singing and dancing, with technical help from clergy in religious topics, minstrels with music and grooms with horses. The teaching of reading to girls took place as well, as we shall see, from an early date. Matthew the grammar master of Henry II had previously been tutor to Henry's aunts, the sisters of Count Geoffrey of Anjou,[131] but later such teaching was probably done by non-specialized men and women whose names have not survived. The first professional schoolmasters who are known to have taught noble

---

[128] Theophania mistress of Isabella of France was buried in the Grey Friars church, London (Kingsford, *The Grey Friars of London*, p. 100; *CPR 1317–21*, p. 66), and Joan mistress of Isabella of Castile countess of Cambridge is mentioned in 1377 (PRO, DL 28/3/1).

[129] She occurs as mistress in 1379–80 and as former mistress in 1382 (*John of Gaunt's Register, 1379–83*, ed. Lodge and Somerville, ii, 93, 302–3, 366).

[130] Chaucer, *Works*, ed. Robinson, p. 145 (C 72–82); cf. pp. 131–2 (F 374–83).

[131] Richardson in *EHR*, lxxiv (1959), p. 194.

girls appear in the royal family in the early sixteenth century. Henry VIII's younger sister Mary was being instructed by his own ex-schoolmaster, William Hone, in 1514, and his daughter Mary I was learning Latin, apparently from Thomas Linacre, in 1523.[132] In this way the professional teaching of reading and grammar, which we have traced for boys since the reign of Henry VI, became extended to girls as well, but not until almost a hundred years later.

THE EDUCATION OF CHILDREN

It is well known that the medieval aristocracy lived in public rather than private, alongside a crowd of household retainers of all ranks from knights of the chamber down to laundresses and turnspit boys of the kitchen. The word 'family' in the Middle Ages meant not only the kindred group of parents and children but the retainers who lived beneath the roof, shared the parental authority and received the same protection in return as did the children. It followed that most noble boys and girls grew up at home in a sociable environment, in close proximity to servants as well as to parents, masters or mistresses. The Oxford author of a set of school exercises in about 1500 imagines the spoilt son of wealthy parents waited on hand and foot by his family's retainers. None of them dares to wake him up, however late he sleeps. He stirs when he pleases, calls them to lay out his clothes and orders his breakfast to be brought to his bedside, so that frequently he is fed before he is dressed.[133]

The princes and princesses of the royal family had their own separate households of chaplains, minstrels and servants with whom they settled down or travelled about independently of their parents. There were often other noble children in these households. The sons of the aristocracy were regularly drafted in to be companions for the princes of the blood-royal and to share their education. Edmund Crouchback, the younger son of Henry III, had five or six noble children dwelling with him at Windsor Castle in 1254, and his nephew Edward II had ten with him in 1301, including the future earl of Gloucester Gilbert de Clare, and the notorious Piers Gaveston.[134] When Henry VI was 4 in 1425, all the noble boys in the king's wardship who held the rank of baron or above were ordered to

[132] *LPFD, Henry VIII*, i part i, no 2656 (p. 1162); *BRUO*, ii, 1148.
[133] *A Fifteenth Century School Book*, ed. Nelson, p. 2.
[134] *Close Rolls, 1253–4*, p. 75; Tout, *Chapters*, ii, 172.

stay about the person of the king and in his household.[135] Edward V was brought up in the 1470s, chiefly at Ludlow, in the company of 'sons of nobles, lords and gentlemen', who studied grammar, music and other exercises just as he did himself.[136] Henry VIII's sons Henry Fitzroy and Edward VI were reared in a similar way.[137] There were parallel groups of boys and girls in the households of the greater aristocracy, as well as those of the royal family. As for the lesser nobility, who could not afford to maintain such gatherings themselves, they sent their children away to be equally sociable in the households of the greater, or to other places of resort like abbeys, schools and universities.

The gatherings of children in noble households lacked homogeneity by modern standards. The boys and girls concerned were often of disparate ages, so that the grouping resembled that of a large modern nuclear family rather than that of a class at a modern school. Edward II was 16 in 1301 but Gilbert de Clare was only 5, and Henry VI in 1426–8, when he was aged between 5 and 7, was accompanied by the duke of York and the earl of Oxford who were both 17 and by Lord Roos who was 20.[138] Yet the parallel even of a modern family is inadequate, since noble children growing up together were of different ranks with different privileges, and were often attended by their own servants as well as those of the household where they were staying. The noble boys accompanying Edward II in 1301 all had their own masters to look after them, except for Gaveston – perhaps because of his lower rank and wealth.[139] John of Gaunt, when sending his son and daughter to stay in the houses of other aristocracy between 1369 and 1380, despatched a retinue with each of them.[140] When Sir John Pilkington of Wakefield arranged for his son and heir to be brought up in the household of the lord chamberlain in 1478, he likewise provided for the boy to be attended by two of his own servants and specified their names.[141] Notwithstanding these anomalies, close friendships might be made between boys growing up together.

---

[135] *Proceedings of the Privy Council*, ed. Nicolas, iii, 170.
[136] Orme in *BIHR*, lvii (1984).
[137] Ellis, *Original Letters*, 3rd series, i, 333–7; Nichols, *Edward the Sixth*, i, p. lvi.
[138] Wolffe, *Henry VI*, p. 37.
[139] Tout, *Chapters*, iii, 172.
[140] PRO, DL 29/262/4069; *John of Gaunt's Register, 1379–83*, ed. Lodge and Somerville, i, 106–7.
[141] *Testamenta Eboracensia*, ed. Raine, iii, 239–40.

Edward II met Piers Gaveston as a result of the latter's being brought up as a ward in his household, and Henry Courtenay earl of Devon was for a time a close friend of his first cousin, Henry VIII, for the same reason.[142] Both boys did well initially from their royal connections; one got an earldom and the other a marquessate, but they were less fortunate in the long run. Gaveston's favouritism by Edward II led to his death at the hands of Edward's enemies, and Courtenay's links with Henry did not stop the king from killing him, on suspicion of treason, in 1539.

The proximity of noble children to one another and to servants of inferior rank solved one abiding problem of education: the need to accustom the young to the company of other people. A boy, says the thirteenth-century friar and educationist Vincent of Beauvais, benefits from companions both better and worse than himself, for he strives to imitate the better and to keep ahead of the worse.[143] The growing up of an aristocratic child in public, with a recognized status and surrounded by companions and retainers also prepared it for its maturity in which it would live the same kind of life and play the same kind of role on a larger scale. A royal baby, in its earliest days, was attended to the font by squadrons of squires and yeomen, as it would be on its journeys in adulthood. It took its rest in a great cradle emblazoned with the royal coats of arms, anticipating the splendour of the beds and chairs it would use on growing up.[144] Royal parents in particular gave their sons honorific titles when they were quite young, to emphasize their importance and prepare them for their adult careers. Henry II contemplated crowning the Young King as early as 1162 when he was 7, and the coronation was finally carried out eight years later. Of Henry's younger children Geoffrey was installed as count of Brittany in 1169 when he was 11, Richard I as duke of Aquitaine in 1172 when he was 14, while John was proclaimed king of Ireland in 1177 at the age of 10. Throughout the rest of the Middle Ages, royal princes were given knighthoods and peerages while they were young, and even nominal posts of responsibility. The Black Prince and his brother Lionel were each named as keeper of the realm at different times in the 1330s and

---

[142] Tout, *Chapters*, iii, 172; *A Collection of Ordinances*, p. 154; Cockayne, *Complete Peerage*, iii, 433–4; iv, 330–1.

[143] *De Eruditione Filiorum Nobilium*, ed. Steiner, pp. 123–8.

[144] *A Collection of Ordinances*, pp. 125–7.

1340s when they were 7, to give status to the government in England during the absence of their father overseas. The sending by Edward IV of his eldest son to be brought up at Ludlow Castle reflected a similar policy to provide a royal presence to back up the administration of Wales and the Marches, and its usefulness was so apparent to Henry VII that he repeated it in the 1490s by sending his own son Arthur to Ludlow for the very same purpose.

The drawback of a public life and social integration was that they increased the exposure of children to coarseness and vice. Aristotle had warned of the need to shield the young from hearing rude words, seeing indecent practices or watching comic plays, until they were old enough to join the company of adults.[145] Giles of Rome urged that boys be prevented from seeing paintings or carvings of naked women.[146] As far as medieval England was concerned, the chief danger of corruption, no doubt rightly, was identified with the household retainers around the young, who were always liable to undermine discipline, distract from education and lead into temptation. In 1432 the earl of Warwick complained to the privy council of England that persons unnamed had 'stirred' the 10-year-old Henry VI 'from his learning' and told him about 'diverse matters not behoveful'.[147] Three years later the council discovered that the 20-year-old duke of Norfolk, John Mowbray, who was in the king's wardship and staying at court, was leading a disorderly life with members of his retinue. The council removed the offenders and substituted new squires to advise and attend on the duke, one of whom was ordered to stay in his company all the time.[148] When Edward IV arranged for the education of his son in 1473, similar careful provisions were made for the proper conduct of his household. Gates were to be shut at night and dishonest people excluded; household servants guilty of violence were to be put in the stocks, and no one was to sit at the prince's table without his governor's permission. While the prince ate he was to hear noble stories, and the conversation in his presence was to be 'of virtue, honour, knowledge and deeds of worship, and of nothing that should move or stir him to vice'.[149] The seclusion of girls was

---

[145] *Politics*, book vii, chapter 17.
[146] *De Regimine Principum*, book ii, part ii, chapter 10 (ed. Molenaer, pp. 206–8).
[147] *Proceedings of the Privy Council*, ed. Nicolas, iv, 135–6.
[148] Orme in *BIHR*, lvii (1984).
[149] ibid.

especially emphasized by writers, and probably also practised. Giles of Rome devotes a chapter to the subject.[150] If men are guarded to protect their innocence, he says, how much more must we do the same for women. Women have less sense and reason than men, and are more inclined to do evil. When they are accustomed to men they become intimate with them, 'as we see with savage beasts'. Girls must be carefully supervised so that they have no time or place for such familiarity, be prevented from going about the streets or the countryside and be secluded from men. If they are shy and unused to the opposite sex, they will better guard their bodies and their chastities. Chaucer agreed with this. In 'The Physician's Tale' he described a noble girl so modest and retiring that she would feign sickness when asked to feasts and dances, lest she got involved in foolish things. All this he much approved; company and revelry make children ripe too soon, and a girl will learn boldness soon enough when she is married.[151]

The exposure of children to company on the one hand and their seclusion on the other formed a pair of contrasting principles in medieval education. In the bringing up of individual boys and girls the two principles would have been mixed in different, changing proportions, which are now impossible to quantify. Discipline and its counterpart indulgence formed a similar pair of policies, technically opposite yet inextricably entwined. Medieval educationists and moralists placed much emphasis on the need to use firm discipline to make children study and learn and to deter them from vices. A father's love for his child, says Bartholomew Glanville, consists not only in feeding him and teaching him, but in chastising him with beating. In the words of Trevisa's translation,

> The more the father loveth his child, the more busily he teacheth and chastiseth him, and holdeth him the more strait under chastising and lore. And though the father love him most, it seemeth that he loveth him not, for he reproveth and beateth him often, lest he draw to evil manners and habits.[152]

Langland makes Reason itself commend the beating of children, quoting Solomon's famous proverb that 'he who spares the rod

---

[150] *De Regimine Principum*, book ii, part ii, chapter 19 (ed. Molenaer, pp. 225–7).
[151] Chaucer, *Works*, ed. Robinson, pp. 145–6 (C 43–7, 93–104).
[152] *De Proprietatibus Rerum*, book vi, chapter 14 (ed. Seymour, i, 311).

hates his child'.[153] In practice, the corporal punishment of children was widespread in medieval society – and not only that of children, what with the beating of wives by husbands, penitent sinners by clergy, and minor criminals by secular officers. The beating of children was therefore not a special punishment for them; rather it signified their inclusion in the world of adult values and practices. It was possible for medieval people to imagine the beating even of a royal prince. In the thirteenth-century chanson de geste *The Story of Fulk Fitz-Warin*, King John is portrayed as a child attacking a friend with a chessboard in a fit of temper, upon which his father Henry II orders him to be beaten by his master – an amusing but apocryphal story.[154] Henry VI may really have been beaten in his childhood. In 1424 his lady mistress Alice Butler was commissioned to chastise him reasonably from time to time, and similar power was given to his master, the earl of Warwick, in 1428.[155] Since the word 'chastise' applied to verbal as well as to physical discipline, however, we cannot be quite sure which was used. Beating was certainly in use among the lower aristocracy, both for girls and boys. Agnes Paston, one of the famous Norfolk family of letter writers and a hard-hearted woman, was beating her daughter Elizabeth in about 1449, when Elizabeth was 20, 'once in the week or twice, and sometimes twice in one day, and her head broken in two or three places'.[156] Later, in 1458, Agnes commanded the master of her 16-year-old son Clement, studying in London, that he 'truly belash him' if he had not done well, for 'so did the last master, and the best that ever he had'.[157] Sir William Carew of Mohun's Ottery in Devon preferred punishment by public humiliation. When his son Peter played truant from school in Exeter in about 1526 and got up to dangerous pranks on the city wall, Sir William had the boy tied up and led by a servant round Exeter and all the way home, 'like a dog'. When they reached home, Peter was shackled to one of the family hounds to emphasize the point, until his father relented.[158]

That writers and preachers insisted so much on the beating of

---

[153] *Piers Plowman*, B, v, 34–41.
[154] Ralph of Coggeshall, *Chronicon Anglicanum*, ed. J. Stevenson, RS, 1875, pp. 324–5.
[155] *Proceedings of the Privy Council*, ed. Nicholas, iii, 143, 296–8.
[156] *Paston Letters*, ed. Davis, ii, 82.
[157] ibid., i, 41.
[158] Hooker, *Life of Sir Peter Carew*, ed. Maclean, pp. 4–5.

children, however, when they ignored so many other aspects of childhood and growing up, should make us cautious of assuming that the practice was really quite so well established. Often, indeed, the moralists make it clear that they are recommending corporal punishment because it is not being carried out to a sufficient degree. Langland, as has been mentioned, thought that the deaths of children in the plagues made parents too indulgent of their offspring.[159] The Oxford author of school exercises in about 1500 refers contemptuously to the tender-heartedness of a mother whose small son tastes the rod at his ABC school:

> And if he come weeping after his master hath chared [i.e. driven] away the fleas from his skin, anon his mother looketh on his buttocks if the stripes be seen. And the stripes appear, she weepeth and waileth and fareth as she were mad; then she complaineth of the cruelty of teachers, saying she had liefer see her child were fair buried than so to be entreated.[160]

Tender-heartedness and simple negligence must often have dulled the edge of discipline. So, perhaps, did aristocratic status. The master in charge of the noble youths in the royal household in 1471–3, though empowered to discipline them, did so privately 'in their chambers, according to [the status of] such gentlemen'.[161] Furthermore, from at least the thirteenth century, voices began to be raised by liberal educationists who sought to modify the use of corporal punishment on moral and rational grounds. Some of their number were friars, whose tolerance in matters of sin (though often attacked by anti-clerical writers) was ancestral to that of liberal educationists today. Vincent of Beauvais, writing in France in about the 1250s, had urged that warnings should precede punishments and that masters should bear in mind the nature of their pupils, since it was wrong to do violence against the good-natured.[162] Similar pleas were made in fourteenth-century England by the friars John Bromyard and Robert Holcote.[163] Since friars were much in the company of the aristocracy as their spiritual advisers and confessors,

---

[159] *Piers Plowman*, B, v, 34–41.
[160] *A Fifteenth Century School Book*, ed. Nelson, pp. 13–14.
[161] Myers, *Household of Edward IV*, pp. 126–7.
[162] *De Eruditione Filiorum Nobilium*, ed. Steiner, pp. 92–5.
[163] Owst, *Literature and Pulpit*, pp. 423–63; Beryl Smalley, *English Friars and Antiquity*, pp. 192, 332.

such ideas may well have percolated into aristocratic households. Chaucer in his one clear discussion of the beating of children implied that its use was unnecessary,[164] and a century later the theme began to be taken up again by the educationists of the Renaissance. As the English schoolmaster John Anwykyll remarked in the 1480s, adapting Terence, 'it is better to hold children under with shame and gentleness, softness or easiness, than by fear or dread'.[165]

There were two other positive ways in which a special indulgence was extended to aristocratic children: food and play. In the fifteenth-century royal household, though adults were limited to two meals a day (dinner and supper), children were allowed an extra breakfast, no doubt as a concession to their appetites and need for growth.[166] Early-Tudor schoolbooks tell of presents of food conveyed by parents at home to their sons away at school, especially of fruit: raisins, figs and pears.[167] 'Children love games and vanities', says Bartholomew Glanville, and educationists saw play as an element of childhood which should be encouraged and might be turned to good account. Aristotle, followed by Giles of Rome, considered that play helped to develop the limbs and should be organized to prepare children for the functions of adult life.[168] Edward IV's ordinances for his son in 1473 specified that he should have periods of exercise and recreation twice a day, after dinner and supper.[169] We know a little about the games that medieval children played. Gerald of Wales describes how he and his brothers used to play on the sands near Manorbier, their father's castle in Wales, in the 1150s. While his brothers erected towns and palaces, he built churches and monasteries which led his father, after much cogitation, to set him to study letters and prepare for an ecclesiastical life.[170] There is a good list of the quieter children's games in the fifteenth-century Scottish or northern-English poem, *Ratis Raving*.

---

[164] Chaucer, *Works*, p. 249 (I 670–3).
[165] *Vulgaria quedam abs Terencio traducta*, Oxford, 1483, f 3ᵛ.
[166] Myers, *Household of Edward IV*, p. 83.
[167] *A Fifteenth Century School Book*, ed. Nelson, p. 16; Orme in *Renaissance Quarterly*, xxxiv (1981), p. 33.
[168] *Politics*, book vii, chapter 17; *De Regimine Principum*, book ii, part ii, chapters 15–16 (ed. Molenaer, pp. 216–20).
[169] Orme in *BIHR*, lvii (1984).
[170] Gerald of Wales, *Autobiography*, trans. Butler, p. 35.

This tells how children then, like Gerald and his brothers, built houses out of sticks, containing hall, buttery and chamber like a real noble house. They would make a white horse from a peeled wand – presumably bestriding it like a hobby horse, a sailing ship from pieces of broken bread, a sword from a sedge, or a beautiful lady from a cloth adorned with flowers.[171] In the early sixteenth century Thomas More depicts the more violent games of a schoolboy: whipping the top, quoit throwing, and the hurling of a 'cockstele' in the cruel game of killing cocks and hens with weighted sticks.[172] As boys grew older, they were encouraged to imitate their elders in their games, and swords, bows and arrows were bought for their use. Play insensibly developed into formal physical exercises.[173]

CAREERS AND CONFLICTS

The planning of children's careers involved a third pair of contrasting principles: what may be called rigidity and flexibility. We have already seen how medieval kings conferred honours and offices on their sons at early ages, thereby proclaiming long before their sons grew up the roles they were to play in adult life. There are many other examples of parents planning the careers of their sons and daughters, when they were only a few years old and quite incapable of giving their consent. Such planning was a matter of prudence as well as of power. It was not simply that parents claimed the right to decide their children's futures, but advisable that this be done early on, lest the parents should die and the children be left unprovided for and at the mercy of others. Child marriage was a common institution among the medieval aristocracy. The Church, as has been mentioned, allowed the marriage of children from the age of 7, but in practice boys and girls were sometimes married when they were even yonger. Henry the Young King was betrothed to Margaret of France at the age of 3 and the marriage was ratified two years later. A marriage was proposed for King John when he was 4; the contract was signed a year later, and although this marriage came to nothing, he was again betrothed at the age of 9 to the girl whom he married properly when he reached adulthood. Records of child

[171] *Ratis Raving*, ed. R. Girvan, Edinburgh and London, Scottish Text Soc., 3rd series, xi (1939), pp. 32–3.
[172] *The English Works of Sir Thomas More*, ed. Campbell, i, f ciii.
[173] Discussed below, chapter six.

marriages among the gentry in the sixteenth century show that such unions were solemnized in church between partners of only a few years old. At one ceremony between a boy of 3 and a girl of 2, the parents spoke the words of consent themselves since the infant bride and groom could not do so in person.[174] Other children were committed at equally early ages to careers in the Church. In Anglo-Saxon and early Norman times young boys and girls were placed in religious houses in order that they should stay there all their lives as monks and nuns. Archbishop Lanfranc's constitutions for Canterbury Cathedral describe the bringing of such 'oblates' or boy-monks by their parents into the monastery church. The boy's hands were wrapped in the altar cloth as a sign of dedication, his parents promised that they would not cause him to forsake the monastic life, and the promise was written down and witnessed. Finally, the child exchanged his secular cloak for a monk's cowl, before being taken away to be shaved and clad in full monastic dress.[175] These practices fell out of use in the twelfth century as far as boys were concerned, but continued in the case of some girls. Edward I in 1283 promised the nuns of Fontevrault in France, a house long associated with the English royal family, that his 5-year-old daughter Mary should become a nun there, though in the outcome, two years later, she entered Amesbury Priory in Wiltshire instead and died there in her fifties.[176] After boys had ceased to be offered as oblates, it remained quite common among the aristocracy for them to be given secular ecclesiastical benefices: cathedral canonries and parish churches. Henry II's eldest and bastard son Geoffrey was given a canonry of St Paul's and the archdeaconry of Lincoln in about 1171, when he was probably in his late teens, and much earlier instances can be found in later centuries.[177] Thomas Courtenay, son of the earl of Devon, was only 9 in 1341 when he received a canonry of Crediton in Devon, and Robert Nevill, son of the earl of Westmorland, became a canon of Auckland in Durham at a similar age in 1413.[178] William Percy,

---

[174] *Child Marriages*, ed. Furnivall, p. 26.
[175] *The Monastic Constitutions of Lanfranc*, ed. D. Knowles, London, 1951, pp. 110–11, and below, p. 61.
[176] *Rôles Gascons*, ed. C. Bémont, vol ii, Paris, 1900, p. 178; *VCH Wiltshire*, iii, 247.
[177] J. Le Neve, *Fasti Ecclesiae Anglicanae, 1066–1300*, vol iii; *Lincoln*, ed. Diane E. Greenway, London, 1977, p. 25.
[178] *BRUO*, i, 502; ii, 1350.

whose father was earl of Northumberland, was a canon of York at the age of 8 in 1436.[179] These examples were rather unusual, but the conferring of benefices on 13- and 14-year-olds was quite common. Alexander Nevill, archbishop of York 1374–88, William Courtenay, archbishop of Canterbury 1381–96, and Lionel Wydeville, bishop of Salisbury 1482–4 are all examples of sons of peers who got their first preferment at about that age.[180]

At first sight the practices of child marriage and child entry into the Church, whatever the prudence involved, seem to entail the subjection of children to a system of planning intolerably rigid by modern standards. Closer inspection, however, reveals more flexibility. The canon law of the Church allowed the dissolution of child marriages up to the age of 12 for girls and 14 for boys, provided the marriage had not been consummated. The child holders of ecclesiastical benefices could not begin to take major holy orders involving celibacy until they were 17. Parents who arranged for their sons to hold such benefices probably thought of the latter as scholarships to fund their education as much as commitments to a clerical career. It was, of course, unwise for parents to plan their children's futures too rigidly too soon. A child might not develop any aptitude for the role in which it was cast, or might rebel against its destiny. Even if this were ignored, deaths among children frequently upset the plans which parents made for them and their surviving brothers and sisters. A second, third or even fourth son for whom a clerical career had been envisaged might come to be heir to the family property through the deaths of his elder brothers. Such an eventuality might happen at any stage of childhood or adolescence, and even in adulthood. It followed that parents were wise to keep open their options for as long as possible, and when they laid plans to arrange them in such a way that they could be altered. Child marriage and child entry into the Church were both provisional after the twelfth century, and changes could be made to them, at least up to the early teens.

In practice we find many examples of parents arranging their children's futures in a flexible way. When Richard FitzAlan earl of Arundel drew up his will in 1393, he expected his sons Thomas (aged 11) and Richard (a year or two older) to remain laymen and to

[179] *BRUC*, p. 450.
[180] *BRUO*, ii, 1346; i, 502–4; iii, 2083–4.

marry, but he also provided for one of the churches in his patronage to be held available in case either of them wished to enter the Church and to occupy it.[181] In 1415 Sir Walter Hungerford procured a papal dispensation for his son Walter, aged 8, to hold a benefice when he was 14, presumably with a clerical career in mind.[182] Yet Walter grew up as a soldier, and fought at the battle of Patay. So too Margaret Paston, when her fourth son Walter went to study at Oxford in his mid-teens in about 1473, counselled him not to be too hasty in taking holy orders that would bind him to celibacy. This could be done at 17, but she wished him to leave such a decision until later, for as she put it, 'often rape rueth': a hasty action is regretted. She would love him better, she said, as a good secular man than as a bad priest.[183] Nor did boys alone benefit from this flexibility. Examples occur of fathers and mothers faced with death when their girls were young making arrangements for them either to be married or to enter a nunnery. Sometimes the girl's consent was not thought necessary, and the alternative was to be chosen by her guardians. Sir John Daubriggecourt left forty marks in 1415 for his daughter Margery if she should marry, or £10 and an annuity 'if she were caused' to receive the veil and become a nun.[184] Lady Beatrix Constable, on the other hand, though she put her daughter Elizabeth into Watton Priory in Yorkshire at the age of 8 in 1505, gave orders that she was to choose her future herself when she was 12. If she were willing to become a nun, the nunnery authorities were to have money to pay for the cost of admitting her, but if she would not agree to this, she was to receive an annuity for two years and the sum of £20 towards her marriage.[185]

The need for flexibility in planning careers meant that noble education remained general rather than specialized in nature. As far as girls were concerned there was little difference between the knowledge and behaviour required of a nun and those of a secular lady, and there was consequently little need to shape their upbringing to either career in particular. The difference between a knight and a male cleric ought to have been greater, but here too specialization was unwise, at least until the mid or late teens, for the

[181] *Testamenta Vetusta*, ed. Nicolas, i, 131–2.
[182] *Calendar of Papal Letters*, vol vi: *1404–15*, p. 461.
[183] *Paston Letters*, ed. Davis, i, 370.
[184] A. Gibbons, *Early Lincoln Wills*, London, 1888, p. 177.
[185] *Testamenta Eboracensia*, ed. Raine, iv, 238.

reasons that have just been described. We need not imagine the eldest son of a nobleman or gentleman spending his childhood purely in riding and hunting, while his younger brother went to church or sat in school. What we know of the interests and accomplishments of adult noblemen, both laymen and ecclesiastics, rather suggests that they all studied a wide curriculum, at least up to their early teens, in which worship, study, etiquette and athletics all received attention. Gerald of Wales, though he was singled out for clerical training at an early age, confesses in his autobiography how he joined his brothers in playing at knights, to the detriment of his progress in learning. In later life, though a redoubtable scholar and ecclesiastic, he retained a deep interest in tournaments and military events, and once wrote 'would I were strong enough to despise all this as vanity'![186] Gilbert Marshal, the third son of the great William Marshal, born in about 1200, was intended to enter the Church and held benefices, but at a late age in 1234 he inherited the earldom of Pembroke, married and took up the life of a knight. Though reckoned to be weak and unskilful in warlike exercises because of his clerical past, he did well at a tilting-match at Hereford in 1241, and was agreed to have shown both skill and valour.[187] It hardly looks as though his earlier life had been an unathletic one, entirely removed from contact with horses and arms.

The adult cleric who wore secular dress, rode great horses, had women and went to war is a frequent figure in the pages of bishops' registers and anticlerical writings, and seems to have been only too common. Henry Burghersh, third son of a baron, who became bishop of Lincoln at the age of 28 in 1320, was sarcastically described by the chronicler Robert of Reading as 'a notable jouster with a tilting shield'.[188] Another baronial bishop, Henry Despenser of Norwich (1370–1406), was said to have fought in Italy during his youth and certainly led a military expedition to Flanders as bishop in 1383.[189] We might think that such secular habits in adult life were the mark of unusually corrupt or ill-suited ecclesiastics, but we

[186] Gerald of Wales, *Autobiography*, trans. Butler, p. 36; Bartlett, *Gerald of Wales*, pp. 27–8.
[187] Cockayne, *Complete Peerage*, x, 371–4; Paris, *Chronica Majora*, ed. Luard, iv, 135.
[188] *Flores Historiarum*, ed. H.R. Luard, vol iii, RS, 1890, p. 192.
[189] *BRUO*, iii, 2169–70; John Capgrave, *The Chronicle of England*, ed. F.C. Hingeston, RS, 1858, p. 226.

should have to include most of the clergy in that category if we thought so. Archbishop Thomas Cranmer, born in 1489, was not a warrior, but he was an active and strenuous athlete.

> And albeit his father was very desirous to have him learned, yet would he not that he should be ignorant in civil and gentleman-like exercises, insomuch that he used him to shoot and many times permitted him to hunt and hawk and to exercise and to ride rough horses. So that now being archbishop, he feared not to ride the roughest horse that came into his stable.... And when time served for recreation after study, he would both hawk and hunt ... and would sometime shoot in the long-bow.[190]

So too John Major, describing the students of Oxford and Cambridge in the early sixteenth century, most of whom were still intended to become ecclesiastics, said 'they are all of them no longer boys; they carry swords and bows'![191] The secularity of the aristocratic clergy and its counterpart, the religious devotion and bookishness of the lay aristocracy, reflect a wide curriculum in youth, the result of necessary flexibility about pupils' adult careers. It was not only evil nature which caused the secularity of so many clergy, as their opponents asserted, but the fact that there was so little specialized clerical education. Childhoods spent in largely lay surroundings, following lay pursuits, instilled lay habits which those concerned found hard to shake off when they took up clerical careers in later life.

The co-existence of several contrasting policies in the education of aristocratic children shows that the process was a complex one, not easily to be summarized in a simple formula. Within the extremes of policy which we have described, there may have been much variation in practice from one noble family to another. It follows that the relationships between parents and their children may also have varied widely, between the poles of harmony and discord. Such personal relationships are especially hard to recon-struct, since they have generally been preserved only in the

[190] J.G. Nichols, *Narratives of the Days of the Reformation*, London, Camden Soc., lxxvii (1859), pp. 238–40.
[191] John Major, *A History of Greater Britain*, ed. A. Constable, Edinburgh, Scottish Text Soc., x (1892), pp. 26–7.

conventional forms of literature and documents, behind which personal emotions can rarely be discerned. Many noble parents apparently took an interest in and trouble over the bringing up of their offspring. The employment of nurses, masters and mistresses to look after them cannot have been a mere shifting of responsibility, nor can the sending of children away from home to other households, schools and universities which we shall deal with next. The purchase of medicine and the hiring of doctors betokens an anxiety that children should survive and grow up to play the roles in life that their parents planned for them. Letters like those of the Pastons show a concern by parents for the welfare of their children: that they should work hard, gain influential patrons, marry well and keep up their status.[192] The love of children for their parents and guardians is harder to establish, for children have left few records of their feelings. One adult writer, however, tells how the 14-year-old Edward I stood on the shore at Portsmouth in 1253 when his father departed for Gascony, and wept until the fleet had borne him out of sight.[193] Another in 1500 imagined a child coming home to his parents from boarding school and the parties weeping for joy, for, says the author, mothers and fathers are as comforted by seeing their child as a sick man by kind words from a physician.[194] When founding a chantry it was usual to include prayers for the health of one's parents' souls as well as one's own; parental names were sometimes re-used for one's own children, and the English kings, as we have seen, rewarded their nurses and other servants who had helped to bring them up. These actions can hardly have been entirely conventional.

We know more certainly that family ties came under strain as children entered adolescence, for the strains have left more traces. The recalcitrance of teenage sons and daughters is a common theme in literature. Chaucer's Franklin tells how he chid his son for playing dice and preferring the company of servants to that of gentlemen.[195] The pseudo-Chaucerian 'Tale of Beryn' describes how its noble hero diced in his youth while his mother lay dying, and struck the girl who came to call him home.[196] There are real

[192] E.g. *Paston Letters*, ed. Davis, i, 27, 42, 199–200, 234, 370.
[193] Paris, *Chronica Majora*, ed. Luard, v, 383.
[194] *A Fifteenth Century School Book*, ed. Nelson, p. 15.
[195] Chaucer, *Works*, ed. Robinson, p. 135 (F 682–94).
[196] *The Tale of Beryn*, ed. F.J. Furnivall & W.G. Stone, EETS, es, cv (1887), pp. 29–33.

examples of bad behaviour by noble boys, and mutiny by them against the rule of parents and guardians. Edward I is best remembered as a crusader, warrior and parliamentarian. In 1256, however, when he was 17, the boy who had cried for his father travelled about the Thames valley with a disorderly retinue, seizing the horses, carts and provisions of other people for his own use. As he was passing through one peaceful area, his servants seized a young man – it is not clear why – cut off his ear and blinded him in one eye at Edward's order and without any serious pretext or rule of law. Those who heard about it, noted Matthew Paris, recalled a bloody injury that he had done to another nobleman when he was younger, and people began to despair of his future, since they said 'if this occurs when the tree is green, what can be hoped for when it is old and dying'?[197] When Henry VI was 11, he was already beginning to 'grudge' and 'loathe' the discipline enforced on him, so much that the earl of Warwick felt it wise to report the fact to the privy council and get its declared support, in case he should incur the king's displeasure in the future.[198] Edward V is most familiar as the hapless child victim of Richard III. Yet even in his case, when the ordinances for his education were revised in 1483 (he was then 13), a new clause was put in to specify that he should keep the code. He was forbidden to do anything against the advice of his council, and if its members were aware of any 'unprincely demeaning' on his part, they were to tell the king or queen at once on pain of deep displeasure.[199] It looks as though trouble was anticipated even from Edward, or at least required to be borne in mind. Medieval English history has its quota of unruly princes. The sons of Henry II and subsequently Edward II and Henry V all had notably bad relations with their fathers, but some of them went on in due course to be successful adult rulers. Clearly, education did not wholly override character, and character in the stormy years of adolescence was by no means mature, or typical of what it would become in later life.

---

[197] Paris, *Chronica Majora*, ed. Luard, v, 593–4, 598.
[198] *Proceedings of the Privy Council*, ed. Nicolas, iv, 134.
[199] Orme in *BIHR*, lvii (1984).

Two Away from the family

LEAVING HOME

In 1416–17 the children of Michael de la Pole, the earl of Suffolk who was killed by dysentery at the siege of Harfleur, were all away from their Suffolk home at Wingfield. William the eldest was a ward of the king, and about to attain his majority. Thomas was at Oxford with a clerical tutor, studying for a career in the Church, his thoughtful mother sending him money for clothes, a purse of 3s 4d for his small expenses and a gift of 20s for the tutor. Alexander was a boarder with the town schoolmaster of Ipswich. Men of the de la Pole household rode with him there in September 1416 and brought him back again in July for the summer holidays. In the meantime he stayed at Ipswich, and bills were paid for his clothes, shoes, board, school-fees and candles for use in class. Philippa was at Bungay Priory, a local nunnery, and payments were directed to the prioress for her clothes and her board and that of the gentlewoman who attended her. She came home for a fortnight at Christmas in 1416, escorted by retainers either way, but spent the whole of the summer in the nunnery.[1] Such evidence reminds us that the bringing up of noble boys and girls was not confined, as we have hitherto confined

---

[1] BL, Egerton Roll 8776, m 5, first brought to notice by McFarlane, *Nobility of Later Medieval England*, p. 245.

it, to the households of their own parents. Children were also sent away from home to be educated, and often so. Many spent long years of their childhood in other institutions, under the care and control of other people.

A custom that boys should leave their families to learn and be trained elsewhere can be traced back to very early times. The hero of *Beowulf*, written down in the mid-eighth century, recalls how he went from his father's house at the age of 7 to live with his mother's father, Hrethel king of the Geats, who fostered him and gave him food and treasure.[2] His counterpart Cuchulainn in the *Tain Bo Cuailgne*, the ancient Irish epic preserved in texts of the twelfth century but much older, travelled from Ireland to Britain when he was young to learn athletic feats and military skills.[3] The Tristan stories of the twelfth century also describe the journeys of a boy prince and his tutor from Britain to France in search of learning and accomplishments abroad.[4] In the period with which we are dealing, from 1066 to 1530, such goings away became very common, not only by boys as in heroic times but by their sisters too. The process could begin at any age. Even an infant could be left with relatives or in a religious house, if its parents wished to move on quickly elsewhere. Henry II's daughter Joan and her younger brother John were both deposited at Fontevrault Abbey during their tender age in the late 1160s.[5] John of Gaunt's son Henry (IV) was sent to stay with his great-aunt Lady Wake in 1369 at the age of 3,[6] and his sister Katherine can only have been about 7 in 1380 when she went to live with Lady Mohun at Dunster Castle in Somerset.[7] Other children left home when they were older. If it were wished to 'finish' the education of a son or daughter by sending them to another noble household, to a school or university, or later on to the inns of court in London, this was more appropriate to adolescence, after basic training had been done at home. We shall encounter plenty of examples of such practices in the following pages.

[2] *Beowulf*, lines 2428–31.
[3] *The Tain*, trans. Kinsella, pp. 28–31.
[4] Thomas, *Le Roman de Tristan*, ed. Bédier, ii, 194–6; *Le Roman de Tristan en Prose*, ed. Curtis, i, 135–8.
[5] Green, *Lives of the Princesses*, i, 309; A. Richard, *Histoire des Comtes de Poitou, 778–1204*, 2 vols, Paris, 1903, ii, 375.
[6] PRO, DL 29/262/4069.
[7] *John of Gaunt's Register, 1379–83*, ed. Lodge and Somerville, i, 106–7, ii, 259.

But not all medieval education was planned. Like aristocratic life as a whole, it was a mixture of design and accident. Just as a noble father could experience sudden and violent changes of fortune through capture in war or political downfall, so too the education of his sons and daughters could be disrupted by adventitious factors, thereby resembling adult life as in so many other ways. Even in Anglo–Saxon times it was possible for a child to lose its parents through death, and pass into the care of relatives or some superior lord. With the coming of the Normans in 1066 this possibility was extended and regularized through the introduction of the Norman system of wardship. Wardship arose when a member of the aristocracy who held his land by feudal tenure died while his eldest son, or his daughter if he had no son, was under the age of majority. The care of his land and children immediately returned to the hands of his superior feudal lord, who might be variously an abbey, a bishop, a lay magnate or the king. The children were taken away from their own family and brought up by the lord, who was free to grant or sell their custody to someone else, in which case they were brought up by that person. Wardship endured until the eldest son attained the age of 21 or until the daughter was married, the marriage lying also in the power of the custodian. The institution led to the movement of thousands of children from their own to other households throughout the Middle Ages and the Renaissance, for it was not abolished until the Civil War of the 1640s.

The effects of wardship were increased by political upheavals. A father's exile or imprisonment led more than once to the taking of his children into the king's hands for reasons of security or simply out of charity. In 1307 Edward I commanded the sheriff of York to pay 3*d* a day for the upkeep of Marjorie Bruce, the daughter of his Scottish enemy, who was staying in the nunnery of Watton near Beverley.[8] When Roger Mortimer was in prison in 1324, his daughters were despatched by Edward II to three East Anglian nunneries and allocated money for their board and one new gown each year.[9] The Wars of the Roses in the fifteenth century disturbed the educations of several young men for longer or shorter periods. The death of Richard duke of York in 1460 forced Richard and George, his younger sons aged 8 and 11 respectively, to flee to Utrecht until the

[8]   *CPR 1301–7*, p. 503.
[9]   *CCR 1323–7*, pp. 88–9.

victory of their brother Edward IV in March 1461 allowed them to come back. That victory in turn obliged their enemy Edward, the 7-year-old Lancastrian prince of Wales, to go into exile first in Scotland and later in France, where he spent most of the rest of his short life. When the wars broke out again in 1470–1, the future Henry VII passed first from the wardship of the earl of Pembroke into the care of his uncle, Jasper Tudor, and then into a long residence in France which lasted for most of his adolescence. In measuring these misfortunes it must not be forgotten that the education of all medieval children was liable to disturbance through deaths of parents, shortage of money, lack of schoolmasters and the closure of schools through plague. The special troubles of the aristocracy would have seemed less startling and less to be pitied in the Middle Ages than they do today.

The motives of those who sent their children away from home were probably as varied as modern ones. Parental convenience must have been a factor. When the Venetian traveller who wrote the well-known account or 'Relation' of England in about 1500 examined what was to him the unusual custom of putting children 'to hard service in the houses of other people', he concluded, 'I for my part believe that they do it because they like to enjoy all their comforts themselves, and that they are better served by strangers than they would be by their own children.'[10] In other words, the sons and daughters of one's neighbours were more biddable and hard-working than one's own. Those who defended the system, however, argued that it benefited the children. A tradition of writing as old as the thirteenth century asserted that wealthy parents overindulged their offspring, and pointed to the fate of Eli and his sons in the First Book of Samuel as God's punishment on a lax father and his two spoilt children.[11] 'All the richest men's children everywhere', wrote an Oxford educationist in about 1500, 'be lost nowadays in their youth at home, and that with their fathers and mothers.' Mothers, he complained, played with their children as if they were dolls, and parents laughed when their offspring called them 'whore' and 'cuckold'. He painted a lurid picture of the outcome: naughty

[10] *A Relation of England*, ed. Sneyd, pp. 24–5.
[11] Legge, *Anglo-Norman Literature*, pp. 213–14; *Robert of Brunne's "Handlyng Synne"*, ed. F.J. Furnivall, part i, EETS, os, cxix–cxxiii (1901–3), pp. 161–6; Langland, *Piers Plowman*, A, v, 32–3; B, v, 34–5; C, i, 104–15; vi, 137–8.

children grew up into criminals, some were hanged and some beheaded, and they died cursing their parents for having misruled them in their youth.[12] Sending one's children away was therefore seen as putting them into more disinterested hands and leading them into a better way of life. Sir John Fortescue, in his treatise on English law of the 1460s, applauded the system of wardship on the grounds that it took boys from smaller households to larger ones, and from relatives of comparatively rustic behaviour to lords of higher rank who would better ensure the teaching of manners and military skills.[13] The Venetian author, when he asked why people sent their children away, says 'they answered that they did it in order that their children might learn better manners'.[14] Clearly, there were many advantages in children leaving home, and not only ethical ones. The training of a boy as a cleric or a lawyer was best done in a religious community, a school, a university, or an inn of court. If he wanted to pursue a career in a household or go to war, or if a girl were to be married, the necessary patronage and contacts often stood to be better gained by going away into the service of a great magnate or his wife than by staying at home with all its limitations.

THE ROYAL HOUSEHOLD

Fortescue, in his account of wardship, had no doubt that the best of all households in which a young man could be educated was that of the king.[15] In the first place, he says, the household of the king is noted for its magnificence and grandeur – a judgment that need not be questioned. It was always the largest English household in the number of its staff, and grew in size throughout the Middle Ages. Contemporary estimates put its permanent strength at about 200 in 1136, 300 or more in 1318, and about 600 in the 1450s, excluding casual visitors.[16] Its personnel included more men of high rank than elsewhere, visitors from a wider range of places, and practitioners of

---

[12] *A Fifteenth Century School Book*, ed. Nelson, pp. 13–14.
[13] Fortescue, *De Laudibus Legum Anglie*, ed. Chrimes, pp. 108–11.
[14] *A Relation of England*, ed. Sneyd, pp. 24–5.
[15] Fortescue, *De Laudibus Legum Anglie*, ed. Chrimes, pp. 110–11.
[16] For 1136, see FitzNigel, *Course of the Exchequer*, ed. Johnson, pp. 128–35; for 1318, T.F. Tout, *The Place of the Reign of Edward II in English History*, Manchester 1914, pp. 244–72; and for 1471–3, Myers, *Household of Edward IV*, p. 9.

more varied cultural pursuits: clergy, musicians, physicians and teachers. Secondly, Fortescue noticed and paid tribute to its educational function. 'It is', he averred, 'the supreme academy for the nobles of the realm, and a school of physical activity [*strenuitas*], behaviour [*probitas*] and manners [*mores*], by which the realm gains honour, flourishes and is secured against invaders'.[17] The tone is idealistic, but the substance is correct.

The royal household had long been a place for the training of youths, and not simply of noble ones. Besides the aristocracy, each of its departments came during the later Middle Ages to employ and train young men, who finally totalled a tenth or more of the whole personnel of the household. By the early fourteenth century there were already children of the royal chapel who were thought of as undergoing education, since Edward II in 1317 began the establishment of King's Hall at Cambridge so that they could continue their studies there when their chapel service was over.[18] There were boys in some other household departments too, at least unofficially, since the household ordinances of 1318 forbade them to be there except in the kitchen, where the grooms were allowed to employ one boy between two of them.[19] References to the lost household ordinances of Edward III, which occur in later documents, show that during his reign pages began to be allowed in the two wardrobe departments of the household and the chamber,[20] and by the middle of the fifteenth century boys were officially tolerated in nearly every other department. In 1445 there were at least sixty-two, including eight noble boys attending the king and queen, seven choristers in the chapel, and forty-seven in the other departments: hall, cellar, kitchen, scullery and so on.[21] In 1454 the household was reduced in size for reasons of economy and the number of boys fell to forty-four,[22] but it rose again under Edward IV, and the 'Black Book' of 1471-3 which gives an incomplete description of the household suggests that the likely total of boys was then in the fifties.[23] Like Fortescue, the author of the 'Black Book' was conscious of the

---

[17] Fortescue, *De Laudibus Legum Anglie*, ed. Chrimes, pp. 110–11.
[18] A.B. Cobban, *The King's Hall . . . Cambridge in the Later Middle Ages* Cambridge, 1969, p. 9.
[19] Tout, *Place of the Reign of Edward II*, p. 308.
[20] Myers, *Household of Edward IV*, p. 121, which qualifies the statement on p. 118.
[21] ibid., pp. 70–4.
[22] *Proceedings of the Privy Council*, ed. Nicolas, vi, 220–33.
[23] Myers, *Household of Edward IV*, pp. 118–95, *passim*.

household as an educational institution. Not only does he describe the training of noble youths and the choristers of the chapel, but he says that the sergeants or heads of departments were allowed 'to draw forth' servant boys 'to cunning' (in other words to give training), and to choose and take in 'young apt persons to learn to serve'.[24] He is one of the earliest writers to note, as a modern observer would do, that the employment of young people in a working institution can be educational. If we consider education in its widest sense as including training for an occupation, the royal household is seen to have been deeply concerned with it in all its departments by the fifteenth century, though as in all households this education was only one activity which went on and was by no means the main one.

The recorded history of aristocratic boys in the royal household goes back much further than that of servant boys, for it is mentioned in Saxon times. Asser relates that King Alfred maintained children of noble and ignoble birth in his household, that he spent a quarter of his income on them, and that he arranged for their training in letters and good manners.[25] The introduction of wardship under the Normans meant that noble boys came regularly to be brought up in the king's household or those of the queen and the royal children. When Waleran count of Meulan, one of the trusted counsellors of Henry I, died in 1118, the king, who had been closely attached to him, brought up his sons Waleran and Robert 'as affectionately as his own children', and 'girded them with the arms of knighthood' when they reached adolescence.[26] Historically, the number of wards in royal households must have fluctuated. As we have seen, when the eldest son of the king was young it was felt desirable to keep the high-ranking wards together to be his companions,[27] but at other times wardships were sold or granted away and the children were brought up elsewhere by the grantees. The order of the privy council in 1425 that all the royal wards of the rank of baron and above should stay with the young king Henry VI in his household suggests that their keeping had hitherto become dispersed into other places.[28] The tendency to make ad hoc arrangements for royal wards

---

[24] ibid., p. 118.
[25] Asser, *Life of King Alfred*, ed. Stevenson, pp. 60, 88–9.
[26] Orderic, *Ecclesiastical History*, ed. Chibnall, vi, 328–9.
[27] Above, pp. 28–30.
[28] *Proceedings of the Privy Council*, ed. Nicolas, iii, 170.

and the wide disparities between their ranks and ages hampered their growth as an organized group in the royal household. In the household ordinances of 1318, in which they are first mentioned, it is only said of them that they must be given wages, liveries and necessaries 'according to their estate and at the advice and discretion of the steward and treasurer'.[29] The 'Black Book' of 1471-3, which is elaborate in its descriptions of other household institutions, simply repeats this clause without embellishment.[30] The wards of the royal household consequently failed to develop as an institution, and their history is little more than the sequence of their names and dates.

In other respects, however, the education of the aristocracy in the royal household certainly developed institutionally as the Middle Ages wore on. First, there emerged a second group of educable boys with a more regular status than that of the wards: the henchmen. The word 'henchman' in the later Middle Ages meant a servant, usually someone of high rank with ceremonial rather than menial duties.[31] The king, the queen, members of the nobility and the lord mayor of London are all known to have employed henchmen, either on single occasions or on a long-term basis. In the royal household, 'henchmen of the king' are first mentioned in records in 1345-9, and by 1368 there seem to have been two of them permanently.[32] By 1445 their number had risen to eight: six for the king and two for the queen,[33] and although in 1454 those of the king were reduced to three,[34] the number of six was re-established by 1471-3, or more if he pleased.[35] Later, in about 1480, we hear of a henchman of the prince of Wales (Edward V) which suggests a similar group in his own household.[36] In 1471-3 the henchmen of the king clearly held their posts for long periods. They were noble youths who might be wards or not. Each had at least one servant to attend him, and more if his rank so required. Their names have not been systematically

[29] Tout, *Place of the Reign of Edward II*, p. 280.
[30] Myers, *Household of Edward IV*, p. 141.
[31] For early usages, see *Middle English Dictionary*, ed. Kurath and Kuhn, sub 'hengest-man'.
[32] N.H. Nicolas, 'Observations on the Institution of the Most Noble Order of the Garter', *Archaeologia*, xxxi (1846), p. 92; PRO, E 101/395/10.
[33] Myers, *Household of Edward IV*, pp. 71-2.
[34] *Proceedings of the Privy Council*, ed. Nicolas, vi, 223.
[35] Myers, *Household of Edward IV*, p. 126.
[36] Below, note 37.

recorded, but what we know of them shows that they came both from the higher or peerage nobility and from the lower or knighthood. Edward Audley (d. about 1478), henchman to the prince of Wales, was the son of a peer,[37] and so were Henry Lord Morley and Thomas Dacre, henchmen to Edward IV in 1483.[38] Thomas Howard, who served Edward in the same capacity, and Robert Knolles and Peter Carew, henchmen respectively of Henry VII and Henry VIII, were the sons of knights.[39] The institution thus developed continued well into the sixteenth century until Elizabeth I, to the surprise of some of her court, disbanded it.[40] Up to that time it was evidently a matter of distinction to be a henchman, since at least three holders of the office: Audley, Howard and Richard Lord Grey of Wilton (d. 1518) had the distinction recorded on their tombs.[41]

The emergence of the henchmen was accompanied by the appearance of permanent masters to teach them. No doubt there were teachers of a sort in the household from early times. Wards had their own knightly masters, and possibly chaplains or clerks to teach them grammar.[42] The children of the chapel must also have had an instructor in song by at least the early fourteenth century, and in 1401 a man named John Bugby is recorded teaching them grammar with a regular salary of £5 a year.[43] The first clear mentions of permanent masters with the professional title of 'schoolmaster' or 'grammar master', however, come in the mid-fifteenth century, as

[37] He was described on his memorial brass, formerly at Eton, as the prince's *cyronomon* (Bodleian Library, MS Ashmole 1137, f. 152ᵛ). *Cyronomon* (correctly *chironomon*, one who moves his hands) is best explained as an attempt to Latinize 'henchman' (often spelt and pronounced 'hansman' at that time).

[38] Nichols, *Edward the Sixth*, i, p. lxxv.

[39] For Howard, see J. Weever, *Ancient Funeral Monuments*, London, 1631, p. 834, or London, 1767, p. 554; for Knolles, see *Materials for the Reign of Henry VII*, ed. Campbell, ii, 383–4; and for Carew, Hooker, *The Life of Sir Peter Carew*, ed. Maclean, p. 13.

[40] E. Lodge, *Illustrations of British History*, 2nd edn, 3 vols, London, 1838, i, 438. On the henchmen in the sixteenth century, see Nichols, *Edward the Sixth*, i, pp. lxxv–vi.

[41] For Audley and Howard, see above, notes 37 and 39, and for Grey, T.W. King, 'Observations on the . . . Inscription to . . . Lord Grey de Wilton', *Archaeologia*, xxxii (1847), pp. 58–9.

[42] Thus four noble wards each with a master occur in the royal household in 1325 (PRO, E 101/381/11 no 42).

[43] Wylie, *England under Henry the Fourth*, ii, 487; iv, 208.

they do in the case of princes' education. The *Liber Regie Capelle*, which describes the working of the chapel in about 1449, talks of the grammar master as a regular officer attached to the chapel, teaching not only the children there but 'the noble boys being brought up in the court of the king' – in other words the wards and henchmen.[44] At about the same time a second permanent office developed, that of the master of the henchmen, to deal with their general non-scholastic education in the tradition of the old knightly masters. The 'Black Book' of 1471–3, which gives us our fullest information about the teaching in the household, relates that the master of the henchman was a squire of the household, and therefore of gentle rank.[45] He had to see that the henchmen attended divine service each day and to teach them a wide variety of things: 'sundry languages' (presumably French), music and dancing, etiquette and good manners, and military skills (riding, jousting and how to wear armour). The only subject that he did not teach was grammar, for which the henchmen went to the grammar master.[46] From this time onwards the offices of master of the henchmen and grammar master can be traced until the middle of the sixteenth century, the former including some well-respected squires and knights and the latter, from at least the 1520s, a series of university graduates.[47] One of the grammar masters, Robert Whittinton, was the author of an important grammar book for schools. In this way the royal household developed permanent, professional teachers for its noble boys, and there is every reason to think that a high standard of teaching was available for most of the Yorkist and Tudor periods.

A distinction should be made between the household, a permanent body of staff, and the king's court, which included those who came on visits for political or social purposes. Attendance at court as a visitor could also be educative for a young man who was not able to become a permanent member of the household. Even an onlooker with no household status had the opportunity to absorb court life and courtly fashions of speech, dress and behaviour. The sending of boys to court in the mid-fourteenth century was attacked by the Dominican friar, John Bromyard, on the grounds that the education

[44] *Liber Regie Capelle*, ed. Ullmann, p. 57.
[45] Myers, *Household of Edward IV*, pp. 126–7.
[46] ibid., pp. 137–8.
[47] Orme, *English Schools in the Middle Ages*, pp. 218–19.

that they got there was of little benefit to their souls. Rather, he said, they learnt oaths, follies, bad manners and how to keep dissolute company.[48] In 1461 John Paston I sent his eldest son John II to court, in the hope that he might gain a permanent post in the household. The youth made very slow progress. His uncle Clement wrote on 25 August that he had not yet been accepted as a member of the household and was not entitled to meals. The trouble was that 'he is not acquainted with nobody but with Wekys, and Wekys had told him that he would bring him to the king, but he hath not yet done so'. Clement's first reaction was that John should be brought home, 'till ye had spoke with somebody to help him forth, for he is not bold enough to put forth himself'. On second thoughts he felt that John should stay, lest he lose face and favour by withdrawing, and suggested that his father should send him another £5 to support him.[49] The advice bore fruit, and by the following March John II was travelling with the king and asking for yet more money to pay his expenses.[50] In the early sixteenth century the attack on the sending of boys to court was renewed by the satirist Alexander Barclay:

> Of great estates there is a blinded sorte
> Which cause their sonnes unto the court resorte,
> That they may in court themselfe dayly frequent
> In learning vertue and maners excellent,
> But better might they say to learne all malice.

Like Bromyard he sees them instead becoming proud, disdainful, envious and ribald. One man boasts of gluttony, another of seducing a virgin, a third of slaying a foe:

> Nor thinke not in court to find a yonge stripling
> Chast, sober, shamefast or maners ensuing;
> All sueth vices, all sue enormitie.[51]

The writings of Bromyard and Barclay, of course, are evidence for their authors' own views, not for the state of the institution they were attacking. They are interesting, none the less, as contrasts to the favourable picture of the royal household given by Fortescue

[48] Owst, *Literature and Pulpit*, p. 466.
[49] *Paston Letters*, ed. Davis, i, 199–200.
[50] ibid., pp. 205, 392.
[51] *The Eclogues of Alexander Barclay*, ed. Beatrice White, EETS, os, clxxv (1928), pp. 128–30.

and the author of the 'Black Book', and remind us that education was not always for the better. Given the failings of human nature, some noblemen were bound to pick up vices at court, just as others would return from court more courteous than when they had gone there.

ARISTOCRATIC HOUSEHOLDS

For those who did not have the wealth or importance to gain admission to the royal household or the court, there were plenty of similar opportunities for education in the households of the great lay aristocracy: magnates, peers and important knights. Though we cannot be sure that every such household received children to be educated, many undoubtedly did so, what with the lord's relatives, his wards, and others who were sent or came to serve him at their own expense. Some of the most famous English boys of the Middle Ages were educated in this way. The young Henry of Anjou (Henry II) was partly brought up at Bristol Castle in the household of his uncle, Robert earl of Gloucester, in about 1142–7 when he was between 9 and 14.[52] His loyal and trusty warrior, William Marshal, was likewise trained as a squire in the 1160s in the household of his father's cousin, William lord of Tancarville in Normandy.[53] A little later the satirist Walter Map tells us of one of his relatives, a boy of good qualities, who crossed the Channel in his late teens to offer himself to Philip count of Flanders, 'to learn of him the art of chivalry'.[54] Similar practices persisted during the later Middle Ages. Chaucer himself served in the household of the countess of Ulster in 1357, when he was aged between 12 and 17, no doubt despatched there by his merchant father to acquire aristocratic status and connections, as in due course he certainly did.[55] Henry duke of Lancaster (d. 1361) was thought a century later to have taken in young knights from as far away as France and Spain 'to be doctrined, learned and brought up in his noble court in school of arms and for to see noblesse, courtesy and worship',[56] and the French poetess Christine of Pisa certainly sent her 13-year-old son

---

[52] Gervase of Canterbury, *Historical Works*, ed. W. Stubbs, vol i, RS, 1879, p. 125; *Materials for the History of Thomas Becket*, ed. Robertson, iii, 104.
[53] *L'Histoire de Guillaume le Maréchal*, ed. Meyer, i, 28.
[54] Map, *De Nugis Curialium*, trans. James, pp. 155–6.
[55] M.M. Crow and C.C. Olson, *Chaucer Life Records*, Oxford, 1966, pp. 13–18.
[56] Worcester, *The Boke of Noblesse*, ed. Nichols, p. 77.

Jean to England in 1397 to become page to John Montagu earl of Salisbury.[57] When Sir John Pikington planned the education of his son in 1478, he commended him to two of the most powerful lay magnates in England at that time: the duke of Gloucester (Richard III) and the lord chamberlain (Lord Hastings), with the request that the boy might stay in Hastings's household until he was 16.[58] A safe and sensible plan – with anyone other than Richard III. Five years later Richard murdered Hastings, and if Pilkington's son was still in the victim's service, he must have experienced the political disruption which upset the educations of other, nobler boys in the course of the Wars of the Roses.

Equally popular was the sending of boys to the households of bishops and other great ecclesiastics. They too were aristocratic in status, if not in birth; they were almost equally involved in the affairs of the world, and with their trains of knights, squires and menial servants, they led a life-style similar in many ways to that of the lay nobility. Thomas Becket, for example, while archdeacon of Canterbury and a cleric, was also chancellor of the king and a rich potential source of patronage for secular boys. Henry II sent his own eldest son, the Young King, to be brought up in Becket's household in the 1160s, along with masters, servants and boy companions, and we are told that other magnates entrusted their children to him too, 'whom he educated in gentlemanly upbringing and teaching. When they had been given the belt of knighthood, he sent some back to their fathers and families with honour and kept others with him.'[59] The pattern of a great cleric presiding over noble children, deputing their day-to-day teaching to subordinate masters and giving them a good enough secular education to be knighted, was often repeated down to the Reformation. A generation after Becket, William Longchamp bishop of Ely and chancellor of Richard I, so overawed the noble youths residing in his household that they did not dare look up unless he called them, and if their attention wandered elsewhere William (whose grandfather had driven oxen at the plough) would prick them with a goad kept handy for the purpose.[60] Robert Grosseteste, bishop of Lincoln (d. 1253) had such a

[57] Christine de Pisan, *Oeuvres Poétiques*, ed. M. Roy, 2 vols, Paris, 1886–96, i, 232–3.
[58] *Testamenta Eboracensia*, ed. Raine, iii, 238–40.
[59] *Materials for the History of Thomas Becket*, ed. Robertson, iii, 22.
[60] Roger of Howden, *Chronica*, ed. W. Stubbs, vol iii, RS, 1870, p. 142.

reputation as a master of learning and courtesy that he too attracted noble boys to be educated in his household, notably Henry de Montfort, Simon's son, who became a warrior like his father.[61] In the fifteenth century Cardinal Beaufort appears to have taken in boys, since James Lord Berkeley sent him his 13-year-old son and heir to stay in his household in 1439,[62] and Cardinal Wolsey certainly did so. His household in the 1520s contained nine or ten young lords with an instructor to teach them, including the teenaged earl of Derby, Edward Stanley, who had five servants to attend him, and the young adult Henry Percy, son and heir of the earl of Northumberland.[63] It mattered little that some of these figures – Longchamp, Grosseteste and Wolsey – were men of humble birth. They were men of power, whose high standing with the monarch impelled other men to keep well in with them, and the sending of a son to their household may have been one means of doing so. Equally, with their patronage and connections, they were in a good position to forward the careers of young men who came to serve them and who acquired their favourable notice.

The institutional history of boys' education in aristocratic households parallels that of the royal household. During the fifteenth century permanent groups of youths were established and professional schoolmasters were retained to teach them. There were henchmen in the retinues of the secular aristocracy by the end of the fourteenth century (Henry earl of Derby had two or three in his service in 1388),[64] and by the second half of the fifteenth they were acquiring the same educational character as those of the king. George duke of Clarence had five henchmen in his household in 1468, with a squire 'to be master of them and to see their rule' exactly like that of his brother Edward IV.[65] The earl of Northumberland maintained three henchmen in 1512, besides two other 'young gentlemen at their friends' finding', and a grammar master to teach

[61] William Lyndwood, *Provinciale*, Oxford, 1679, ii, 122; *Monumenta Franciscana*, ed. J.S. Brewer, RS, 1858, pp. 110, 129, 163; R.W. Hunt, 'Verses on the Life of Robert Grosseteste', *Medievalia et Humanistica*, new series, i (1970), pp. 242, 248.

[62] J. Smyth, *The Lives of the Berkeleys*, ed. J. Maclean, 3 vols, Gloucester, 1883, ii, 100.

[63] George Cavendish, *The Life and Death of Cardinal Wolsey*, ed. R.S. Sylvester, EETS, os, ccxliii (1959), pp. 18–21, 29–30.

[64] PRO, DL 28/1/2 ff 16, 26ᵛ.

[65] *A Collection of Ordinances*, pp. 98–9.

them.[66] Edward Stafford duke of Buckingham also had henchmen, wards and a grammar master in 1521, though we do not know their numbers.[67] Sir Thomas Lovell, knight of the garter, presided over the education of several noble youths in his house at Enfield. When he died in 1524 two henchmen rode in the chariot bearing his body and nine young gentlemen were given funeral clothes, along with their yeoman 'keeper' and their writing master.[68] The specific mentions of grammar masters show that full-time teachers were taking the place of part-time clerics. Some of them were university graduates. One, Maurice Westbury, was engaged in 1494 by Lady Margaret Beaufort 'to apply him to the erudition and doctrine of certain young gentlemen at our finding'.[69] Another, John Holt, worked for Cardinal Morton as schoolmaster of his household at Lambeth Palace in the 1490s, the household in which the young Thomas More was brought up. It was here in about 1496 that Holt drew up his Latin grammar for children, *Lac Puerorum*.[70] Buckingham's household schoolmaster, Robert Broke, was sent to Oxford at the duke's expense in the 1510s and graduated BA there in 1521.[71] In the outside world, free schools were being endowed and growing numbers of graduates were being attracted to teach in them. The evidence of the royal household and these other great institutions shows that they were by means surrendering the function of education to the public schools. On the contrary, they too were supporting salaried graduate professional masters, as good as those in the schools.

The education of girls in noble households is less well recorded than that of boys. In the case of prelates, even the worldlier ones, the lord's vocation and the absence of noble ladies seem to rule out the presence of aristocratic girls, even in wardship. Among the lay magnates, on the other hand, who had wives with bevies of ladies and especially where a widow herself presided over the household, good facilities existed for receiving female wards and girls sent from elsewhere, and these were probably used from early times. Little is

---

[66] *Regulations of the Household of Henry Algernon Percy*, ed. Percy, p. 44.
[67] *LPFD, Henry VIII*, iii part i, p. 500.
[68] *HMC, MSS of the Duke of Rutland*, vol iv (1905), pp. 260–1, 263; *LPFD, Henry VIII*, iv part i, no 366.
[69] *Epistolae Academicae Oxon*, ed. Anstey, ii, 614.
[70] *BRUO*, ii, 953.
[71] ibid., iv, 73.

known in detail about the subject, however, until the second half of the fifteenth century, when it is clear that a well-established custom had developed by which aristocratic parents paid to board out their daughters in the households of other members of the nobility for the sake of the life-style and patronage to be acquired. Nunneries were popular places for the education of girls until they were 14, and their boarding out in aristocratic households probably formed a sequel to that, taking place in adolescence or early adulthood. Elizabeth the daughter of William Paston I must have been in her late twenties in 1458, when her mother Agnes wrote to tell her 'to use herself to work readily as other gentlewomen do' for her hostess, Lady Pole, and sent her £1 6s 8d to pay for her board. Indeed, Elizabeth married later that year.[72] At about the same time Margaret the wife of John Paston I was approached by her cousin Sir John Heveningham to take in a protegée of his called Agnes Loveday. Sir John had laboured to place her elsewhere without success, and pleaded with Margaret to have her to stay until another mistress could be found, concluding with a promise to pay for her board.[73] In 1466 Sir John Howard, later duke of Norfolk, sent his daughter Jane to London to stay with the countess of Oxford, with a man to escort her, and payments appear later on for her 'gear' in Sir John's accounts.[74] Lady Oxford came to the mind of Margaret Paston, too, when her 19- or 20-year-old daughter Margery fell in love with the family bailiff in 1469, and Margaret wanted to get her away from the scene. Can it be arranged, she writes to her eldest son John II, for Margery to stay with Lady Oxford or Lady Bedford 'or in some other worshipful place whereas ye think best, and I will help to her finding, for we be either of us weary of [each] other'?[75] Meanwhile, Margery's younger sister Anne was already living away from home with another 'good lady', probably with Lady Calthorp of Burnham Thorpe whose husband Sir William asked for Anne to be removed in 1470, as he was reducing the size of his household.[76]

The domestic correspondence of the fifteenth century is valuable not simply in showing the system of boarding girls out, but for revealing some of the feelings of those it involved. Just as a mother,

[72] *Paston Letters*, ed. Davis, i, 42, lvi.
[73] ibid., ii, 350–1.
[74] *Manners and Household Expenses*, pp. 338, 355.
[75] *Paston Letters*, ed. Davis, i, 339.
[76] ibid., i, pp. lxii–lxiii, 339, 348.

like Margaret Paston, might wish to rid herself of a headstrong daughter into someone else's care, so a girl like Agnes Loveday might grow unhappy or homesick in her boarding place and plead to be removed. There is a letter of about 1472 among the Stonor correspondence, perhaps written by Jane Stonor to one of her daughters who seems to have been placed in a household by the queen, Elizabeth Wydeville, and not to like it. The writer says that the girl may certainly come home if 'they' are weary of her, but the queen must give her approval; clearly, so grand a lady, having taken an interest in the girl, must not be offended.[77] A similar story is that of Dorothy, one of the many children of the Yorkshire knight Sir Robert Plumpton. She was living with Lady Darcy in the early sixteenth century at Temple Hirst in Yorkshire when, in evident unhappiness, she sent a message to her father asking to be called home. But this episode had a happy outcome. Lady Darcy got to hear of the message and, a little later, a much more cheerful Dorothy wrote to her father to say that her ladyship had become

> a better lady than ever she was before, insomuch that she hath promised me her good ladyship as long as ever she shall live, and if she or ye can find anything meeter for me in these parts or any other, she will help to promote me to the uttermost of her puissance.[78]

The Venetian writer may have convinced himself of the heartlessness of the English in sending their children away to 'hard service', but the letters of those involved show more variety of feelings. Agnes Paston, a hard woman, might simply tell her daughter to get on with her work, but a Jane Stonor was willing for hers to come home rather than be unhappy, and a Lady Darcy to clear up a misunderstanding and to make very handsome amends.

RELIGIOUS HOUSES

There was no great gulf between the aristocratic household and the monastery or nunnery. Religious houses paralleled households in their communal life, their hospitality and their employment of servants, and their connections with the aristocracy were close ones.

[77] *The Stonor Letters and Papers, 1290–1483*, ed. C.L. Kingsford, vol i, Royal Historical Soc., Camden 3rd series, xxix (1919), pp. 122–3.
[78] *Plumpton Correspondence*, ed. Stapleton, pp. 202–3.

Nobility had founded them, helped choose abbots and abbesses, came to stay in them, burdened them with the support of aged retainers, and finally were buried in them. Equally, they made use of them for educational purposes. Let us begin with the monasteries. In Saxon England the monastic life was itself an acceptable career for a nobleman.[79] The leaders of the English monastic revival in the tenth century, Dunstan, Ethelwold and Oswald, all came from distinguished families. On the eve of the Conquest Abbot Fritheric of St Albans was a kinsman of King Cnut, Abbot Leofric of Peterborough the nephew of Earl Leofric, and Abbot Wulfric of Ely a relative of the Confessor. Up to the mid-twelfth century, when the custom flourished of placing boys in monasteries as 'oblates', aristocratic boys were also offered in this way. The records of Abingdon Abbey show sons of knights as well as of ordinary people being given to the house, along with gifts of property, to spend their lives there. The twelfth-century chronicle of Ramsey Abbey tells a story of four young noble boys who came to be educated in the abbey in the early eleventh century. They were probably meant to become monks, since they lived under the monastic rule and had monks to look after them, but as a concession they were allowed to play outside the cloister, and in the way of boys they ran races and got involved in pranks. One day they pulled at the ropes of the great bells in the west tower, and not having the strength to control them succeeded in cracking one. The monks were angry at this, but the abbot took a more lenient view and did not punish them because, he said, the damage was done by accident not by malice. He also observed that since the boys were noblemen, they would doubtless recompense the abbey a hundredfold when they grew up.[80]

During the twelfth century the recruitment of monks underwent change. Increasing respect for human individuality made it seem undesirable to impose lifelong monastic vows on children, and the growth of town schools outside the monasteries made it feasible to recruit young adults who had already gained their education elsewhere. The admission of child oblates died out, and in 1216 it was formally forbidden by the Lateran Council. At the same time, the taking of monastic vows by the nobility was in decline. The Norman aristocracy who settled in England were less attracted to do so than the Saxons had been, and though there were some Norman

---

[79] On what follows, see Knowles, *Monastic Order in England*, pp. 417–25.
[80] *Chronicon Abbatiae Rameseiensis*, ed. W.D. Macray, RS, 1886, pp. 112–14.

monks of good family in English monasteries in the early and mid-twelfth century, most of them had come from overseas. By the end of the century the recruitment of monks had fallen below the high aristocracy into the middle ranks of society, where it remained for the rest of our period.[81] Some sons of the gentry continued to become monks, but the aristocratic presence was no longer so strong or influential. What did remain, however, was the sending of noble boys to monasteries to stay there temporarily, as a preparation for life in the world as laymen or as secular clergy. Boys of this kind no longer lived in the cloister with the monks, as pre-twelfth-century boys had done; instead, they were accommodated in the worldlier surroundings of the abbot's household. This, being detached from the cloister and staffed by gentlemen and lay servants, differed little in nature from that of a bishop. John of Hertford, abbot of St Albans (d. 1263), was still remembered in the fifteenth century as a man renowned for his courtesy and open-handedness. 'Whence', says the abbey historian, 'many noblemen of the kingdom commended their children to his custody to be educated.'[82] Thomas Bromele, abbot of Hyde at Winchester, had eight gentle boys with him 'for reason of study' in about 1450, eating at his personal table and supplied with grooms of their own to wait upon them.[83] Sir John Stanley of Honford in Cheshire, arranging for the education of his 3-year-old son John in 1527, laid down that he should stay in the keeping of the abbess of Barking until he was 12, and then in that of the abbot of Westminster. Twenty pounds a year was set aside for his maintenance, and he too was to have his private servants.[84] There were three young gentlemen in Woburn Abbey in the 1530s with their own schoolmaster, a good old conservative who made the memorable remark that 'he could never assent to the New Learning',[85] and when after the Reformation a Catholic writer tried to recall the former glories of Glastonbury Abbey, one of the points that struck him was the great size (as he

[81] Knowles, *Monastic Order in England*, p. 424.
[82] *Gesta Abbatum Monasterii Sancti Albani*, ed. Riley, i, 397; for a fifteenth-century picture of him, see BL, Cotton MS Nero D.viii, f. 18.
[83] T. Warton, *History of English Poetry*, ed. W.C. Hazlitt, vol iv, London, 1871, p. 9.
[84] J. Burtt, 'Will of Sir John Stanley of Honford, Cheshire', *Archaeological Journal*, xxv (1868), pp. 81–2.
[85] *LPFD, Henry VIII*, xiii part i, p. 361.

thought) of the abbot's household and the many sons of the nobility who had studied letters there.[86]

The role of the monasteries in noble education was equalled, indeed exceeded, by that of the nunneries.[87] There was the same strong aristocratic element among nuns as there was among monks in the eleventh and early twelfth centuries. Gunhild the daughter of Harold II was a nun at Wilton for a time, and Edgar the Atheling's sister Christina was a long-term inmate of Romsey. In the twelfth century one of the daughters of Robert earl of Gloucester, Avicia, became abbess of Romsey and another, Cecilia, abbess of Shaftesbury. Cecilia's successor Mary was the half-sister of Henry II. Aristocratic girls were vowed to the veil in childhood, as their brothers were to the cowl, and stayed in their houses all their lives. The nunneries differed, however, in retaining childhood oblation and also a strong aristocratic membership after the twelfth century. Oblation of nuns remained tolerated even by the Church authorities, and in 1282 the archbishop of Canterbury himself urged the nuns of Stratford near London to veil a small girl because, 'by reason of her minority' she was better able to learn the discipline of their rule.[88] Not all nuns necessarily took the veil as children, but child-nuns can be traced in houses down to the eve of the Reformation. Some of them were aristocratic, like Mary the ninth child of Edward I, who entered Amesbury Priory when she was 7.[89] Katherine the daughter of Sir Guy de Beauchamp went into Shouldham Priory at about the age of 6 in 1359, and was still there in 1400.[90] Thomas of Woodstock's daughter Isabel was placed as a young child with the Minoresses of Aldgate, London, in about the 1380s and remained there to become abbess.[91] So one abiding relationship of the nunneries with the aristocracy was the taking in of daughters to be nuns, and their education specifically for the religious life.

The role of nunneries, however, was wider than this. They had obvious merits too as places for noble children to stay on a temporary basis, as a prelude to lay careers in adulthood. There was

---

[86] C. Reyner, *Apostolatus Benedictorum in Anglia*, Douai, 1626, p. 224.
[87] On the history of nunneries to 1200, see Knowles, *Monastic Order in England*, pp. 136–9, and after 1200, Power, *Medieval English Nunneries*, passim.
[88] ibid., pp. 26–7.
[89] *VCH Wiltshire*, iii, 247, 249.
[90] Power, *Medieval English Nunneries*, p. 26.
[91] ibid.; *VCH London*, i, 518.

a need for nurseries for tiny children, boys as well as girls, who were still at the stage of being looked after by women. Repositories were in demand for older girls as well, whom schools did not yet cater for and who could therefore only be placed away from home in a household or nunnery. Teaching was almost the only pastoral role allowed to nuns, and the income from boarding children and teaching them must also have been an attraction, especially to the poorer houses. So we find the aristocracy eager to send their children, both the younger and the older, to stay and be educated in nunneries, and the nuns just as glad to receive them. Bungay Priory took in three girls of the de la Pole family in 1416–17,[92] and Sopwell Priory had the daughter of Lady Anne Norbury at commons in 1446.[93] Jane and Elizabeth Knight, the daughters of a gentleman of Devon, entered Cornworthy Priory in about 1460, so that the nuns might 'teach them to school', and the prioress was trying to recover their unpaid debts years later.[94] Henry VI's half-brothers, Edmund and Jasper Tudor, were brought up in their tender years at Barking Abbey in the 1430s,[95] and Barking, as we have seen, was the choice of Sir John Stanley for his son in 1527. Thomas Cromwell himself in the 1520s, before he organized the dissolution of the nunneries, put his son Gregory into one, probably at Little Marlow, with a private schoolmaster to teach him.[96] Generally, however, the nuns themselves were the teachers, and it may be significant that Chaucer begins his portrait of the Prioress by listing accomplishments of the kind that girls in nunneries might learn: deportment (modelled on that of the court), good table manners, and French of the Anglo-Norman dialect. The use of the words 'scole' and 'y-taught' in his description suggests that nuns and teaching were associated in his mind.[97]

So widespread was the invasion of nunneries by children that bishops were frequently moved to regulate the practice, and a long series of episcopal injunctions on the matter survive from the mid-

[92] BL, Egerton Roll 8776, m 5.
[93] *VCH Hertfordshire*, iv, 425.
[94] PRO, C 1/44/227.
[95] Rymer, *Foedera*, x, 828.
[96] *LPFD, Henry VIII*, v, pp. 7–8.
[97] Chaucer, *Works*, ed. Robinson, p. 18 (A 122–41). There is also, however, a satirical dimension in these lines: below, pp. 139–40.

thirteenth century down to the Reformation.[98] Authority was worried by the distraction to the religious life posed by the presence of children, and tried to limit their presence to an acceptable level. In a few cases bishops laid down that no children be admitted at all without their special permission, but usually they were more liberal. Normally their regulations provided that the nuns should confine themselves to a certain number of children, e.g. one each. Children were not to sleep in the nuns' dormitory but to be housed elsewhere. Some bishops disliked the presence of boys in nunneries and a few forbade them altogether, but it was more common to lay down an age beyond which boys might not be kept. This was fixed by the more austere legislators as low as 5 and by the more indulgent as high as 12, but never higher. Girls too were ordered to leave the houses by a certain age, variously fixed between 10 and 14, presumably because they could be boarded in a lay household after that age. The regulations show that the desire for children to be educated in nunneries was a strong one – stronger in the view of the bishops than the religious life of the communities could afford. It remained strong even on the threshold of the Reformation. The king's commissioners in 1536 reported that thirty or forty gentlemen's children and students were 'right virtuously brought up' at Polesworth Abbey,[99] and St Mary's Winchester in the same year housed twenty-six girls from local knightly and gentry families, headed by Bridget Plantagenet, daughter of Viscount Lisle.[100] The dissolution of the nunneries left an educational gap, and a Protestant as convinced as the puritan Thomas Becon could look back on them afterwards not merely as places of superstition but of good religious education. The girls they received, he thought, were not constrained to live the life of the nuns, but they were taught to pray in their mother tongue when the Holy Ghost so moved them, and 'all that they were commanded to do of their schoolmistresses and governesses was nothing else than the doctrine of the gospel, and matters appertaining unto honest and civil manners'.[101]

---

[98] These are admirably summarized in Power, *Medieval English Nunneries*, pp. 563–81.

[99] Dugdale, *Monasticon Anglicanum*, ed. Caley, ii, 363.

[100] *VCH Hampshire*, ii, 125.

[101] Thomas Becon, *The Catechism*, ed. J. Ayre, Cambridge, Parker Soc., 1844, pp. 376–7.

SCHOOLS AND UNIVERSITIES

The institutions mentioned so far were all primarily domestic or religious ones, in which the pursuit of education, though often significant, was a secondary or ancillary matter. Most education in the Middle Ages, if we consider the population as a whole, was of this kind, taking place alongside the pursuits of daily life in homes and workshops, rather than being segregated into separate places. This situation began to be modified in the twelfth century with the growth of schools in the English towns, open to the general public. Here for the first time were specialized institutions, taught by professional masters and occupied with teaching alone, unmixed with other concerns. Some of the twelfth-century schools, at least in the cathedral cities, offered a range of teaching to students of all ages, from reading and Latin grammar up to the liberal arts, theology and canon law. Later, in the thirteenth century, a two-tier system of education began to develop. Most of the town and city schools confined themselves to teaching younger boys in reading and grammar, and the higher subjects and the older students became concentrated at Oxford and Cambridge in the form of universities. It is still very often assumed that the English aristocracy did not make significant use of these new specialized institutions until the Renaissance. The entry of gentlemen and noblemen into grammar schools tends to be associated with the rise of the modern kind of 'public schools' in the fifteenth, sixteenth and seventeenth centuries, and their arrival at university with the reign of Elizabeth I after the Reformation. It cannot be stressed too much that these assumptions arise from too narrow a definition of aristocracy. Those who associate the nobility with the universities after the Reformation are thinking of youths who, in their adulthood, would remain laymen. There were plenty of aristocratic youths at Oxford and Cambridge before the Reformation, but they were intended to become clerics. The difference was not really that great. The aristocratic pedigrees of the pre-Reformation university scholars were just as good as those of their post-Reformation successors, and their life-styles at university were also aristocratic. As we have seen, the distinction between adolescents who might become laymen or clerics was not a sharp one, and the same kinds of clothes, horses, games and servants were common to both. The change of the sixteenth century was not a change of the presence of the aristocracy; rather, it was one of their long-term career ambitions.

The entry of the nobility into schools and universities began, on the contrary, almost as soon as those institutions were founded. Were they not already well practised at infiltrating the religious houses? In the twelfth century the leading schools of the Anglo-Norman world were those of northern France, and it is there that noble boys are first recorded going to prepare themselves for clerical careers. The sons of Ranulf Flambard, bishop of Durham, and the nephew of Roger bishop of Salisbury were all sent to schoolmasters at Laon in the early twelfth century.[102] Gerald of Wales, of the noble family of Barri, was studying at Paris in the 1160s,[103] and Henry II sent his bastard son Geoffrey, later archbishop of York, to the schools of Tours a decade later.[104] With the rise of the English universities in the thirteenth century, the aristocracy turned their attention to Oxford and Cambridge. Indeed, the secure establishment of Oxford as a university may well be measured not only by the organization of a corporation of secular clerks and by the arrival of the friars, but by the coming of Aymer de Lusignan, half-brother of Henry III, to study there in the late 1240s.[105] This signified that Oxford had 'arrived' in the eyes of the royal family itself, and encouraged a regular flow of wealthy noble youths marked out for the highest posts in Church and state. At first such youths were often sent in pairs, a boy and his younger brother, no doubt because it was almost as cheap for their fathers to pay for two as for one, while the second provided a hedge against the premature death of the first. We find among others the Cantilupe brothers at Paris in the 1240s, the Clare brothers (sons of the earl of Gloucester) at Oxford in the 1250s, the Grandisson brothers there in the early 1300s, and the Nevill brothers of Raby in the 1340s.[106]

These noble youths enjoyed at university the kind of privileged and comfortable life they were accustomed to at home. The Cantilupes rented a whole house at Paris and installed their personal

---

[102] H.G. Richardson, 'Gervase of Tilbury', *History*, xlvi (1961), p. 103; *Patrologia Latina*, ed. Migne, vol clvi, Paris, 1853, cols 977, 983.

[103] Gerald of Wales, *Autobiography*, trans. Butler, p. 37.

[104] *Gesta Regis Henrici Secundi*, ed. W. Stubbs, vol i, RS, 1867, p. 93.

[105] *BRUO*, ii, 1179–80.

[106] ibid., i, 347, 423–5; ii, 800–1, 1346, 1351.

household inside.[107] At Oxford Henry III made rooms in the castle available for Walter Giffard and his mother in 1256, and Edward I provided royal houses for Edmund Mortimer two decades later.[108] Licences for noble scholars to have private oratories in their lodgings are suggestive of other spacious premises, with hired chaplains officiating in them. Some were favoured with gifts of oak trees from the king's forests to fuel their fires, others with deer to grace their tables. To supervise them they had tutors, either brought with them like Master Vincent of Tours, the tutor of Aymer de Lusignan, or perhaps chosen from an MA already resident in the university. As colleges developed, with better accommodation and facilities than elsewhere, the aristocracy duly began to move into them, their wealth and status making them welcome guests. They were not at first members of colleges, which were originally meant for the less wealthy, but rather the private tenants of vacant rooms. Henry Beaufort lived at Peterhouse, Cambridge, and then at Queen's College, Oxford, between 1388 and 1393.[109] William Scrope resided at Oriel in the 1410s, and Humphrey de la Pole at Gonville Hall in the 1490s.[110] The custom was institutionalized by William Wainfleet, the founder of Magdalen College, Oxford, who laid down in the college statutes (by 1486) that twenty commoners of noble birth might live there at their own expense under the control of tutors, for whom he employed the new word *creditores* in Latin or 'creancers' in English.[111] The dwindling number of halls and hostels during the fifteenth century, together with increasing prohibitions against living in private houses, tended to concentrate the aristocracy by 1500 into the colleges and the few remaining halls, with college fellows or hall principals as their creancers. The term 'creancer' seems to signify a new concept of an old function. The creancer looked after the young man's money, disciplined him and perhaps gave him some teaching, though the youth went also to the

---

[107] ibid., i, 347.

[108] ibid., ii, 762, 1316.

[109] ibid., i, 139–40.

[110] ibid., iii, 1660; *BRUC*, pp. 46, 180.

[111] *Statutes of the Colleges of Oxford*, ii, 60. The use of the terms *creditor* and 'creancer' in an educational sense seems to have begun at Oxford in the 1480s. For other early references to them, see *Statuta Antiqua Universitatis Oxoniensis*, ed. S. Gibson, Oxford, 1931, p. 587; The *Winchester Anthology*, ed. E. Wilson, Cambridge, 1981, f. 69^v; *OED* sub 'creancer'.

1 (left) Alexander the Great shown as a medieval royal baby, his mother in a luxurious bed, and visitors bringing presents.

2 (below) The baptism of Richard Beauchamp, later earl of Warwick, in 1382. A bishop officiates, and the godparents (right) include Richard II and Richard Scrope, later archbishop of York; the baby was given their name.

1

2

PARENTS AND TEACHERS   3 (top)   Noble parents might teach their children personally, as St Anne is shown teaching the Virgin Mary to read. Much teaching, however, was deputed to masters and mistresses.   4 (bottom)   Richard Beauchamp, earl of Warwick, takes up his post as knightly master of the 7-year-old Henry VI in the presence of parliament, 1428.

5

Noble children were variously brought up in the households of the king, lay magnates, bishops and abbots.   5 (above)   Robert Grosseteste (d. 1253), bishop of Lincoln, famous for his learning and good manners. Only the ruins now stand of his palace at Lincoln (6, below), where he brought up Simon de Montfort's son Henry and other noble boys.

6

EDUCATIONAL WRITERS: THE FRIARS

The modern development of theories and writings about lay education owes much to the friars in the thirteenth century. Here are three of the most famous of them, conventionally portrayed: Bartholomew Glanville (7, top), Vincent of Beauvais (8, centre), and Giles of Rome (9, left).

lectures provided by the university and later by the colleges. 'They do wisely that send no children to the university', observed an Oxford writer in about 1500, 'except they put them under creancers to have the rule of them and their money.' If boys were not under such control, he argued, they would waste their money at cards and dice, especially at Christmas time![112]

As records increase it becomes apparent that the acquisition of a nobleman's son could be a matter of general interest and self-congratulation among the university's leaders. The chancellor and masters of Oxford wrote officially to Edward IV and the bishop of Salisbury in 1480 to express their pleasure at the arrival of Edward's nephew, Edward de la Pole, in order to study.[113] John Bourchier, the son of Lord Fitzwarin, was entertained to wine in All Souls College when he came up in 1468–9, and the sons of the marquess of Dorset were greeted with wine and wafers in 1495.[114] The degree registers, which survive at Oxford and Cambridge from the middle of the fifteenth century, show that the favour displayed to noble boys outlived their coming and lasted until they completed their studies. They were allowed to graduate on easier terms, abridging the times laid down, omitting certain studies, and being freed of obligations to reside and to lecture. When they graduated, some gave feasts and had more royal venison given them for the purpose. Many of these noble boys were already beneficed clerics when they came to the university, and enjoyed the status and profits of canonries and rectories for which ordinary students could only cherish a hope. Some, on leaving university, were promoted to archdeaconries and bishoprics, others to further clutches of parish benefices. Here Bogo de Clare, the 'incubator' rather than the incumbent of churches, as one contemporary called him, achieved particular success and notoriety.[115] But it was not all taking rather than giving. Several of the nobility were able men who did good service to their fellow scholars. Men like William Courtenay and Lionel Wydeville at Oxford, and Henry Beaufort and Richard Scrope at Cambridge, served as chancellors of their universities, gave benefactions, and after becoming bishops were in a position to

---

[112] *A Fifteenth Century School Book*, ed. Nelson, p. 25.
[113] *Epistolae Academicae Oxon*, ed. Anstey, ii, 453–7; *BRUO*, i, 564.
[114] ibid., i, 229–30; ii, 824.
[115] ibid., i, 423–4.

promote poor scholars to ecclesiastical benefices. Both universities gained from the wealth and influence which their noble alumni brought with them.

When did young noblemen first go to Oxford and Cambridge to study, not with the purpose of entering the Church but as a preparation for life as a courtier, knight or landowner? As early as the thirteenth century there were those who dropped out of the universities and took up secular careers, because the deaths of elder brothers left them heirs to the paternal property or (perhaps less often) because they themselves refused the fate proposed for them. Thomas de Clare, a younger son of the earl of Gloucester, who studied at Oxford in the 1250s was knighted in adult life and led a military career in Ireland.[116] Edmund Mortimer, after spending several years at the university in the 1270s and occupying ecclesiastical benefices, gave up the clerical life on the death of his elder brother and inherited the family barony.[117] William Beauchamp, the fourth son of the earl of Warwick, was beneficed at fourteen and spent at least three years at Oxford between 1358 and 1361, before he too became the heir and left to make a successful career as a warrior.[118] There may have been more such cases, but they are exceptions to the rule rather than modifiers of it. No clear examples survive in the thirteenth and fourteenth centuries of boys who were definitely going to lead secular careers engaging in university study. The earliest such boys whom we hear of were those who came to Oxford and Cambridge not to study in the universities, but in the grammar schools and business schools which also flourished there and over which the university authorities exercised a loose control. Thomas Sampson ran a popular commercial school at Oxford between about 1350 and 1409, in which he taught how to write letters, cast accounts and convey property as a training for lay careers.[119] Some of Sampson's pupils may have been gentlemen's sons, since one of his model letters features a young man who has become steward of a noble household, while another recommends a father to take his son away from Oxford and place him in the court of

---

[116] ibid., i, 425.
[117] ibid., ii, 1316.
[118] ibid., i, 138–9.
[119] ibid., iii, 1636–7.

the king or the duke of Lancaster.[120] Chaucer's son Lewis was apparently studying in Oxford in 1391, when he was 10, and subsequently held a post as squire in a noble retinue.[121] Alexander de la Pole, on leaving Ipswich school in 1417, went to Cambridge 'to go to school there', and he too became a squire and was eventually knighted.[122] Of neither boy, however, is it clear that he learnt university studies (Lewis, his father said, knew only a 'little Latin'), and entry into the Church may well have been in mind for them, albeit unfulfilled.

It is in the 1430s and 1440s that we find the first clear cases of noble boys at Oxford and Cambridge who were definitely intended to follow secular careers. In 1437–8 the 9-year-old Robert Hungerford and his tutor lodged for three terms in rooms belonging to University College, Oxford.[123] Soon afterwards in 1441–4 John Tiptoft, then in his early teens, occupied rooms in the same college, again with a tutor of his own.[124] At Cambridge, Henry Holland stayed with a train of servants at the King's Hall for ten weeks in 1440–1 and eleven in 1441–2, at the age of 11 or 12.[125]. All three of these boys were eldest sons and heirs to peerages: Hungerford, Tiptoft and Huntingdon, and there is no likelihood that any of them was destined for the Church. University residence in their case was evidently meant to be part of their training as secular aristocrats. Their presence takes on an extra significance because of the high contemporary interest in professional education in court circles. Activities by courtiers in founding schools and patronizing university institutions can be traced back to the 1420s and 1430s among men such as Walter Lord Hungerford, Robert's grandfather, and Humphrey duke of Gloucester.[126] In 1440 the young Henry VI began the foundation of Eton College, and during the next twenty years several other schools were endowed by his bishops and lay

---

[120] Richardson in *Formularies which Bear on the History of Oxford*, ed. Salter and others, ii, 371, 415–16.

[121] *BRUO*, i, 396–7.

[122] BL, Egerton Roll 8776, m 5; McFarlane, *Nobility of Later Medieval England*, p. 245.

[123] *BRUO*, ii, 985.

[124] ibid., iii, 1877–9.

[125] *BRUC*, p. 321.

[126] This matter is discussed in Orme, *Education in the West of England*, pp. 142–3.

nobility.[127] The sending by some of the latter of their heirs to be taught professionally in a university setting was another dimension of this activity. The significance once stated, however, must immediately be qualified. Hungerford and Holland were so young that they can scarcely have studied more than grammar. Tiptoft indeed was older; in later life he studied at Padua and became a fluent Latinist, capable of making an oration before the pope himself. To him, perhaps, belongs the palm of being the first English peer deliberately to follow true university studies and to fuse the worlds of scholarship and lay nobility. But he and his contemporaries had few imitators. Casual visits by eldest sons of peers to the universities may easily have escaped record, but even allowing for that, there is a notable absence of such youths at Oxford and Cambridge from the 1440s until after the Reformation. Most aristocratic parents seem to have preferred their eldest sons to follow the traditional pattern of education in a household, where the growth of bodies of henchmen and professional schoolmasters, though not providing the highest scholarship, offered good teaching and companionship and more useful patronage than could be gained for laymen at the universities.

It was instead at a lower social level that the aristocracy penetrated the universities with lay careers in mind. In 1440–1, at about the time that Henry Holland was living in the King's Hall, John Paston I, the son and heir of a royal justice and Norfolk landowner, also spent a year or two at Cambridge, first at Trinity Hall and then at Peterhouse, before going on to London to study the common law.[128] This practice, unlike that of the higher aristocracy, became more frequent as the century wore on. John Paston's studies seem to have been worthwhile, since in 1444 his father William the justice provided for his second son Edmund to read logic for half a year and civil law for one year – both university subjects – in preparation for studying the laws of England.[129] His third son William read grammar and logic at Cambridge in 1449, and the youngest Clement was there some nine years later, both of them subsequently taking up lay careers.[130] By the end of the century

---

[127] Orme, *English Schools in the Middle Ages*, pp. 200, 202.
[128] *Paston Letters*, ed. Davis, i, p. liv.
[129] ibid., pp. 22–3.
[130] ibid., pp. 22–4, 41, 234.

knights and gentlemen from the north of England were arranging to send their sons on similar schemes of training. Sir Thomas Markenfield bequeathed money in 1497 to keep his son and heir Ninian at Oxford for three years,[131] Robert Constable provided for his son Marmaduke in 1501 to be maintained at Cambridge for a similar period,[132] and Matthew Wentworth arranged for his son Thomas in 1505 to be sent to grammar school for two years and to Cambridge for one.[133] Each of these boys was to conclude his education by studying the common law in London. Plans of this kind imply a regard for university residence in the eyes of gentlemen, but as a preparation for the study of common law rather than an end in itself. The sons in question were enabled to broaden their knowledge by going to university, and perhaps to partake of university life, but it is not clear that even they embarked on university studies to any great extent. Their ages, often less than 15, and the shortage of time allotted to them suggest the contrary. Even in the early sixteenth century the arts course – the core of the universities' curricula – provided an education chiefly for future clerics as far as the aristocracy was concerned, and hardly at all for future gentlemen or common lawyers.

As for the English schools, which after the rise of the universities were left with the teaching of grammar in local towns and villages, they (as we would expect) attracted boys from the lesser rather than the greater aristocracy. We do encounter the occasional son of a magnate or a peer. John de Balliol, the future king of Scotland, studied at Durham school in the 1260s,[134] as Alexander de la Pole did at Ipswich in 1416, but such examples are rare, no doubt because most parents of such boys could assign a household chaplain to teach them at home, or later on hire a private schoolmaster. It was rather the gentry, whose means were more slender, who followed the cheaper plan of using the ordinary schools. Some of the boys they sent there were intended to become clerics, others to remain gentlemen. We hear of Hugh de la Tour, son of a small landowner in Hampshire and Somerset, at Taunton school in the 1290s, and Roger Standlake of similar rank in Oxfordshire at Witney school in

---

[131] *Testamenta Eboracensia*, ed. Raine, iv, 125.
[132] ibid., pp. 196, 237.
[133] ibid., p. 238.
[134] *Historiae Dunelmensis Scriptores Tres*, ed. J. Raine, Durham, Surtees Soc., ix (1839), p. 74.

the middle of the fourteenth century.[135] The grammar exercises of a Bristol schoolmaster in the 1420s feature 'a gay squire of Devonshire' who goes to school above the New Gate of the town and, since he is soon to be married, will evidently have a lay career.[136] There are many later examples. Gentle boys who went to school took lodgings with the master, like Alexander de la Pole, or in the private houses of people of suitable rank. Nicholas Lestrange of Hunstanton apparently stayed with the vicar of North Elmham in 1524,[137] and Peter Carew with an Exeter alderman a year or two later.[138] The rise of colleges at the universities was paralleled among the schools, to a much smaller extent, with the foundation of Winchester College (1382) and Eton College (1440). Though primarily for children of modest wealth, each college permitted the entry of fee-paying commoners of noble birth – ten at Winchester and twenty at Eton – who were allowed to partake of the teaching, food and accommodation at their own expense.[139] We know the names of one or two of the higher nobility who took advantage of these schemes. John Bourchier was at Winchester in 1468–9[140] and Edward Audley, son of Lord Audley, at Eton in the 1470s.[141] In general, however, the early commoners of Winchester and Eton do not seem to have belonged to peerage families, but to have been the sons of knights, esquires or gentlemen.[142] Once again, what the two colleges provided in terms of education had less appeal for the higher aristocracy, who could do as well or better through the traditional household institutions.

THE INNS OF COURT

The growth of a system of education in London, centred upon the study of the common law, can be traced back to at least the end of the

[135] *Calendar of Inquisitions Post Mortem*, vol v (1908), p. 126; vol xiii (1954), pp. 264–5.
[136] Orme in *Traditio*, xxxviii (1982), pp. 309, 315–16.
[137] D. Gurney, 'Extracts from the . . . accounts of the Lestranges of Hunstanton', *Archaeologia*, xxv (1834), p. 466.
[138] Hooker, *The Life of Sir Peter Carew*, ed. Maclean, pp. 3–5.
[139] Kirby, *Annals of Winchester College*, p. 490; *The Ancient Laws . . . for King's College, Cambridge, and . . . Eton College*, ed. J. Heywood and T. Wright, London, 1850, p. 535.
[140] *VCH Hampshire*, ii, 273; *BRUO*, i, 229–30.
[141] His memorial brass, formerly at Eton, said in Latin 'here he learnt grammar' (MS Ashmole 1137, f 152ᵛ).
[142] Kirby, *Annals of Winchester College*, pp. 109–16.

thirteenth century.[143] We begin to hear of young men training to become common lawyers by attending the king's courts of law in London during the 1290s and early 1300s. By the middle of the fourteenth century, these lawyers, both the young learners and the older practitioners, were dwelling together in hostels in the Temple area immediately outside the west gate of the city, like the house containing thirty of them which is mentioned by Chaucer in his portrait of the Manciple.[144] By the beginning of the fifteenth century, some of these hostels or 'inns' had grown into larger, more formal communities whose members governed their own domestic affairs and possessed common facilities for eating and studying together. The Middle Temple is mentioned in 1404, Lincoln's Inn in 1422, the Inner Temple in 1443 and Gray's Inn in 1454. By the late 1460s, when Fortescue wrote his famous account of legal education in London, these four principal 'inns of court' had acquired an institutional form and a predominance over the ten or so lesser communities called 'inns of chancery'. Fortescue asserted that in his time the inns together accommodated 1,800 students, but this was a large overestimate.[145] The best modern reckoning, that of Dr E.W. Ives, suggests that the inns housed 700–800 lawyers in the second half of the fifteenth century, of whom about 400–500 were practising lawyers and the remaining 200–300 were students.[146]

The study of the common law in London was originally an informal one, centred on the king's courts. During the four legal terms when the courts were in session, students attended them to observe the barristers plead and listen to the judgments delivered by the justices. Mention is made in the early fourteenth century of a place in the courts called the crib, apparently an enclosure in which the students stood.[147] Later, in the fifteenth century, the inns developed educational facilities of their own, supplementing the practical experience of the courts. 'Readings' or lectures on statute

---

[143] On the history of legal education in London and the inns of court, see Holdsworth, *History of English Law*, ii, 315, 493–512; Ives in *TRHS*, 5th series, xviii (1968), pp. 145–73; Simpson in *Cambridge Law Journal*, xxviii part ii (1970), pp. 241–56; and Ives in *Profession, Vocation and Culture*, ed. Clough, pp. 181–217.

[144] Chaucer, *Works*, ed. Robinson, p. 22 (A 567–86).

[145] Fortescue, *De Laudibus Legum Anglie*, ed. Chrimes, pp. 116–19.

[146] Ives in *TRHS*, 5th series, xviii (1968), pp. 146–7.

[147] *Year Book of Edward II*, ed. F.W. Maitland and G.J. Turner, vol iv, Selden Soc., xxii (1907), pp. xli–xlii.

law began to be given by senior members of the inns at certain times of the year. An 'autumn reader' is mentioned at the chancery inn, Furnivall's Inn, as early as 1408, and manuscripts of readings survive from the 1420s.[148] 'Moots' in which students pleaded mock cases before their seniors are recorded at Lincoln's Inn in 1428 and at Furnivall's by the 1450s.[149] Gradually, what began as informal occasions of legal education grew into a formal system. An important milestone at Lincoln's Inn was the order in 1436 that two 'learning vacations' should be observed outside the legal terms: a month in Lent and a month at harvest time, at which both senior and junior members of the inn should keep residence, evidently so that they could join in educational exercises.[150] The developed system is described in an account of the inns drawn up in 1539 for presentation to Henry VIII.[151] By that time, a moot was held at each inn every evening during term, in which the students pleaded before the barristers. Outside term, there were two learning vacations, one in Lent and one in August, each lasting for three weeks. During these periods a lecture was given at each inn of court every morning by a senior barrister. He analysed a legal problem, this was followed by discussions and debates on the matter by other barristers, and in the evening a moot again took place as happened in term. When a student had stayed at an inn for three years, studying the law and engaging in the moots, he was eligible to be chosen an 'utter barrister' of his inn and to plead in the courts.

Fortescue observed that those who studied law at the inns were chiefly nobility, because of the cost involved.[152] In fact, of those who came to study law professionally, the gentry predominated, not the peerage nobility. From early times sons of the gentry went to London to make careers as professional lawyers, whereas the sons of the peerage nobility had no need to take up law as a profession and are unlikely to have been present as professional students. By the 1460s, however, Fortescue was also noting that 'knights, barons and other magnates and noblemen of the realm' were placing their sons at the inns 'although they do not desire them to be trained in the

---

[148] Ives in *Profession, Vocation and Culture*, ed. Clough, p. 201.
[149] ibid., pp. 201–2.
[150] ibid., pp. 203–4.
[151] E. Waterhouse, *Fortescutus Illustratus, or a Commentary on . . . De Laudibus Legum Anglie*, London, 1663, pp. 543–6.
[152] Fortescue, *De Laudibus Legum Anglie*, pp. 116–19.

science of the laws, nor to live by its practices, but only by their patrimonies'.[153] In other words, by the middle of the fifteenth century aristocratic boys were being sent to the inns simply to get a liberal education as a preparation for inheriting property and spending their lives as independent landowners. Actually, gentry seem to have predominated over peerage nobility in this respect as well. The records of Lincoln's Inn, the best surviving evidence from the fifteenth century, do mention the admission of one or two sons of peers: William Herbert aged 13 in 1468 and George Dinham at about the age of 20 in 1485.[154] But these are exceptions. Most of the peers and sons of peers who feature in the admission registers were adults whose admissions were a mark of honour by the inn to them, and vice versa. The vast majority of aristocratic boys admitted to the inns were the sons of knights and gentlemen, like the Constables and Markenfields already mentioned.[155] A peer had little need to study law, even superficially, since he could hire professional lawyers to advise him whenever he needed. A gentleman landowner, on the other hand, had the same need as the peer to defend his interests, but fewer resources to do so, and depended more on his own knowledge. William Paston I, his widow recalled, 'said many times that whosoever should dwell at Paston should have need to con [i.e. know how to] defend himself', meaning at law.[156] It was this, no doubt, that prompted him to send his eldest son John, the inheritor of his property, to study law, as well as his younger sons for whom the law might offer professional careers.[157]

There were other advantages too, besides the study of law, to lead a knight or gentleman to send his sons to the inns. Their residential facilities were already well developed in the mid-fifteenth century, rivalling those of Winchester, Eton, or the colleges at the universities. Lincoln's Inn, for example, contained chambers for accommodation, a chapel and (by 1475) a library. A hall, buttery and kitchen provided communal meals, and two grades of diet were available: masters' commons and clerks' commons. A private

---

[153] ibid.
[154] *The Records of the Honorable Society of Lincoln's Inn*, vol i: *Admissions, 1420–1799*, [ed. W.P. Baildon], London, 1896, pp. 16, 23.
[155] ibid., *passim; A Calendar of the Inner Temple Records*, ed. F.A. Inderwick, vol i: *1505–1603*, London, 1896, *passim.*
[156] *Paston Letters*, ed. Davis, i. 27.
[157] ibid., pp. liv–lvi, 22–3.

servant could also be kept.[158] The senior lawyers who governed the inns exerted discipline over the juniors, which must have found favour with parents afraid of the temptations of life on the outskirts of London. Dicing and playing at cards were forbidden, and so was the bringing in of women at night.[159] Activities of a cultural kind, on the other hand, were tolerated and even encouraged. Fortescue says that the inns were

> like a school of all the manners that nobles learn. There [the students] learn to sing and to exercise themselves in every kind of harmony. They also practise dancing and all the games proper to noblemen, just as those in the king's household are accustomed to practise them.[160]

This evidence finds support from the records. The 'Black Books' of Lincoln's Inn show that revels were held at Christmas from at least 1444, involving the appointment of a master of the revels and the hiring of minstrels.[161] Military exercises took place too. In 1467 Edward IV ordered the four chief inns each to provide four armed men to attend him at the tournament between Lord Scales and the Bastard of Burgundy. Lincoln's Inn paid £5 to erect a scaffold from which its members could view the jousts, and did the same on another occasion in 1477–8.[162] It all goes to show that a gentleman's son with independent means could have a comparable education at the inns to that at the king's court. He was near Westminster, the chief royal residence, able to attend court and observe its fashions. He was in a community of learned men (to satisfy his father) and young men (to please himself), with whom he could join in noble pastimes. It is not hard to see why the inns attracted lay aristocratic recruits in search of a liberal education in the fifteenth century, and more so than the universities. The latter could offer good school education to younger boys, but their more clerical ethos and their remoteness from the court and its fashions made it hard for them to compete with the inns as places to train intending laymen. The practical skill of law, the contacts to be made at court, and the

---

[158] *The Records of the Honorable Society of Lincoln's Inn: The Black Books*, vol i: *1422–1586*, [ed. W.P. Baildon], London, 1897, pp. i–xl.
[159] ibid., pp. 68, 71, 74, 79, 103.
[160] Fortescue, *De Laudibus Legum Anglie*, pp. 116–19.
[161] *The Black Books*, ed. Baildon, pp. 16, 18, 20–2, *passim*; 106.
[162] ibid., pp. 45, 65.

amusements of London must have been much more compelling to such men than the academic studies which constituted the chief amenity of Oxford and Cambridge.

Historically, the period between 1100 and 1500 saw the growth of a greater variety of educational institutions for men (though not for women). A noble boy in 1100 who needed to leave home to be educated had only two possible destinations: another great household or a religious house. Neither was primarily educational in function, and in each the bringing up of children was done by people who were not solely teachers. The twelfth century saw, by contrast, the appearance of specialized institutions, operated by professional masters and more divorced from ordinary life. First came schools, next universities, and then the inns of court (though there the teachers were also practising lawyers). The aristocracy took advantage of all these opportunities in due course, sending some children to them for professional training and eventually others for a liberal education. The greater nobility only made significant use of the universities, but the lesser resorted to all three. It might have been expected that the rise of specialized places of education would lead to the decline of the non-specialized ones. We ourselves live in an age when the private household has surrendered the giving of formal and technical education to schools and universities. In the Middle Ages, however, the non-specialized households and religious communities proved very resilient against the challenge from outside. The religious houses continued to attract boys and girls for care and training up to the Reformation. The households developed their own educational institutions, and matched the schools with the formation of bodies of henchmen and salaried professional schoolmasters. The education of noble girls remained entirely household-based, even in the early sixteenth century.

In truth, the great households stand up well in the history of education, and deserve a place of honour alongside that of the specialized institutions. They nurtured many subjects of the curriculum, and gave them the sophistication which enabled them to move away into their own independent organizations. Thus literary studies were pursued in the royal household and in monasteries long before the appearance of schools and universities, and likewise secular music, dancing and the teaching of arms before the formation of schools of these arts in the sixteenth century. In the history of teaching in England, the function of knightly master is at least as old as that of schoolmaster, while mistresses of noble girls anticipate schoolmistresses by 150 years or more.[163] So too in the fifteenth century, the first surviving daily plans for the education of individual children are those of a prince and a duke who were growing up in households.[164] Yet another important household contribution appears, from early times, in the sphere of educational writings. We shall find in the twelfth century Hugh of St Victor writing for the novices of his abbey, and John of Salisbury for the lord of the day's most fashionable educational household.[165] In the thirteenth we shall see great educational pioneers – Bartholomew Glanville, Vincent of Beauvais and Giles of Rome – centring their work on noble boys in noble households,[166] and Robert Grosseteste devising his famous poem on etiquette, *Stans Puer ad Mensam*, for boys in the same environment. Courtesy, by definition, modelled itself on courts and households throughout the Middle Ages, and most of the writings on manners, like Grosseteste's, described or were influenced by household conventions.[167] The first major English treatise on French was written by a knight for a lady to use with her children at home, and the earliest independent work to circulate in England on the education of women had a similar household audience and setting.[168] It would therefore be a mistake to measure the culture of the medieval aristocracy by the scale of its involvement with schools and universities alone. These institutions did not even monopolize literary studies, much less compete effectively in other fields. Those noble families who did not frequent them need not be judged to have lacked an interest in education. Rather, they may remind us how much, even in the 1530s, education still flourished in the great households and religious houses, its ancient homes.

---

[163] For mistresses, see above p. 26, and for schoolmistresses, Orme, *English Schools*, pp. 54–5.
[164] Below, pp. 116–17.
[165] Below, pp. 88, 136.
[166] Below, pp. 90–4.
[167] Below, pp. 135–9.
[168] Below, pp. 95, 107–9.

Three The literature of education

The two previous chapters have established the practice of education by the medieval aristocracy. This raises the question how far the practice was conceived, described and taught in writings. To what extent was there a literature of aristocratic education in the Middle Ages, who wrote it and for whom, and what does it tell us about the theory and practice of children's upbringing? Well before the Renaissance, and indeed from the twelfth century, a series of texts began to be written and diffused which took as their subject the principles and methods of aristocratic education. They set out the ethics, the behaviour, the knowledge and the techniques which kings and noblemen should learn. The best of them have an ambition and a range equal to that which is normally associated with the Renaissance, and are landmarks in the history of European education. In the following chapter we shall examine the texts which dealt with education in general. Works also evolved on specific topics, such as grammar, courtesy, war, hunting and chess, but these will be considered alongside the topics to which they refer, in later chapters of the book.

NARRATIVE LITERATURE

In practice, a great part of all the literature of medieval England (Latin, French and English) probably had some impact on the bringing up of children. The literature of the Church – theology and canon law – defined a code of Christian behaviour and this was expounded to the laity in sermons, devotional handbooks and through the confessional. Apart from the rites of baptism and confirmation, the literature of the Church contained little or nothing specifically addressed to children or concerned with their development, but that does not mean that it had no impact on them. Religious writing, like most medieval literature, was addressed to the population generally, not to adults or children separately, and could be heard or read by either group. By forming the ideas and methods of parents, guardians and masters it must have had a consequent influence on the upbringing of children. With the narrative literature of the Middle Ages – histories, saints' lives, epics, chansons de geste and romances – we come closer to a specific concern with children, since the births of heroes and heroines, their rearing and their training, were common subjects of such literature from an early period. The reference in *Beowulf* to the bringing up of the hero from the age of 7 in the household of the king of the Geats has already been mentioned.[1] In the Irish stories of the *Tain* cycle, the court of Conchobor king of Ulster is portrayed at some length as the training place of noble boys in arms and athletics, where the hero Cuchulainn gets part of his own upbringing.[2] As adult warriors both Beowulf and Cuchulainn can be called models for education, since they enshrine the best aristocratic values and accomplishments of their authors' times: loyalty, comradeship, bravery, skill in arms, eloquence and generosity. They too cannot have been without some impact on the education of the young.

The educational content of the epics continued in the new genres of twelfth-century literature: chanson de geste and romance. It is especially apparent in the stories of Tristan, which first survive in literary form in the second half of the century and were subsequently very popular in different versions. Not all of these exist in complete form, but all agree (or seem to have done) that Tristan was educated in his youth by a wise tutor, originally called Gorvenal but later often corrupted to Governayl (perhaps through association with his role as governor). The boy learnt various studies and techniques, all

[1] *Beowulf*, lines 2428–31.
[2] *The Tain*, trans. Kinsella, pp. 76–84.

of which he mastered superbly.[3] In Gottfried von Strassburg's German *Tristan* of about 1210, the earliest full account of the education, Tristan is said to have learnt books, languages, stringed instruments, riding and military arts, athletics (wrestling, running, jumping and throwing the javelin), tracking and hunting, and courtly pastimes including chess. So much is said indeed, that the narrative comes near to describing a plan for a prince's education.[4] The French prose *Tristan* of 1215–1235, which would have been the commonest version read in England up to the fifteenth century, places less emphasis on the hero's education, though the matter is not overlooked. Here Tristan is educated partly in the household of his own father, King Melyadus, and partly away from home in that of Faramon king of Gaul. Gorvenal is as usual the tutor; the boy learns chess, 'tables' or backgammon, riding and self-defence with weapons, and is good at everything.[5] The prose *Tristan* was improved on in the first surviving version of the story in English, the anonymous fourteenth-century poem *Sir Tristrem*, written in the north of England. This describes a more varied curriculum. Tristan is brought up for fifteen years by a knight called Rohand. He learns the study of books, Rohand teaches him how to sing and play every kind of music; he can play chess and goes hunting so often that he learns more of the art than anyone.[6] When Sir Thomas Malory translated the French prose *Tristan* into English in the fifteenth century, he also stressed the hero's education more than the French original had done. Tristram's father appoints him a tutor, Gover-nayle, who 'was well learned and taught'. His training lasts for more than seven years. He studies 'language' (evidently French), 'nurture' (which usually means good manners), and deeds of arms. He learns to harp and to play other instruments, so 'that there was none such called in no country.... And after, as he growed in might and strength, he laboured in hunting and in hawking – never gentleman more than ever we heard read of.'[7] Right from the start, the Tristan writers established the romantic hero as a well-educated

[3] On the postulated original form of the story, see Thomas, *Le Roman de Tristan*, ed. Bédier, ii, 194–6.
[4] Gottfried, *Tristan*, trans. Hatto, pp. 68–71.
[5] *Le Roman de Tristan en Prose*, ed. Curtis, p. 138.
[6] *Sir Tristrem*, ed. McNeill, lines 278–97.
[7] Malory, *Works*, ed. Vinaver, i, 375.

man, whose tutor and curriculum were worth mentioning as part of his story.

The same was true of other such heroes in the literature of England from the twelfth century onwards. The romance of *Horn* by Thomas, a French poem written in England in about the third quarter of the twelfth century, spends several lines describing its hero's education. Horn, the son of a king, is entrusted to the care of his father's seneschal, Sir Herlant. He learns to play all the instruments under heaven, to hunt in wood and by river, to manage a horse and to defend himself. He also acquires good qualities: humility and loyalty.[8] *Ipomedon* by Hue de Rotelande, also composed in French in England in about the 1180s, recounts a similar kind of education. The hero, handsome, courteous, valiant and son of a king is brought up by a master named Tholomeu, a man skilled in courtly things. He learns much of birds and dogs (in other words hawking and hunting), he is taught to serve at feasts and he is well lettered, the author adding the comment that a man is worth more if he learns 'clergie', meaning literary studies.[9] A third French poem, *Guy of Warwick*, was probably written in England during the 1230s. This features the upbringing not only of a noble boy but a noble girl: Felice, daughter of the earl of Warwick, and Guy the son of the earl's steward, the lord of Wallingford. Guy has a master to look after him; he is courteous, experienced with dogs and falcons, and generous with his money to poor knights and prisoners; nothing, however, is said of his studying letters. Felice on the other hand is highly educated in this respect, and masters of the Premonstratensian order of white canons come from 'Tulette' (Toledo or Toulouse) to teach her astronomy, arithmetic and geometry.[10] Nor is she the only case of a learned lady in literature. The early thirteenth-century French prose version of the *History of Merlin* had already featured women with similar power in Morgan, King Arthur's half-sister, and Viviane, Merlin's mistress. Morgan, a great 'clergesse' or lady clerk, learns astronomy and necromancy,

[8] *The Romance of Horn*, ed. Pope, i, 12–13; Legge, *Anglo-Norman Literature*, pp. 96–104.
[9] Hue de Rotelande, *Ipomedon*, ed. Kölbing and Koschwitz, lines 194–212; Legge, *Anglo-Norman Literature*, pp. 85–96.
[10] *Gui de Warewic*, ed. Ewert, lines 63–8, 147–56; Legge, *Anglo-Norman Literature*, pp. 162–71.

while Viviane can write and learns all Merlin's craft. The wizard is the tutor of them both.[11]

The motif of the education of the young nobleman or noble-woman found in these early romances continues to turn up frequently in later ones. The works we have mentioned and others like them were read in French by the English aristocracy until the middle of the fifteenth century, and in English versions from the thirteenth, the episodes of education being generally preserved (though sometimes reshaped) in the translations.[12] The motif was adopted by original writers in English as well. Here it will be sufficient to refer to two well-known examples in Chaucer's *Canterbury Tales* of about the 1390s. Chaucer does not exactly say that the squire was taught by a master, but he gives him a list of accomplishments which is fully in the tradition of the well-educated youths of earlier romances:

> Syngynge he was, or floytynge, al the day. . . .
> Wel koude he sitte on hors and faire ryde.
> He koude songes make and wel endite,
> Juste and eek daunce, and weel purtreye and write. . . .
> Curteis he was, lowely and servysable,
> And carf biforn his fader at the table.[13]

This portrait is balanced in 'The Physician's Tale' by the picture of a well-educated girl, Virginia, the 14-year-old daughter of a knight. Here the emphasis is on character not on accomplishments. She is humble and quiet, modest in clothes, behaviour and speech, and wary of idleness, wine and foolish company.[14] It was into this appreciation that Chaucer inserted his exhortation to mistresses of noble girls, already mentioned, confirming the engagement of his mind at this point with girls' education. No doubt the educational

[11] *The Vulgate Version of the Arthurian Romances*, ed. Sommer: *L'Estoire de Merlin*, ii, 211–12, 253, 338. Cf. the English *Merlin* of *c*.1450, ed. H.B. Wheatley, vol i, EETS, os, x, 1865, pp. 121–2; vol iii, ibid., xxxvi, 1869, pp. 418, 507–8.

[12] *King Horn*, ed. Hall, pp. 14–15; Hue de Rotelande, *Ipomedon*, ed. Kölbing, pp. 7, 258–9, 324; *The Romance of Guy of Warwick*, ed. Zupitza, part i, pp. 3–5; part ii, pp. 6–7.

[13] Chaucer, *Works*, ed. Robinson, p. 18 (A 91–100).

[14] ibid., p. 145 (C 5–82).

element in medieval fiction was partly a reflection of the activities and aspirations of real nobility, but equally it must have helped to establish and maintain a concern for education in return. Readers of medieval fiction regularly encountered appreciative descriptions of the teaching of the young, and a wide range of values and pursuits were commended as being the accomplishments of the best people.

DIDACTIC LITERATURE

Medieval England, however, did not depend for its ideas of education on the outlines provided by fiction. The twelfth century also saw the development of serious didactic works of instruction for princes and knights, especially those who were young, on the ethics and techniques desirable in adulthood. Such works were not, of course, entirely new. The authors of classical Greece and Rome had established a literature of the education of children, mainly concerned with the noble elites who governed the societies of their day. Medieval educationists drew on these authors, especially on Aristotle, and followed them in concentrating on the ruling elites of the day, in this case the clergy and the nobility, rather than on society as a whole. This is not hard to understand. The clergy and the nobility, being the governing orders of society, were obviously the most important targets in the eyes of educationists. Educating them would benefit society the most, they had the best resources for the purpose, and they consequently offered the widest scope for advice. They were also interested in educational ideas, not merely receiving advice in a passive way but commissioning writings about it on their own initiative. The educational writings directed at the clergy and scholars, works like the *Didascalicon* of Hugh of St Victor (d. 1141) and the early thirteenth-century *De Disciplina Scolarium* ascribed to Boethius, are the more pedagogical in nature.[15] They give the greater attention to the definition of knowledge and the techniques of teaching and learning, but are more limited in aiming at adults rather than children, and adults who lived a restricted way of life. The works directed at the nobility, on the other hand, are closer to general life in the range of qualities and accomplishments with which they deal, and more often display a specific concern with children. The best and most comprehensive of them, the works of

[15] Hugh of St Victor, *Didascalicon*, trans. Taylor; Pseudo-Boethius, *De Disciplina Scolarium*, ed. Weijers.

Vincent of Beauvais and Giles of Rome, are the first great modern (as opposed to ancient) writings on the education of the laity. In the general history of European education, the importance of the medieval nobility is that they stimulated such works to be written, and helped to establish the aims and methods which subsequent educationists have been able to apply to the whole of society.

One of the first twelfth-century writers to show an interest in the education of the nobility was Peter Alfonsi (d. *c*.1140), a Spanish Jew by birth, a Christian by conversion and physician by profession to Alfonso I of Aragon. He also made one visit to England on a mission to the court of Henry I. Peter compiled between 1106 and 1140 the *Disciplina Clericalis*, a collection of didactic stories chiefly from Arab sources and aimed primarily at teaching wisdom and self-discipline to the clergy.[16] The author chose his title, he said, because his work 'renders a cleric disciplined', but its relevance extends to the lay nobility as well. In one of his chapters Peter tells how an Arab youth requested his father to give him a definition of true nobility. The father referred him to the advice of Aristotle to Alexander the Great on choosing councillors: select a man well versed in the seven liberal arts, the seven rules for good conduct and the seven knightly skills; such a man is truly noble. Further explanation reveals that the seven liberal arts consist of logic, arithmetic, geometry, medicine, music, astronomy and (depending on opinions) necromancy, philosophy or grammar.[17] The seven knightly skills are riding, swimming, archery, boxing, hawking, chess and the writing of poetry. The seven rules for good conduct are prohibitions not to eat or drink too much, live loosely, harm anyone, tell lies, be envious or keep bad company. The popularity of the *Disciplina Clericalis* was considerable. Latin copies are found in medieval religious libraries, and translations of the work were made into Anglo-Norman towards the end of the twelfth century, continental French in the thirteenth, and middle English (a single copy only) in the fourteenth or fifteenth.[18] The book may well have come into the hands of the English aristocracy, but if so, it seems to

---

16 Peter Alfonsi, *Disciplina Clericalis*, ed. Hilka and Söderhjelm; trans. Hermes and Quarrie, especially pp. 112–16.
17 This list differs slightly from the more usual later schemes of the seven liberal arts.
18 For the French translations, see the edition by Hilka and Söderhjelm, and for the English, W.H. Hulme, 'A valuable Middle-English manuscript', *Modern Philology*, iv (1906–7), pp. 68–9.

have lacked distinctive results. We do not hear in later English literature of Peter's group of seven knightly skills, and the most unusual of them, swimming, seems never to have become very popular in noble circles.[19]

More important for the history of noble education was the appearance, from the middle of the twelfth century onwards, of a genre of works which are called by historians 'mirrors of princes'.[20] The 'mirror' can be defined simply as a work of advice and instruction for kings and princes on how to rule virtuously and successfully. The earliest English example, the *Policraticus* by John of Salisbury, was written not later than 1159 and dedicated to Thomas Becket, chancellor to Henry II and the educator, as we have seen, of noble children including (later on) the eldest son of the king.[21] It is a wide-ranging survey of manners, politics and learning, of which books four and five are specifically concerned with the duties of kings and book six with those of knights. A second work from England, *De Principis Instructione* by Gerald of Wales, was begun in 1191 and completed in about 1216.[22] A third, coeval with them, came to England from abroad: the famous *Secretum Secretorum* or 'secret of secrets', reputedly the advice of Aristotle to Alexander on the art of how to be a king.[23] This work, which began life as an Arabic text in the tenth century, was partially translated into Latin by Johannes Hispaniensis in the mid-twelfth century and completely by Philip of Tripoli in the first half of the thirteenth. From this time onwards, examples of mirrors are common. They were written, translated and rewritten throughout the rest of the Middle Ages and through the Renaissance as well. One well-known late example of the genre, the *Basilikon Doron* written by James I for his son Prince Henry, was published several times in the early seventeenth century, and others were written in France by Bossuet and Fenelon as late as the reign of Louis XIV. Originally and primarily, the mirrors were a royal genre. Their chief concern was to

[19] Below, p. 207–8.
[20] For a good brief summary of the genre, see Genet, *Four English Political Tracts*, pp. ix–xix.
[21] John of Salisbury, *Policraticus*, ed. Webb.
[22] Gerald of Wales, *Opera*, ed. Brewer & others, vol viii, discussed by Bartlett, *Gerald of Wales*, pp. 69–100.
[23] For a brief history of the work, see *Secretum Secretorum*, ed. Manzaloui, i, pp. ix–xlvii.

expound the art of being a king or a prince, and most of the surviving examples were written in the first place for specific monarchs or the heirs to their thrones. In practice, however, the authors often made mention of the nobility as well, and the aristocracy became avid readers of the mirrors. As we shall see in the following pages, they acquired copies of the works and commissioned translations to be made, in an evident desire to learn the knowledge and functions of kings and thereby to share in the same kind of expertise and culture. In consequence the mirrors became effectively an aristocratic genre as well as a royal one.

They also became a genre of education. Throughout their history it was common for mirrors to be produced in the first instance for young men in their adolescence or their early manhood. Parts of the *Disciplina Clericalis* were based on the advice of fathers to their sons, and the *Secretum Secretorum* was supposedly addressed to Alexander by his tutor. Gerald of Wales dedicated his mirror to posterity, but said that if it were meant for any prince, it was for Prince Louis, the 25-year-old heir to the throne of France and Gerald's candidate to be king of England. Within their works the authors of the mirrors sought to convey a good deal of instruction and information. The *Policraticus* surveys the ethics which a king should follow, his relationship to God and the clergy, his obligation to rule justly and according to law, and his conduct in war. Gerald's *De Principis Instructione* examines the qualities which a prince should observe: moderation, generosity, magnificence, justice, boldness, religion and devotion. The *Secretum Secretorum* has a more practical emphasis, which helps to explain its popularity. Its ten discussions cover the different kinds of kings, how a king should look after his body (health, medicine and diet), justice, how to choose ministers and servants, war, the lore of the stars, precious stones and herbs. The mirror-authors often illustrated their advice with literary references, allusions to historical events and moral stories, reminding their readers of the triumphs of virtuous rulers and the downfall of foolish and wicked ones. As a result the mirrors collectively covered a wide range of subjects: religion and ethics, politics, military matters, history, literature and medicine. There was also much diversity within the genre, some works being primarily scientific and analytical, while others were little more than anthologies of moral stories intended to offer amusement as well as instruction.

John of Salisbury and Gerald of Wales, curiously, failed to found a tradition in England. Instead, after 1216 the writing of mirrors shifted to France, and for the rest of the Middle Ages it was French authors of the genre whose works were chiefly read in England, either in Latin, French or English versions. Even John and Gerald do not seem to have had much impact on the English kings or their nobility after the twelfth century. The *Policraticus*, like the *Disciplina Clericalis*, is found in religious libraries rather than noble ones, and although it was eventually translated into French in the late fourteenth century, this took place in France and it seems not to have circulated in England.[24] So it is to France and French writers in the thirteenth century that we must now turn, to find the authors on education of most importance for England during the thirteenth, fourteenth and fifteenth centuries. The English, as we have seen, were good practitioners of education, but the French far surpassed the English in perceiving education as a subject for theory and writing. Nearly every king of France from Philip Augustus (d. 1223) onwards had a mirror written for him, either as a child or an adult, but this did not become the rule in England until the fifteenth century. Indeed King Louis IX (d. 1270) actually dictated his own instructions for his children, the *Enseignements de Saint Louis*, which acquired written form and circulated in France for long after his death.

The most important authors of political and educational treatises in medieval France were clerics. They were chiefly friars: Bartholomew Glanville, Vincent of Beauvais and Giles of Rome being the most famous figures. They were associated with the university of Paris and with the new university learning of the thirteenth century, which was dominated by the works of Aristotle, and it was from his writings that they derived much of the inspiration and material for their own works. The twelfth century had possessed the spurious advice of Aristotle to Alexander which came through Arab sources; in the thirteenth century, the text of Aristotle's *Politics* became generally available in Latin and began to be widely studied in the universities. The *Politics*, as has been mentioned, has a specific concern with the bringing up of children. Book seven discusses their physical care: food, warmth, movement and exercise. Book eight sets out a curriculum of studies and activities, nominally for

[24] Genet, *Four English Political Tracts*, p. xi.

children but actually for boys alone, from the ages of 5 to 21. The work was studied in the English universities, as well as those of France, and one fourteenth-century English scholar, Walter Burley, wrote a Latin commentary on it which was widely read.[25] It is possible that the English aristocracy absorbed Aristotle's ideas on the bringing up of children straight from the *Politics*, via the members of their families who studied at university or through the graduate friars who often served as their confessors. The evidence of writings, however, does not encourage this view. The *Politics* was twice translated into French in fourteenth-century France,[26] but there is no evidence that the translations came into the hands of the English nobility and no English version was published until the end of the sixteenth century. The Aristotelian ideas that we know to have reached the English aristocracy did so at second hand, through the works of the educational writers in France.

Three of these writers call for particular attention in the thirteenth century because of the originality or influence of their works. The first, Bartholomew Glanville, was in fact an Englishman, but very little is known of his life.[27] He evidently studied at Oxford, joined the Franciscan order, went to Paris, and was sent from there by his superiors in 1230–1 to Magdeburg in Germany. In about the 1240s he produced his great encyclopaedia of knowledge, *De Proprietatibus Rerum*, 'on the properties of things', which reflects the teaching of Oxford but was probably written on the continent.[28] We have already noticed its valuable account of the bringing up of children, partly derived from Aristotle and partly based on current practices. Book six contains chapters on the baby, the child (both boy and girl), the mother, the father and the nurse, and although many of the author's remarks are applicable to children in general, the chief concern is clearly with the families of the aristocracy, and hence part of the mainstream educational tradition. At the same time that Bartholomew was working on his encyclopaedia, the French Dominican Vincent of Beauvais (d. 1264) was producing his

---

[25] S. Harrison Thompson, 'Walter Burley's Commentary on the *Politics* of Aristotle', *Mélanges Auguste Pelzer*, Louvain, Université de Louvain, Recueil de Travaux d'Histoire et de Philologie, 3rd series, xxvi (1947), pp. 557–78.

[26] Genet, *Four English Political Tracts*, p. xv.

[27] On Bartholomew's life, see *BRUO*, ii, 771–2.

[28] There are early printed Latin editions. For John Trevisa's English translation of 1398, see *On the Properties of Things*, ed. Seymour and others.

Speculum Majus, an even larger compilation put together during the 1240s and completed in the following decade.[29] The *Speculum Majus* or 'greater mirror' consists of three divisions: the *Speculum Naturale* describing heaven and earth, the *Speculum Historiale* on the history of the world from the Creation to the middle of the thirteenth century, and the *Speculum Doctrinale*, a survey of knowledge divided into seventeen books. The twelfth of these books, like Bartholomew's work, includes a chapter on 'the rule of boys', covering their upbringing from birth to adolescence, again directed generally in principle but in practice mainly concentrating on the nobility. It includes instructions on choosing a nurse, feeding and bathing the baby, play, schooling and physical education. Later, perhaps as late as 1260–1, Vincent also produced a specialized treatise on education, *De Eruditione Filiorum Nobiliorum* 'on teaching of noble children', at the request of Queen Margaret of France for the benefit of her eldest surviving son, the future Philip III.[30] This is an unusual and original work. It is entirely devoted to the upbringing of children, instead of partially so, and a large proportion of it is concerned with the theory and techniques of teaching and learning, which had hitherto only figured in treatises for the clergy or for scholars. The work begins by discussing the noble pupil's schoolmaster, the qualifications of life and knowledge he should possess, and the teaching methods he should adopt. It then turns to the pupil, how he is to listen, take notes and judge his master's teaching. The subject of discipline is discussed, and whether it should be harsh or gentle, concluding in favour of the latter. Attention is given to boys' psychology, their need to have companions of their own age, and the problems which arise during their adolescence. Most of the book is concerned with boys but the last ten chapters discuss the education of girls, and this too is unusual compared with the small space given to them in other educational works.

The originality of the *De Eruditione Filiorum Nobilium* is undeniable. It brought to the education of kings and noblemen the high standards and sophisticated concepts which had previously

---

[29] On what follows, see A.L. Gabriel, *Educational Ideas of Vincent of Beauvais*, *passim*.

[30] Vincent of Beuavais, *De Eruditione Filiorum Nobilium*, ed. Steiner. The editor, like some other scholars, prefers a date in the mid-1240s.

been confined to the educations of clerics and scholars. Its impact, however, was less. Its theoretical and psychological interests were probably beyond the taste or the needs of most princes and noblemen, who were more accustomed to the traditional kind of mirror, and its circulation in later times seems to have been limited. Instead, its approach gained currency in a more modified and acceptable form through Giles of Rome (d. 1316), the third great friar-educationist of the thirteenth century. Giles, born Egidio Colonna of a noble family of Rome, entered the order of Augustinian friars and subsequently studied and taught theology at Paris. In about the 1270s he was commissioned by Philip III, for whom Vincent had written, to produce a new treatise for his own eldest son, the future Philip IV. The work, *De Regimine Principum*, 'the rule of princes', was written in the 1270s or early 1280s.[31] In form it is large, comprehensive and methodical like Vincent's works, but cast in the more familiar mould of a princely mirror. It contains three books. The first discusses how a king or prince should govern himself: the virtues at which to aim, the emotions to be felt, and the habits to be adopted. Book two is concerned with the government of the prince's family: his relationship with his wife, children and household retainers. Book three surveys the state over which he must rule: its nature, how best to govern it in peace, and how in time of war. Giles's work fuses the older mirror tradition with that of the new child-consciousness of Aristotle and Vincent. Not only is it addressed educationally to a young prince, but it describes at length how children should be educated, which earlier mirrors had not done. The section on their bringing up comprises the second part of book two, and contains twenty-one chapters.[32] It is aimed primarily at kings and princes, but frequent references to what is proper for the nobility [*nobiles*] show that the author had in mind the aristocracy as well. He begins by discussing the duty of fathers in general and kings in particular to see to the careful rearing of their offspring. They are to choose suitable nurses and masters for this purpose. Advice is given on how to bring up children to the age of 7, and on the studies and exercises for them to learn when they are

---

[31] There are early printed Latin editions. The late thirteenth-century French translation by Henri de Gauchy has been edited by Molenaer: *Li Livres du Gouvernement des Rois*.

[32] ibid., pp. 188–230.

older: religion, letters, behaviour, athletics and military skills. Finally, there is a section (shorter than in Vincent's work) on the special problems of the education of girls. In general, Giles's work is less concerned than Vincent's with theories of teaching and studying; it adopts a more tolerant and realistic position in what it expects children to learn, and covers a wider range of skills and accomplishments. It evidently came much closer than Vincent's to the aspirations of contemporary kings and noblemen. The book was extremely popular, as we shall see, and most later mirrors were influenced by it, especially in reproducing its concern with the education of the young specifically.

The works of Bartholomew, Vincent and Giles were primarily academic works in Latin. With the exception of Vincent's *De Eruditione Filiorum Nobilium* they achieved a wide circulation in their original Latin forms, both in France and England, among the clergy in whose possession they can often be found in the later Middle Ages. Even in Latin they were capable of some influence on the education of kings and noblemen, through the medium of latinate clergy, but as time went on versions were made in French which the nobility could read themselves directly and with ease. This also happened to the *Secretum Secretorum*, which was translated into French in both France and England towards the end of the thirteenth century, and circulated in each country in French versions afterwards.[33] Giles's work was turned into French in France by Henri de Gauchy at the request of its recipient, Philip IV, soon after he came to the throne in 1285, and was widely diffused in this form.[34] Vincent was less fortunate. The historical section of the *Speculum Majus* achieved translation but the educational one did not, and the *De Eruditione Filiorum Nobilium* had to wait for this until the second half of the fourteenth century. A French version was eventually made for Charles V of France (d. 1380),[35] and one of Bartholomew for the same monarch in 1372.[36] What impact had these works — originals and translations — on the aristocracy of England? There was already an interest in education among one or

[33] Peter d'Abernon, *Le Secré de Secrez*, ed. Beckerlegge, especially pp. xxii–xxiii; Legge, *Anglo-Norman Literature*, pp. 214–16.
[34] Giles of Rome, *Li Livres du Gouvernment des Rois*, ed. Molenaer, pp. xviii, xxvi–xxvii.
[35] Genet, *Four English Political Tracts*, p. xii.
[36] C. Herfray-Rey, 'Jean Corbechon, traducteur de Barthélemy l'Anglais', *Positions des thèses, Ecoles des Chartes*, Paris, 1944, pp. 59–67.

two of the English knighthood in the thirteenth century, though it is not clearly traceable to France. The treatise of Walter of Bibbesworth on the French language, drawn up in about the 1250s, has already been mentioned for its precepts on the bringing up of children.[37] This interesting work demonstrates that England could produce a layman capable of conceiving and writing an educational treatise as early as Louis IX's *Enseignements* in France. It discussed children in ways that may owe much to personal observation, but equally may reflect the influence of Aristotle and Bartholomew Glanville. The French translation of the *Secretum* made in England in the late thirteenth century was the work of Peter of Fetcham, a clerical member of the knightly family of the D'Abernons in Surrey. Since he also did work for Sir John D'Abernon and for the countess of Arundel, it looks likely that his translation was meant for an aristocratic patron and is another sign of interest in education in knightly circles.[38]

In the fourteenth and fifteenth centuries the greater survival of manuscripts and mentions of them in wills and inventories throws much more light on the diffusion of educational works among the English aristocracy. The evidence suggests that during this period the *Secretum Secretorum* circulated very widely, Giles quite widely, Bartholomew a little, but Vincent not or hardly at all. Guy earl of Warwick in 1306 possessed 'a volume of the teaching of Aristotle addressed to King Alexander' in French (in other words the *Secretum*), and an unidentifiable French book 'in which there is teaching of children'.[39] The treasury of Edward II in 1320 contained a book described as *De Regimine Regum*,[40] and the *Enseignements* of Louis IX were quoted to Edward III by a contemporary English writer in the early 1330s.[41] Edward's youngest son Thomas of Woodstock possessed copies of Bartholomew and Giles in Latin in 1397,[42] and a French Giles was bequeathed by his widow two years later.[43] Thomas Lord Berkeley

---

[37] Above, pp. 18, 15, and below, p. 124.
[38] Peter d'Abernon, *Le Secré de Secrez*, ed. Beckerlegge, pp. xii–xiv.
[39] Madeleine Blaess, 'L'Abbay de Bordesley et les livres de Guy de Beauchamp', *Romania*, lxxviii (1957), pp. 511–18.
[40] *The Antient Kalendars and Inventories of the Exchequer*, ed. F. Palgrave, 3 vols, London, 1836, i, 106.
[41] *De Speculo Regis Edwardi III*, ed. Moisant, p. 150.
[42] Viscount Dillon and W.H. St J. Hope in *Archaeological Journal*, liv (1899), pp. 301–2.
[43] *Testamenta Vetusta*, ed. Nicolas, i, 148.

commissioned John Trevisa to translate Bartholomew into English in 1398,[44] and an English translation of Giles, probably also by Trevisa, was made for Berkeley shortly afterwards.[45] Only one copy of the latter now survives, but the Bartholomew evidently became popular, since eight manuscripts are known of it today and it was printed in 1495. During the fifteenth century a series of English translations of the *Secretum Secretorum* began to be made. One was composed in verse for Henry VI by John Lydgate and Benedict Burgh,[46] a second in prose for Sir Miles Stapleton, sheriff of Norfolk in Henry's reign, and a third in prose by John Shirley, gentleman and translator, in the reign of Edward IV.[47] Edward himself possessed a Latin copy before his accession in 1461,[48] and John Paston II owned a copy of the Lydgate version in 1475–9.[49] The popularity of the *Secretum* long outlived the Middle Ages. It was first printed in England in English in 1528, and versions went on circulating throughout the Tudor period.

Giles too continued to be read in England during the fifteenth century. John Talbot earl of Shrewsbury presented Margaret of Anjou with a French translation in 1445–7,[50] Sir Thomas Charleton of Edmonton, a former speaker of the House of Commons, owned an English version in 1465 (perhaps the Berkeley translation),[51] and Sir Peter Arderne, a chief baron of the exchequer, bequeathed a French copy to his daughter Anne Bohun two years later.[52] A Latin Giles of about the same period, with an inscription of ownership by 'the duke of Gloucester', probably belonged to the future Richard III.[53] Indeed, so closely associated

[44] Bartholomew Glanville, *On the Properties of Things*, ed. Seymour and others, especially ii, 1396. For a Latin copy belonging to a fifteenth-century knight, see M.C. Seymour, 'Some medieval English owners of De Proprietatibus Rerum', *Bodleian Library Record*, ix (1974), p. 162.

[45] Oxford, Bodleian Library, MS Digby 233, ff 1–182b(2).

[46] John Lydgate and Benedict Burgh, *Secrees of old Philosoffres*, ed. Steele.

[47] *Secretum Secretorum*, ed. Manzaloui, i, pp xxxi, xxxvii.

[48] Warner and Gilson, *British Museum: MSS in the Old Royal Collection*, ii, 54–5 (12 E.xv).

[49] *Paston Letters*, ed. Davis, i, 516–18, now BL, Lansdowne MS 285.

[50] Warner and Gilson, *British Museum: MSS in the Old Royal Collection*, ii, 177–9 (15 E.vi).

[51] McFarlane, *Nobility of Later Medieval England*, pp. 237–8.

[52] PRO, Prob 11/5, f 149ᵛ–151 (PCC 19 Godyn).

[53] Ker, *Medieval MSS in British Libraries*, i, 282–3.

with the English aristocracy had Giles's work become by the fifteenth century that the friars of his order at Clare in Suffolk asserted, quite wrongly, that he had originally written it at the request of their patron, Gilbert earl of Gloucester, and had only afterwards dedicated it to Philip of France![54] The accidental nature of all this evidence makes it difficult to identify cases of noble tutors using these educational works in their teaching or of noblemen reading them during their youth, but both practices are likely to have occurred. Sir Simon Burley, the knightly master of Richard II, owned 'a book of the government of kings and princes' in French in 1387–8,[55] and the French Giles bequeathed by the duchess of Gloucester in 1397 was intended for Humphrey her son who was then in his late teens.[56] Fifteen years later in 1411–12 Thomas Hoccleve credited the future King Henry V with having read both Giles and the *Secretum*, when Henry was still in his early twenties,[57] and Edward IV was less than 19 when he owned the *Secretum* in Latin in the 1450s.

But the influence on England of French educational works was not confined to the great productions of the thirteenth century; later works also penetrated north of the Channel and were even translated into English. Jean Golein turned an anonymous Latin treatise *De Administratione Principum* into French for Charles V of France,[58] and one extant copy of this belonged to Sir Robert Roos, the fifteenth-century English soldier and ambassador to France, who gave it to Humphrey duke of Gloucester.[59] A treatise of 1347 in French on the estate and government of princes and lords, dedicated to the future John II, was translated into English in the middle of the fifteenth century with a long title beginning *Three Considerations*.[60] Three copies of this are known, including one belonging to another famous soldier, Sir John Fastolf. Delayed translation was also

---

[54] John Capgrave, *The Chronicle of England*, ed. F.C. Hingeston, RS, 1858, p. 152; J. Weever, *Ancient Funeral Monuments*, London, 1767, pp. 473–5.

[55] V.J. Scattergood, 'Two medieval book lists', *The Library*, 5th series, xxiii (1968), pp. 236–9.

[56] Above, note 43.

[57] Thomas Hoccleve, *Works*, ed. Furnivall, iii, 74–7.

[58] Genet, *Four English Political Tracts*, pp. x, xiv.

[59] Warner and Gilson, *British Museum: MSS in the Old Royal Collection*, ii, 323 (19 A.xx); A. Sammut, *Unfredo duca di Gloucester*, p. 107. On Roos, see Ethel Seaton, *Sir Richard Roos*, London, 1961, pp. 42–9.

[60] Genet, *Four English Political Tracts*, pp. 174–9.

achieved by Christine of Pisa's *Livre du Corps de Policie*, written between 1404 and 1407, and much indebted to Giles of Rome. This was translated into English in the late fifteenth century, a single manuscript copy surviving, and printed in 1521.[61] The manuscript bears the arms of the Haut family of Kent, and may have belonged to Richard Haut, cousin of Anthony Wydeville Lord Rivers, who was controller of the household of Edward V. In the tradition of the great thirteenth-century writers, these later treatises while being generally adult in character include specific mentions of the education of children. The *Three Considerations* tells kings and princes to provide good masters and have their children taught to read and write French and Latin, especially Latin, on the ground that when princes 'have knowledge and understanding of clergy [i.e. letters] and science..., then shall they more royally and sagely govern both themselves and their lordships, and there is not any man that by reason hereof may say the contrary'.[62] Christine of Pisa elaborates on this. Princes are to take care in seeking a master for their sons, and he is to teach them religious observances, good manners and letters. Other boys, the children of barons, are to be brought up with the prince's son under the same master. At a later age the young prince should be put into the care of an elderly knight to be trained in arms and armour. He should also hear sermons from clerics, learn how the different orders of society live, and be taught to have pity on the poor – especially poor noblemen.[63]

THE ENGLISH EDUCATIONAL REVIVAL

So far, the activity of the English themselves in the sphere of educational writings has been a modest one, almost wholly limited after 1216 to the reading and translating of books which originated elsewhere. Setting aside works confined to the academic sphere, like Roger Bacon's edition of the *Secretum Secretorum* in the thirteenth century and Walter Burley's commentary on the *Politics* in the fourteenth, there is little evidence for the production of original works aimed at kings or noblemen in either of these centuries. In the thirteenth we have only Walter of Bibbesworth's treatise, and in the

[61] Christine of Pisa, *Livre du Corps de Policie*, ed. Bornstein, pp. 17–22.
[62] Genet, *Four English Political Tracts*, p. 205.
[63] Christine of Pisa, *Livre du Corps de Policie*, ed. Bornstein, pp. 42–9.

early and mid-fourteenth only two Latin mirrors written for the young Edward III. One, *De Nobilitatibus, Sapientiis et Prudentiis Regum*, was produced for the king by one of his clerks, Walter de Milemete, in 1326–7. It is based on the *Secretum Secretorum* and other sources, and survives in two manuscripts which, interestingly, are illuminated with knightly scenes and heraldic shields. The other, *Speculum Regis Edwardi III*, was probably written in the early 1330s by William of Pagula, rector of Winkfield near Windsor.[64] It is primarily a complaint against the exactions of the king's servants in requisitioning provisions for Windsor Castle from the nearby parishes, but it contains a middle section of general application, advising Edward to live a good Christian life and to rule well. This work also exists in two manuscripts. With these exceptions, however, it was not until the late fourteenth century and in the fifteenth that the English began at last to start producing works on royal and noble education to a significant extent. A major cause of this development was the decline of French as a literary medium in England, and the rise of a new English literature alongside French. First, the disuse of French, as we have seen, led to the making of English translations of the educational works which the nobility had been accustomed to reading in French. Second, there appeared original writers from Langland and Chaucer onwards, prepared to handle in English a wider range than before of topics of current interest in their society. One of these was the education of the young, and in due course it attracted their attention.

Langland, for example, though he rarely singles out the young for extended treatment, makes several allusions in *Piers Plowman* to childhood and education, including aspects of growing up at home, the discipline of children, schooling and apprenticeship. Once, briefly, he mentions his own school education.[65] Chaucer exhibits a stronger interest in the subject than Langland, and the references to it in the course of his work are built up on a larger scale.[66] As well as referring several times to the growing up of children in noble households, he surveys the ideal accomplishments of a young

[64] *The Treatise of Walter de Milemete de Nobilitatibus, Sapientiis et Prudentiis Regum*, ed. M.R. James, Roxburghe Club, 1913; *De Speculo Regis Edwardi III*, ed. Moisant, especially pp. 149–59; also discussed in *Medieval Studies*, xxxii (1970), pp. 329–36.
[65] Orme in *History of Education*, xi (1982), pp. 251–66.
[66] Orme in *The Chaucer Review*, xvi (1981), pp. 38–59.

nobleman in his portrait of the Squire and its antithesis, the story of
Nero and Seneca in 'The Monk's Tale'. The treatment of the
Prioress, as has been suggested, alludes to the education of girls in
nunneries and that of Virginia to their growing up at home under
mistresses. The poet's liking for university scholars and locations at
Oxford and Cambridge is also evident and well known. Gower, too,
in the *Confessio Amantis* describes the education of Achilles by
Chiron in book four, while book seven contains a complete mirror:
the education of Alexander by Aristotle. In it the philosopher
describes to the prince the nature of knowledge and science, rhetoric
or how properly to speak, and in the manner of Giles of Rome how to
rule oneself, one's family and one's kingdom.[67] An interest in
education continued among fifteenth-century writers. Hoccleve
and Lydgate, like Gower, each wrote a mirror in verse,[68] and
Lydgate has left us a poem confessing the sins of his childhood and
his education.[69] Malory in his account of Tristan was moved to
enlarge the description of the prince's education given in his French
source,[70] and the achievements of Caxton, as we shall shortly see,
included both the publication, translation and dedication of works
for educational purposes. There is no doubt that the education of
the young, from the middle of the fourteenth century, was often
present in the minds of English writers, and sometimes emerged as
one of their major themes.

There were at least three important developments in educational
literature during the age of Chaucer and in the fifteenth century.
First of all, we can see the more frequent adoption in England of the
practice long current in France that heirs to the throne should have
mirrors or other works specially written for their education.
Whereas between 1216 and 1400 there is only the single example of
the *Speculum Regis Edwardi III*, between 1400 and 1509 mirrors or
other educational writings were produced for five or six of the seven
heirs to the throne who had a childhood during that period. The
earliest of them, *The Regement of Princes*, was dedicated to Prince
Henry, later Henry V, by Thomas Hoccleve in 1411–12 when

[67] Gower, *Complete Works*, ed. Macaulay, ii, 354–5; iii, 233–385.
[68] Hoccleve, 'The Regement of Princes' in *Works*, ed. Furnivall, vol iii; Lydgate, *Fall of Princes*, ed. Bergen.
[69] Lydgate, *Minor Poems*, ed. H.N. MacCracken part i, EETS, es, cvii (1911), pp. 352–4.
[70] Above, note 7.

Henry was a young adult, and is in verse. It consists of a number of maxims which kings should observe: keeping one's oath, justice, observing the law, pity, mercy, patience and so on, gathered from the *Secretum*, Giles of Rome, and Jacques de Cessoles's moral commentary on the game of chess.[71] These are illustrated by the usual kinds of stories (from the Bible and classical history), which Hoccleve declared would be pleasant for passing the evening when Henry was in his chamber.[72] A year or two later in 1413 the prince's father Henry IV delivered to his son his own, apparently oral, advice on kingship, which got recorded and nearly achieved an independent circulation like the *Enseignements* of St Louis. It was first written down in a Latin poem (or part of a poem) about the death of Henry IV, which was also addressed to Henry V by Thomas Elmham, royal chaplain and prior of Lenton near Nottingham. According to Elmham, Henry IV before he died exhorted his son to love and worship God and to keep his conduct upright, deviating neither to right nor left.[73] Another early writer on Henry IV, John Capgrave friar of King's Lynn, reports that the king moralized on his own decline from a strenuous warrior to a parcel of bones and nerves, and enjoined the prince to choose a wise confessor, ask counsel of good and religious men, avoid idleness and pay his father's debts.[74] The advice, except in Elmham's poem, never gained independent form as Louis's did, but it was incorporated in all the later chronicle accounts of Henry's reign and became well known. The famous death-bed scene in Shakespeare's *Henry IV Part II* is a well developed form of the same tradition.

Henry VI was also the recipient of an educational treatise. A single copy survives of a Latin work called *De Regimine Principum* composed for him by an unknown cleric, probably at the end of the 1430s when the king was in his late teens, since it calls him a young man.[75] The work is in three parts, of which the first two discuss the qualities necessary to a king (mercy, charity, peace, warlike resolution, and so on), while the third surveys the four estates of society: noblemen, prelates, lesser clergy and people. Henry's own

---

[71] For Jacques de Cessoles, see below, p. 179.

[72] Hoccleve, *Works*, ed. Furnivall, iii, 73–8.

[73] *Political Poems and Songs*, ed. T. Wright, vol ii, RS, 1861, pp. 120–1.

[74] John Capgrave, *Liber de Illustribus Henricis*, ed. F.C. Hingeston, RS, 1858, pp. 110–11.

[75] Genet, *Four English Political Tracts*, pp. 40–173.

son Edward prince of Wales (d. 1471) had at least two treatises written for him during his childhood and adolescence. The first, by George Ashby, clerk of the signet to the prince's mother Margaret of Anjou, survives in a single manuscript.[76] It falls into two parts, the first 'on the active policy of a prince' in English verse, and the second on 'the sayings and opinions of various philosophers' consisting of Latin quotations followed by English verse translations. Both parts cover the same ground: deportment, ethics and policy, with some interesting suggestions for the prince's own education. He ought to read the Bible and the chronicles, speak well, cultivate music, and when he grows up take care over the education of his own children and the wards in his governance. Probably later than this, between 1468 and 1471 when Edward was in his late teens and in exile in France, Sir John Fortescue addressed to him his famous Latin treatise *De Laudibus Legum Anglie*, 'in praise of the laws of England'.[77] This is the most original of all such works produced in fifteenth-century England. It is not the usual kind of survey of kingly qualities, but a praise and description of the English legal system, though like Ashby and other works since the thirteenth century it also contains specific passages about the education of the prince and the nobility.[78] Nor was it dedicated to Edward merely as a formality. Fortescue was evidently aware of the prince's warlike and military propensities, and may have been afraid of the effect of absolutist influences on him during his stay in France. The work therefore had a main educational purpose, to instruct the king's son in the English legal system, as well as to describe how the system operated.

The interest in writing works for princes continued under the Yorkists and the Tudors. Just as George Ashby had prepared 'sayings and opinions of various philosophers' for Edward son of Henry VI, so did Anthony Wydeville Lord Rivers for Edward son of Edward IV. Rivers tells us that while on pilgrimage to Compostela in the summer of 1473, he amused himself on board ship by reading a French collection of sayings of ancient philosophers, ultimately derived from an Arab work of the eleventh

---

[76] Ashby, *Poems*, ed. Bateson, especially pp. 17–19, 33, 39, 71.
[77] Fortescue, *De Laudibus Legum Anglie*, ed. Chrimes.
[78] E.g. ibid., pp. 2–5, 16–19, 108–11, 116–19.

century.[79] When in the following autumn Rivers was appointed by Edward IV to be governor to the prince of Wales,

> when I had leisure I looked upon the said book, and at the last concluded in myself to translate it into the English tongue, which in my judgment was not [done] before, thinking also full necessary to my said lord [the prince] the understanding thereof.[80]

Rivers's translation, the *Dicts and Sayings of the Philosophers*, was published by Caxton at Westminster in 1477, and thus achieved a general currency as well. Not surprisingly, we lack evidence of any work specially produced for the next prince of Wales, Richard III's son Edward who was prince for less than a year in 1483–4, but the fashion continued with the *Speculum Principis* compiled by John Skelton in 1501: a short Latin prose collection of maxims and exhortations from biblical and classical sources.[81] Skelton was the earliest schoolmaster of the duke of York (Henry VIII), who was 10 in 1501, and the work which begins with an address to a single prince was probably intended primarily for him. The conclusion, on the other hand, speaks of it being finished 'for noble princes, to whom, perhaps, it is not unsuitable'. This use of the plural, together with the date, makes it possible that the work was also drawn up with an eye to the duke's elder brother, Prince Arthur, who did not die until the following year.

A second parallel development, from the late fourteenth century onwards, was the production or dedication of other works than mirrors for the use of children, both those of kings and of the nobility. Here careful definition is required. There was an ancient tradition of literature being addressed by a father (or occasionally a mother) to a son (or daughter). In the Bible, the books of Proverbs and Ecclesiastes consist of moral and practical advice delivered by fathers to their children. In classical Rome, Marcus Portius Cato is recorded to have written an encyclopaedia and a history for his son;[82] Cicero compiled the *De Officiis* for his son Marcus, then aged

---

[79] On the history of the work, see *The Dicts and Sayings of the Philosophers*, ed. C.F. Bühler, EETS, os, ccxi, 1941, pp. ix–xiii.

[80] Wydeville, *The Dicts and Sayings of the Philosophers*, prologue.

[81] Salter in *Speculum*, ix (1934), pp. 25–37.

[82] Plutarch, *Lives*, ed. B. Perrin, vol ii, London and New York, 1914, pp. 360–3.

21, and Quintilian tells us that Livy wrote advice to his son on the authors whom he should read.[83] In the Middle Ages, the thirteenth-century Italian author, Albertano da Brescia, produced three works in Latin, one on the love of God and one's neighbour, another on speech and silence, and a third on consolation and counsel, for his three sons Vincenzio, Stefano and Giovanni. The writings of Albertano were popular in medieval Europe, and Chaucer's 'Tale of Melibee' is a translation of the third of them.[84] The motif of addressing a treatise to one's son was also adopted by the thirteenth-century English author, Walter of Henley, in his well-known treatise on *Husbandry*, or farming and estate management.[85] The convention is therefore likely to have been well known in late medieval England.

What we find from the late fourteenth century onwards is not an originality in writing such works, but a greater number of them and examples which were clearly meant for children as opposed to adolescents or young adults. The first such example is the most famous one: Chaucer's *Astrolabe*, written in about 1391 for his son Lewis, then aged 10 and probably studying grammar at Oxford.[86] The work is highly technical, but the preface makes four distinct allusions to Lewis's littleness, youth and childishness, and three of the manuscripts of the text entitle it 'bread and milk for children'. It may have fulfilled a wider role in teaching children to read than its author intended. In the early fifteenth century Hoccleve translated 'The Tale of Jonathas' from the *Gesta Romanorum* for the edification of a 15-year-old boy, the son of a friend who was worried by his son's wildness,[87] and in the 1440s or 1450s Benedict Burgh, a beneficed clergyman in Essex and later archdeacon of Colchester, turned the famous Latin school poem, the *Distichs of Cato*, into English verse for another boy, William the son of Henry Viscount Bourchier.[88] It was later published by Caxton in 1483. The chronicler John Hardyng also glances at the education of children in

[83] Cicero, *De Officiis*, ed. W. Miller, London and New York, 1913, pp. 2–7; Quintilian, *Institutio Oratoria*, ed. H.E. Butler, vol iv, London and New York, 1922, p. 25.
[84] On Albertano, see Peter Idley, *Instructions to his Son*, ed. D'Evelyn, pp. 36–44.
[85] *Walter of Henley*, ed. Oschinsky, pp. 308–9.
[86] Chaucer, *Works*, ed. Robinson, pp. 544–6.
[87] Hoccleve, *Works*, ed. Furnivall, i, 216.
[88] Caxton, *Prologues and Epilogues*, ed. Crotch, p. 76.

his history of England. When it was first dedicated to Henry VI in 1457, the author expressed the hope that the queen and the prince (then young) would read it too, and when a year or two later he changed the dedication to Henry's cousin Richard duke of York, he made a similar commendation of the work to the duchess and the duke's heirs who were aged from 17 downwards.[89] Caxton published three works besides the *Cato* with ascriptions to children or for their use. One, Lord River's *Dicts and Sayings* addressed to Prince Edward, has already been mentioned. The second, Caxton's translation of Raoul le Fevre's story of Jason (1477), was also dedicated to Edward, then aged 7, with an overtly educational purpose 'to the intent he may begin to learn read English', not for any beauty of the language (says Caxton modestly) 'but for the novelty of the histories which, as I suppose, hath not been had before the translation hereof'.[90] Lastly in 1490, Caxton dedicated a similar translation, the *Eneydos* or story of Aeneas, to the 4-year-old Prince Arthur, though in this case the motive of educating him is not specifically mentioned.[91]

Two other fifteenth-century works addressed to children call for more detailed treatment. The first is that of Peter Idley, lord of the manor of Drayton in Oxfordshire and a minor household officer of Henry VI, who appointed him gentleman falconer in 1453 and controller of the king's works three years later.[92] He lost the latter post in 1461 when Henry was deposed, and after his death in about 1473 was buried in the abbey of Dorchester-on-Thames. Idley had a large family by two wives, and ten boys and girls were featured on his memorial brass. In about the 1450s he drew up a series of moral *Instructions* for Thomas, his eldest son, because like Hoccleve's friend he feared that his son was 'somewhat wild'. Idley was able to read Latin, and the *Instructions* are based on two of Albertano's Latin works, already mentioned, and two works in English: Robert Mannyng's early fourteenth-century poem *Handling Sin* on the ten commandments and the seven deadly sins, and Lydgate's *Falls of Princes*. Out of these Idley constructed a long poem of over 4,000

[89] C.L. Kingsford, 'The first version of Hardyng's Chronicle', *EHR*, xxvii (1912), pp. 462–82, 740; Hardyng, *Chronicle*, ed. Ellis, p. 23.
[90] Caxton, *Prologues and Epilogues*, ed. Crotch, p. 34.
[91] ibid., p. 110.
[92] Peter Idley, *Instructions to his Son*, ed. D'Evelyn, contains a full biography and text.

lines in two books. Book one enjoins the son to love God, learn while he is young, guard his tongue and be submissive to those he serves. He should observe cleanliness, avoid fantastic clothes, women, taverns and great oaths, and choose the company of good fellows. He is instructed in how to take counsel, when to exact vengeance, and the way to love his wife and rule his servants. Book two, based on Mannyng, is less specifically the advice of a father to a son and surveys the Church's instructions to Christians in general on how to behave. The work is a compilation and not a very sophisticated one at that, but it is a further sign of interest in education among the lesser aristocracy, and it did spread beyond the author's family. The survival of seven manuscripts shows that it met some need or response among its author's contemporaries.

THE EDUCATION OF WOMEN

The other work by a father, important in fifteenth-century England, leads us towards a third development: the literature of women's education. It also takes us back to the writers of France. All the works we have glanced at hitherto were chiefly concerned with the training of boys and men. The education of girls, though of course it existed in practice, lagged far behind that of boys in separating itself from life in general and consequently in attracting the notice of writers. It did so first in the work of the friar-educationists of thirteenth-century France, but even they, though they recognized it, gave it much less attention than they did the teaching of boys. Bartholomew Glanville may have intended his chapters on infants and young children to apply to girls as well as boys, but he discusses them primarily in terms of boys, and though he has two chapters on 'the girl' and 'the daughter', these are concerned with their physiology and character, not with the ways in which they should be brought up and trained.[93]

Vincent of Beauvais shares some of these characteristics. In his *Speculum Majus* he approaches the care of babies in terms of males, and his chapter on the subject is called 'the rule of boys'. In the *De Eruditione Filiorum Nobilium* forty-one of the chapters are on the upbringing of boys and only ten on that of girls. Nevertheless in these ten Vincent goes some way towards creating a treatment of the

[93] *De Proprietatibus Rerum*, book vi, chapters 6, 8 (ed. Seymour, i, 301–2, 304).

subject.[94] He thought that girls should be carefully guarded and secluded, but also wanted them positively to learn a curriculum. This should include intellectual matters (reading, writing, prayer and the study of holy scriptures), good behaviour (chastity, modesty, humility and silence), and the arts of sewing and weaving. They should be prepared for marriage and told how to deal with a husband, mother-in-law, children and domestics. Equally, if they preferred to remain virgins, they should be allowed to do so. Vincent's work, however, had less impact upon the aristocracy than that of Giles, and Giles here as elsewhere toned down the treatment to what one suspects was more in line with current noble attitudes. Only three of the twenty-one chapters of the educational part of *De Regimine Principum* are concerned with girls, and they are more negative in their approach than Vincent's had been.[95] One chapter covers the need for seclusion and control, the second warns against idleness and the third enjoins care in speaking. Hardly any mention is made of a curriculum of activities. In the second chapter (number twenty) Giles, considering what occupations women should pursue, can only say that 'it is convenient to speak as people generally do' and go on to list sewing, spinning and working with silk. He may have taken it for granted that women would learn to read, but he only mentions the fact and stresses it for women of such high rank that they cannot be put to work of a textile nature.

The view of women's education in France, however, did not remain static. It continued to develop, and by the fourteenth century had grown in the consciousness of educationists sufficiently to generate the writing of books wholly, not just partially, on the subject. The two best known of these are the aristocratic treatise *The Book of the Knight of the Tower*, and the bourgeois one *Le Ménagier de Paris*.[96] The only one of them to reach medieval England, as far as we know, was *The Book of the Knight of the Tower*.[97] It was first turned into English during the reign of Henry VI by an unknown

---

[94] *De Eruditione Filiorum Nobilium*, ed. Steiner, pp. 172–219. For discussion of Vincent's view of women, see Tobin in *Journal of the History of Ideas*, xxxv (1974), pp. 485–9.

[95] *De Regimine Principum*, book ii, part ii, chapters 19–21 (ed. Molenaer, pp. 225–30, especially pp. 227–8).

[96] Eileen Power, *The Goodman of Paris*, London, 1928.

[97] Landry, *The Book of the Knight of the Tower*, ed. Offord, contains text and biography.

author in a version surviving in a single and incomplete copy, but it was translated a second time by Caxton in 1483 and printed, from a French text given to him by 'a noble lady' who may have been Queen Elizabeth Wydeville. It was thus the first book on the education of women to circulate in England, though once again it was of French not English make. The author, Geoffroy de la Tour-Landry, was a middle-aged knight of Anjou who began to compose it in 1371 and finished the task a year or two later. He tells us in his prologue that he got the idea in his garden on a spring day towards the end of April. On seeing his young daughters (he had three) come into the garden, he was struck by how important it was for them to learn good examples of living and to be well taught. He knew that a queen of Hungary had written a book for the education of her daughters (probably Elizabeth of Bosnia, wife of the French king Louis I of Hungary, who is known to have done so), and he decided to follow her example.[98] He was not therefore the first to write such a book, even in his own eyes, but his book was the first of its kind to spread widely over western Europe: France, England and Germany.

The knight's book follows a common form among medieval works of instruction in telling a series of stories of virtue and vice, as examples to the reader of how and how not to behave. Some are taken from the author's own experiences and others from the Bible, the deeds of kings, the chronicles of France and England, 'and many other foreign histories'. The work was intended to be read personally by the knight's daughters.[99] Like Vincent, Bartholomew, Chaucer and other writers on the education of women, it concentrates on character and behaviour rather than accomplishments and tech-niques, but it is a disorderly work compared with the academic treatises. The plan of topics is lacking in logic, the knight repeats himself frequently, especially on women's extravagant dresses which evidently irked him, and towards the end, having apparently run out of female material, he digresses into an account of Cato's education of his son. What the book lacks in method, however, it gains as an autobiography. Its insight into the knight's mind and views on education are very valuable. He wished his daughters to be good Christians, to marry well and to make the best of their married life. His advice to avoid extravagance, loose living and answering

[98] ibid., pp. 11–12.
[99] ibid., p. 122.

back were directed towards these ends. He was aware of the temptations to which young women might be exposed, and besought his daughters to beware of the flattery and seduction of young knights which he had witnessed himself in his youth.[100] No surprise need be felt when we find him adopting the strong language of the preachers to whom he would have listened, threatening his daughters with eternal punishment for worldly vanity, as in the story of the woman in hell who is tortured by devils with burning needles and torches for painting her face in life and plucking her eyebrows.[101] It is, however, a sign of the curious balance of morality and frankness in the Middle Ages, even when dealing with children, that the knight not only warns his daughters against fornication but illustrates the warning with explicit stories of sex. A man copulates with a woman, as a dog does with a bitch, under the altar of a church and becomes immovably stuck in the process. A monk plays truant from high mass to lie with a woman in church, with similar results. Two queens fornicate with knights in church on Maundy Thursday, and are put to death for the crime in a leaden box.[102] As John Fitzherbert observed in 1534, the next commentator after Caxton we have on the book, it could well make men and women 'know more vices, subtlety and craft than ever they should have known if the book had not been made'.[103] How many people took this view is impossible to say. Caxton's edition was never reprinted, but the book clearly made some impact in England. Fitzherbert knew of it sixty years later, and it is known to have belonged to gentlemen in both Gloucestershire and Hertfordshire during the sixteenth century.[104]

The works we have encountered show that a good deal of literature in the Middle Ages was devoted to education, in the widest sense of the term. Religious, moral, political and satirical writings all had this end in view. Most medieval writers on education failed to distinguish between adults and children. They directed their writings to people in general, but that included children and in this

[100] ibid., p. 12.
[101] ibid., pp. 76–8.
[102] ibid., pp. 59–60, 165–6.
[103] Fitzherbert, *The Boke of Husbandrye*, f 50ᵛ.
[104] Landry, *The Book of the Knight of the Tower*, ed. Offord, pp. xvii–xviii.

sense there was literature for children before there was a specific children's literature. A distinct concern with children first appears in fiction, and narrative literature may reasonably be said to contain the oldest descriptions of how children were or should be educated. The subject entered serious literature in the thirteenth century through the study of Aristotle in the universities and the educational works it inspired by the friar-educationists centred in France. After this it became common for works on education to include sections specifically devoted to the bringing up of children, and by the late fourteenth century works like Chaucer's *Astrolabe* and *The Book of the Knight of the Tower* were being produced avowedly to be read by children. Even so, genres of literature for children or about them were slow to emerge and had hardly done so by the end of the Middle Ages, excluding the single area of Latin textbooks for schools. Writing about children, even in 1500, remained a part of other genres: the romance, the mirror and the encyclopaedia; except for Vincent's *De Eruditione Filiorum Nobilium* no work had yet been produced solely about children. Such writing as there was for children, too, had not yet acquired a different character from that which was written for adults. Chaucer, Idley and the Knight of the Tower, though they wrote for children in the first place, wrote in an adult way – most notably in the Knight's salacious stories. Their works were also read by adults, and they can be logically classified as general literature, as well as children's literature.

In educational literature France generally led and England followed. This was not so true in the twelfth century when John of Salisbury and Gerald of Wales wrote in England, though both had studied at Paris. But from the thirteenth century down to the end of the fifteenth, a strong French influence is found alike in works on the education of the clergy, scholars and the nobility, and the grammatical textbooks of schools. In this respect it is difficult to object to the French knight who said to Sir John Chandos before the battle of Poitiers in 1356, 'You [English] can never think of anything new yourselves, but when you see something good you just take it'![105] In the theory of lay education, which was practically limited to noble education, the French influence was particularly dominant. Its best writers, Vincent and Giles, reached a height of sophistica-

---

[105] Froissart, *Chroniques*, ed. de Lettenhove, v, 418–19; *Chronicles*, trans. Brereton, p. 132.

tion unequalled in England, with the sole exception of Fortescue's educational treatise on English law. The English, by comparison, were mainly content to reshape, translate or simply to read the works of France. As far as the conception and exposition of lay education was concerned, the role of England must be reckoned small. What it does exhibit is a social history of interest in education by consumers. From the thirteenth century onwards individual noblemen and gentlemen acquired educational books, had them translated, and in a few cases even wrote them. Walter of Bibbesworth, Chaucer and Peter Idley were not great educationists, but they did have strong personal interests in the subject. They bear witness to the same quiet unobtrusive *practice* of education in England as do the institutional records of the households, religious houses, schools, universities and inns of court.

Four Language, belief, behaviour

THE CURRICULUM

We have now considered the environment of noble education, the officers who provided it and the writings in which it appears. Our remaining task is to establish its content. What knowledge and values, techniques and abilities were taught to aristocratic boys and girls? From early times the narrative literature of the Middle Ages portrayed the ideal nobleman as the owner of many and various talents besides the ability to fight. The hero of *Beowulf* is equal to all occasions. He can arrive in a strange land and speak effectively to its king and his courtiers, behave properly in hall, lead his retainers successfully and rule well when he mounts the throne himself. He is not only brave but loyal, deferential, generous and wise. In the literature of the twelfth century onwards, when characters are introduced as it were with testimonials of their accomplishments, there is an equal emphasis on variety. Tristan, Horn and Ipomedon, as we have seen, are all credited with several abilities from the list of reading, writing, eloquence, good behaviour, singing, dancing, playing chess, riding, hunting and fighting. Sometimes, as in Gottfried von Strassburg's *Tristan*, the whole gamut may be attributed to them.[1] In the case of girls the testimonials relate to

---

[1] Above p. 83.

character rather than techniques, and limitations of activity are more apparent with the stress on modesty and seclusion. Even they, however, are shown in the course of romantic stories engaging in various skills – literary, rhetorical, artistic and even athletic – and the effect, if not the intention, is also one of breadth and diversity. The literature of the Middle Ages anticipates that of the Renaissance in its implication that men and women should be trained in a variety of ways, ready for all eventualities.

While width of accomplishments became almost a cliché in literature, the list of what should be learnt remained by contrast relatively undefined. Although the skills ascribed to heroes and heroines were taken from a stereotyped list, the selection from within that list was not stereotyped. One lot of attributes will omit reading or languages, another dance or song, a third hunting. No essential group of noble accomplishments or values seems to have been universally recognized; there was no noble equivalent to the seven liberal arts of academic study. The same is true of the serious writings on education. They also show an awareness and an approval of width and diversity of skills, but they equally fail to arrange these skills into memorable and influential schemes. Aristotle set the tone when he said that mankind was not agreed about the things which should be taught. He proceeded to describe a traditional four-fold scheme of education, consisting of reading-and-writing, gymnastic exercises, music and drawing, but his scheme was not adopted by medieval educationists, even by those who were otherwise Aristotelians.[2] Peter Alfonsi, as we have seen, ascribed to Aristotle the view that the perfect nobleman should be skilled in the seven liberal arts, the seven knightly skills and the seven rules of good conduct.[3] A concept of seven knightly skills seems to have taken root in medieval Germany, where it also occurs in Johannes Rothe's *Ritterspiegel* or 'knight's mirror' in the early fifteenth century.[4] But it does not appear in books that were read in England. Alfonsi's work, as the slender number of translations into French and English indicates, did not circulate widely among the English nobility. Neither Vincent of Beauvais nor Bartholomew Glanville describes a scheme of noble skills, and Giles of Rome only

---

[2] *Politics*, book viii, chapters 2–3.
[3] Above, p. 87.
[4] Johannes Rothe, *Der Ritterspiegel*, ed. H. Neumann, Halle, 1936, pp. 72–3.

does so hesitantly. Like Alfonsi he thinks that princes should ideally study the seven liberal arts, but he is not confident that they will, since he says that if they have no time to learn them all they should concentrate on Latin, and if not Latin, on French.[5] Later, Giles discusses other desirable matters for princes to learn: observation, hearing, speaking, measurable eating and drinking, exercise and the affairs of adult life, but he does not bring them together into a scheme. Indeed, much of his discussion of exercise occurs outside the second, educational book of *De Regimine Principum* in the third, which treats of war. Giles's work, like the romances, draws attention to a wide range of desirable studies and skills, but it does not define a canon of essential balanced elements, nor was the lack supplied by any other writer of the later Middle Ages.

If educationists failed to define the 'what' of the aristocratic curriculum, they were better aware of the 'how': the ways of teaching skills to noble children. Bartholomew, Vincent and Giles each emphasized the need to choose good nurses and masters for this purpose, and spent some time discussing the qualifications and duties of such people.[6] The widely held belief in three ages of childhood led writers, as far back as classical times, to allocate activities to each of the ages, thereby proposing the organization of education in terms of children's years. Aristotle, as we have seen, identified the objectives in bringing up children until they were 5 or 7 as movement, training to endure cold, and seclusion from adult vices. He recognized the other two ages of childhood too, but he had little to say about the activities appropriate to them, except that hard exercise and military training should be left till 'after boyhood': presumably after puberty.[7] The friar-educationists of the thirteenth century made more progress in this respect. True, Bartholomew restricted himself to the topic of children under the age of 7, but Vincent and Giles both allocated tasks to all three ages of childhood, in virtually similar ways.[8] When infancy was over at the age of 6 or 7,

[5] *De Regimine Principum*, book ii, part ii, chapters 7–8 (ed. Molenaer, pp. 197–202).
[6] *De Eruditione Filiorum Nobilium*, ed. Steiner, pp. 8–12; *De Proprietatibus Rerum*, book vi, chapters 4, 9 (ed. Seymour, i, 299, 304); *De Regimine Principum*, book ii, part ii, chapter 9 (ed. Molenaer, pp. 203–6).
[7] *Politics*, book vii, chapter 17.
[8] *Speculum Doctrinale*, book xii, chapters 31, 63; *De Regimine Principum*, book ii, part ii, chapters 15–17 (ed. Molenaer , pp. 216–23); book iii, part iii, chapter 3 (ed. Molenaer, pp. 375–7).

boys should be put to school under a master and learn grammar and logic. They should take gentle exercise but not do hard physical labour. On reaching 12 or 14, they should practise to ride and fight in preparation for a real chivalric career at the age of 18. In adolescence their reasons developed and they became sexually mature. They began to think for themselves and were tempted by lechery, so that special care should be given to teaching them chastity and obedience. Finally, they should be prepared for the duties of adult life: marriage, the rule of a household and the bringing up of children of their own. In short, both Vincent and Giles held that education should be organized in terms of age to take account of physical and psychological development. Frequent allusions to this principle in English writings and documents show that it became widely observed in practice too.[9]

There is another way in which education is adapted to the passage of time: the observance of a regular sequence of activities throughout the day, repeated every day. Daily routines were established in places of ecclesiastical learning at an early date. Novices in monasteries and choristers of cathedrals were trained in the framework of the daily cycle of prayers and observances carried out by their elders. Schools and universities probably had their customary daily patterns of starting, changing and finishing their work as early as the twelfth century, though little or nothing of these patterns has been recorded. Even in noble households, daily life followed predictable lines, marked out by religious devotions, business and meals, around which children's teaching and recreations must have been fitted. The beginnings of an awareness of daily routines can be seen in one or two educationists of the thirteenth century. Vincent of Beauvais in the *Speculum Doctrinale* describes the pattern of activities which belongs to a baby: baths, feeds, play and sleep.[10] The anonymous treatise *De Disciplina Scolarium* written at Paris in about the 1230s discusses the best time of the day for scholars to learn and be taught their work.[11] A consciousness of daily routines, however, developed only slowly.

---

[9] An unusually detailed treatment of the subject is that of John Hardyng in 1457, where he arranges noble education in a biennial sequence: reading at 4, language at 6, dancing and singing at 10 and 12, hunting at 14 and war-training at 16 (BL, Lansdowne MS 204, f. 12; Hardyng, *Chronicle*, ed. Ellis, pp. i–ii, dated by C.L. Kingsford in *EHR*, xxvii (1912), pp. 462–82, 740–53).

[10] *Speculum Doctrinale*, book xii, chapter 13.

[11] Pseudo-Boethius, *De Disciplina Scolarium*, ed. Weijers, pp. 126–8.

Giles of Rome says nothing about them, and it is not until the fifteenth century that a significant interest in the matter appears to have become widespread in English society. The fifteenth century in England is remarkable for the proliferation of mechanical clocks, both in churches, noble households and town communities.[12] Clocks demonstrate the wish of their users to follow daily routines in some detail with small seasonal variations, and consequently to observe each day in much the same way. There are many traces in fifteenth-century records of an increased concern with daily time, both by individuals and institutions, which looks forward to the concern of modern society. In schools, the first clear evidence of routines timed by the clock comes from the foundation statutes of endowed schools from the 1440s onwards.[13] At the universities, the statutes issued for colleges in the fifteenth century are the first to fix the hours at which business should take place and lectures be given.[14] By the reign of Edward IV the household ordinances of the king and his brother Clarence were laying down specific times for meals, meetings of officers, attendance on the king and the opening and shutting of gates.[15] In a private capacity, Edward's mother Cecily duchess of York (d. 1495) and Henry VII's Lady Margaret Beaufort (d. 1509), are the earliest ladies known to have followed timed routines of business, meals and prayer, in units as brief as a quarter of an hour.[16]

The earliest daily plan to survive for a noble child or youth is that of John Mowbray duke of Norfolk, which was probably drawn up in 1435 when he was 19 or 20.[17] It seems to have been unusual to

[12] On the increasing evidence of church clocks in the fifteenth century, see C.F.C Beeson, *English Church Clocks, 1280–1850*, London, 1971, pp. 22–4.
[13] Orme, *English Schools in the Middle Ages*, p. 124.
[14] The statutes of New College, Oxford, 1389–94, prescribe no hours for any activity (*Statutes of the Colleges of Oxford*, i, especially 24, 40–2, 56, 67, 102). Specific hours begin to appear at Oxford in the statutes of All Souls, 1443 (ibid., p. 13); Lincoln, 1480 (ibid., p. 15); Magdalen, 1487 (ibid., ii, 47, 69); and Corpus Christi, 1517 (ibid., pp. 42, 48, 96).
[15] Myers, *Household of Edward IV*, pp. 201–4, 208, 214, 218–20; *A Collection of Ordinances*, pp. 89–105.
[16] For Cecily's timetable, see ibid., pp. *37–9, discussed by C.A.J. Armstrong, 'The Piety of Cecily, Duchess of York', *For Hilaire Belloc*, ed. D. Woodruff, London, 1942, pp. 73–94. For Lady Margaret Beaufort, see Fisher, *English Works*, ed. Mayor, i, 294–5.
[17] Orme in *BIHR*, 000.

prescribe the daily routines of young noblemen in writing at this date, and the plan laid down for Mowbray was the outcome of an abnormal situation, caused by the duke's disorderly conduct while he was still a ward of the king. Norfolk was summoned before the ruling council of the young Henry VI and made to agree to follow a new way of life, partly defined by the clock. He was to get up between six and seven, say prayers and attend the king to mass. In the evening he was to say prayers again, and be in bed by ten. The daily routine of Norfolk was repeated in more detail in the ordinances for the bringing up of Edward V in 1473, when Edward was nearly 3.[18] These represent a further development of educational planning, since they were not a reaction to crisis but prepared deliberately for a number of years to come. They are also wider in scope than those of Norfolk. Edward was to rise 'at a convenient hour, according unto his age', listen to mattins and go to mass. After mass he breakfasted and spent the morning in 'virtuous learning', also adjusted to his age, till mid-day dinner. In the afternoon he had more learning, followed by recreation and exercise. He then went to evensong, ate supper and had recreation again until bed-time which was fixed at eight p.m. That was the only stated time in the original plan, but in 1483 when Edward was 12, the ordinances were revised and further times were inserted.[19] The morning lesson was now fixed at one hour, the afternoon lesson at two hours, and bed-time was postponed until nine. In this way the fifteenth century produces the first documents in England to regulate the daily lives of individual children, though their form is not truly original. Like the devotional timetables of Duchess Cecily and Lady Margaret they were ultimately modelled on the daily routines of the clergy. Religion was a powerful influence on educational forms among the nobility, as it was in schools and universities.

The emphasis on regular routines, increasingly timed by the clock, probably spread more widely among the aristocracy from the Yorkist period onwards. The late fifteenth-century English translation of Christine of Pisa's *Livre du Corps de Policie* advises a prince's schoolmaster 'to set a competent hour and a certain rule and certain space of time in which the child should continue in his school, and after that give him space to play before his dinner'.[20] The

---

[18] ibid.
[19] ibid.
[20] Christine of Pisa, *Livre du Corps de Policie*, ed. Bornstein, pp. 42–4.

appearance in noble households of professional masters, used to school routines, may also have strengthened the planning and timing of noble children's lives. By the late 1520s the daily routines of study in the leading English schools were being committed to writing and copied by schools elsewhere.[21] Coincidentally, we hear of a daily curriculum drawn up for the private education of Thomas Cromwell's son Gregory in about 1530, with 'an order of study' including French, writing, music and athletics, defined in terms of hours.[22] But planning was not always completely effective. John Palsgrave, the schoolmaster of Henry Fitzroy duke of Richmond in 1525–6, complained to Sir Thomas More of the disruptions to his daily routine with his pupil. People came constantly in, says Palsgrave, with projects to tempt the duke away from his studies, 'some to hear a cry at a hare, some to kill a buck with his bow, sometime with greyhounds and sometime with buckhounds...., some to see a flight with a hawk, some to ride a horse'.[23] It was the old problem of balance between accustoming a noble boy to servants and companions, and shielding him from their distracting influences.

We can now summarize the nature of the aristocratic curriculum in medieval times. It was a wide one, covering various skills and values: religious, intellectual, social, artistic and physical. Educationists, by the thirteenth century, approached it primarily in terms of age, and chose from it topics and activities appropriate for each stage of childhood. In practice, children probably followed daily routines, combining more than one activity, but these routines were almost unconscious until the fifteenth century, when they began to be written down and timed by the clock. Educationists also took for granted the scope of the curriculum, and gave little attention to defining what it should contain. That leaves us free to define and arrange it as we ourselves think best. We shall begin, in the rest of this chapter, with three very basic accomplishments, which are acquired widely and early: language, belief and behaviour. Chapter five will deal with what are nowadays called 'the arts': literature, music, dancing and the visual arts. Finally in chapter six, we shall

[21] Orme, *English Schools in the Middle Ages*, p. 114 and note. These are not strictly timetables, as they are not timed.
[22] Ellis, *Original Letters*, 3rd series, i, 341–3.
[23] *LPFD, Henry VIII*, iv part iii, pp. 2593–4.

examine physical education: training for war, hunting, archery and outdoor games.

LANGUAGE

Long before a noble child was taught to read or write it learnt to speak, and gained through speech the oldest and commonest method of acquiring knowledge and communicating with other people. Medieval writers took much about childhood for granted, but they did not overlook the function of mothers and nurses in teaching young children to speak, or the earliest efforts which children made to do so. Bartholomew, as we have seen, portrayed the nurse lulling her child and singing it cradle songs, lisping and lightly sounding her words 'to teach more easily the child that cannot speak'.[24] Medieval carols imagine the Virgin Mary lulling the infant Jesus as he made his first attempts to articulate words:

> He sayd, 'Ba, bay',
> Scho sayd, 'Lullay',
> The virgin fresch as ros in May,[25]

and an Oxford teacher of the late fourteenth century likens the language of young children to that of a cuckoo, endlessly reiterating 'da! da! da!', which the teacher identifies wittily with the Latin imperative, 'give! give! give!'[26] A colder view was that of Sir Thomas Elyot in 1530, who noticed the distorted talk of nurses and children and disapproved of it. The practice was, he said, 'a wantonness, whereby divers noblemen's and gentlemen's children (as I do at this day know) have attained corrupt and foul pronunciation'. Nurses, he thought, should speak no English but that which was 'clear, polite, perfectly and articulately pronounced'.[27]

Medieval observers seem to have been more tolerant of baby-talk than Elyot, but they would have agreed with him that children, as they grew up, should learn to speak correctly and effectively. This

---

[24] *De Proprietatibus Rerum*, book vi, chapters 4, 9 (ed. Seymour, i, 299, 304).
[25] R.L. Greene, *The Early English Carols*, 2nd edn, Oxford, 1977, pp. 85–104, especially p. 89.
[26] Richardson in *Formularies which bear on the History of Oxford*, ed. Salter and others, ii, 389–90.
[27] *The Governor*, book i, chapter 5.

was essential in a noble environment where one encountered many other people: superiors, equals and servants, each requiring different kinds of communication. Medieval advice on etiquette laid emphasis on speaking properly.[28] *The Babies' Book*, a poem addressed to noble children in the fifteenth century, recommends a boy who enters his lord's house to say 'God speed' as he goes in, humbly salute those he meets, and listen to what is said to him. If he is asked to reply, he should first think what to say and then express himself in courteous language and with brevity, for many words are tedious.[29] The knights and ladies of romances are often commended for their good speaking, reflecting ideals which were probably valued in practice. Readers of stories like *Sir Gawain and the Green Knight* would have appreciated the verbal dexterity with which the hero steers himself through awkward situations, from a public affront to his king to a private attempt by the wife of his host to seduce him in his bedroom. Thus when Gawain is moved to intervene between King Arthur and the Green Knight and to take up the latter's challenge, he is careful to defer not only to Arthur himself but to the queen, with whom he is sitting at table, and to his fellow courtiers whom as a gentleman he must not offend through any claim to special valour or importance:

> 'Wolde ye, worthilych lorde', quoth Wawan to the kyng,
> 'Bid me bowe fro this benche and stonde by yow there,
> That I wythoute vylanye myght voyde this table,
> And that my legge lady lyked not ille,
> I wolde com to your counseyl bifore your cort ryche'.[30]

He himself, he goes on, is the weakest person present, and worthy to be praised only because he is Arthur's nephew. There can be little doubt that noble masters and mistresses urged their charges to aim at similar standards when they spoke. A prince's master, says Christine of Pisa, must teach him to greet and speak properly to all

---

[28] On this subject, see also below, pp. 138–9.

[29] *Early English Meals and Manners*, ed. Furnivall, p. 252.

[30] 'If, worthy lord', quoted Gawain to the king, 'you would bid me leave this bench and stand beside you, so that I might vacate the table without discourtesy, and if my liege lady did not dislike me doing so, I would come to give you counsel in front of your noble court' (*Sir Gawain and the Green Knight*, lines 339–60). Gawain's courteous speaking was proverbial: Chaucer, *Works*, ed. Robinson, p. 129 (F 89–104).

men.[31] The life of a noble household with its ceremonies and visitors provided a school for boys and girls to watch the behaviour of their elders, and to learn what was effective in speech and what was not. The history of the language of the medieval aristocracy is dominated by the question 'which language?' The knights who won the battle of Hastings were speakers of Norman French. They brought to England wives and servants from France, and the children born to them north of the Channel grew up among French speakers from birth, learning French as their primary language in childhood and normally using it when they grew up. A hundred years later, by the last quarter of the twelfth century, this situation had undergone change.[32] Marriages had taken place between Norman and English families, Norman households were employing nurses and servants from among the English, and English families anxious to acquire the knightly status of their conquerors were probably adopting French themselves. By 1177–9 the king's treasurer Richard FitzNigel could remark that except for villeins, it was scarcely possible nowadays to say which man was English by birth and which was Norman.[33] The analogy of the British in India in the nineteenth century suggests that Norman children, as soon as they had English nurses and servants, would have learnt two languages from a very early age.[34] While they were in the nursery and chiefly in contact with their nurses and rockers, they would have picked up English and been fluent in it, though they would also have absorbed some French and spoken it more haltingly on the rarer occasions when they were with their parents or other Normans. As they grew older, this situation was probably reversed. They came into greater contact with French-speaking parents, masters and child-companions, and began to develop French as their normal language, relegating English for use when dealing with servants or other inferiors. French could survive as a spoken language in

---

[31] Christine of Pisa, *Livre du Corps de Policie*, ed. Bornstein, pp. 45–8.
[32] On French in England in the late twelfth and thirteenth centuries, see W. Rothwell in *BJRL*, lviii (1975–6), pp. 445–66. In general a most useful survey, it overemphasizes (I feel) the difference between a 'naturally' learnt English and an 'artificially' learnt French.
[33] FitzNigel, *Course of the Exchequer*, ed. Johnson, p. 53.
[34] See, for example, F. Kilvert, *Kilvert's Diary*, ed. W. Plomer, 3 vols, London, 1961, iii, 181 and Rudyard Kipling, *Something of Myself*, London, 1937, pp. 3, 39.

England under these conditions, but its pronunciation and usages tended to be contaminated by English ones, and this must have been especially so among English-speaking families on the fringe of the aristocracy who tried to pick up French for reasons of status. There was already a recognized 'bad French' in England by the end of the twelfth century. Gerald of Wales calls it 'the rude French of the English', and Walter Map 'Marlborough French'.[35] Gerald indeed suggests that it was possible for someone who should have learnt French to avoid doing so, for he censures one of his nephews for not having bothered to master Latin 'or even French'.[36] Such a failure, however, must have been characteristic of the geographical or social fringes of the aristocracy rather than the centre. For French long resisted the challenge of English, and remained a major spoken language of the aristocracy in adulthood. It had many advantages. It was the language of the still-remembered Conquest, the distinguishing mark of the ruling elite and the linguistic link with western Christendom. Already by 1200 it was the medium of romantic fiction and much religious literature, and during the thirteenth century would become increasingly used for writing administrative and legal records.

The royal family probably had the best understanding of French in England during the thirteenth and fourteenth centuries, and learnt the language most naturally. All the English kings from John to Henry VI married a French-speaking queen, and would have conversed more easily with these ladies and their retinues in French than vice versa in English. Most of these queens were also the mothers of the royal children. Members of the English royal family visited France from time to time, French noblemen came to the English court, and several of the men and women in charge of the royal children were natives of France. The daughters of Edward III in the 1340s were brought up by Mary of St Pol countess of Pembroke and by Isabella de la Mote, both ladies born in France.[37] Richard II was born at Bordeaux; his nurse and rocker were natives of Aquitaine,[38] and his knightly master in the early 1370s who

---

[35] Lefèvre in *Etudes à Félix Lecoy*, p. 309; Map, *De Nugis Curialium*, trans. James, p. 271.

[36] Lefèvre in *Etudes à Félix Lecoy*, p. 302.

[37] Leland, *Collectanea*, ed. Hearne, i, 99; *CCR 1337–9*, p. 94; PRO, E 101/389/11.

[38] PRO, E 101/400/4 m 20; *CPR 1377–81*, p. 120.

instructed him in 'noble virtues' was Sir Guichard d'Angle of Poitou.[39] Richard's cousin Henry IV, then heir to the dukedom of Lancaster, had also a master from France in 1376–7: Sir Guillaume de Mountendre, a knight of Aquitaine.[40] As late as the end of the fourteenth century a child in the royal family was likely naturally to absorb French of a continental dialect, through direct contact with French speakers. Froissart describes how Richard II took up and perused a French book which he, Froissart, gave him in 1395, 'for he spoke and read French very well',[41] and the remark of Henry IV, when his men captured James I of Scotland on his way to be educated in France, points to a similar knowledge. 'He said jokingly that the Scots should certainly be thankful that they have sent the young man to me to be instructed, for I myself know French!'[42]

The households of the rest of the aristocracy were less able to retain the services of native-born French personnel. How did they keep up the language? In the first place, parents, chaplains and senior household servants could pass on to children their own inherited knowledge of French, a knowledge that was renewed and improved through the visits of the aristocracy and their retinues to France which went on frequently up to the end of the Hundred Years War in 1453. Gerald of Wales informs us that a young man whom he knew called John Blund learnt excellent French without leaving England from uncles of his who had lived and studied in France,[43] and many later children must have profited from contact with Englishmen who had learnt the French of the continent. Boys in their turn could better their language when they too grew up and went to France, on campaigns or on embassies. Those who never left England and were not even in contact with visitors to France could learn French of an Anglo-Norman kind more formally from schoolmasters, chaplains or clerks who spoke or wrote the language in its anglified form. The English writers of the 1320s, Ranulf Higden and Robert Holcote, concur in observing that the school-masters of England traditionally taught Latin through the medium of French, and that schoolboys did their translations from Latin into

[39] Froissart, *Chroniques*, ed. de Lettenhove, viii, 137, 379.
[40] PRO, DL 28/3/1; *CPR 1374–7*, p. 471.
[41] Froissart, *Chroniques*, ed. de Lettenhove, xv, 167; *Chronicles*, trans. Brereton, p. 408.
[42] T. Walsingham, *Historia Anglicana*, ed. H.T. Riley, vol ii, RS, 1864, p. 273.
[43] Lefèvre in *Etudes à Félix Lecoy*, p. 303.

French.[44] It followed that until the middle of the fourteenth century when this tradition changed, the clergy and the literate clerks who staffed the chapels and administrations of the aristocracy and are often likely to have acted as tutors to noble children, had themselves learnt a fair degree of French during their studies and could pass it on to their charges.

It seems evident that French was a major language of speech and writing among the aristocracy up to the second half of the fourteenth century, although English must have been known and used in speech as well from the twelfth century onwards. Knowledge of French remained an emblem of nobility for a long time. Robert of Gloucester writing in about 1300 says that the 'high men' of the land still hold to French and that unless a man knows the language, he is little reckoned of.[45] Ranulf Higden agrees in the 1320s. Gentlemen's children are taught to speak French from the time that they are rocked in their cradles, and rustic men who wish to be likened to gentlemen busily endeavour to speak French so as to be the better reputed.[46] The language was not so strongly based in England as it was in France, however, since artificial textbooks were being produced as early as the mid-thirteenth century, to help those (including the nobility) whose access to good oral French was limited.[47] One of the first such texts was Walter of Bibbesworth's *Tretiz de Langage* of about 1250, written to help Denise de Mountchesney teach her children. She evidently knew some French but was limited in her vocabulary, and Walter's *Tretiz* provided a supplement in this respect, listing large numbers of words relating to various aspects of everyday life, and distinguishing homonyms and homophones: words which might lead to confusion because they were written or pronounced in the same way. Other French textbooks made their appearance during the late thirteenth and fourteenth centuries, describing the grammar and spelling of words, but all presuppose a background of spoken French and simply aim

[44] *Fourteenth Century Verse and Prose*, ed. Sisam, p. 148; Smalley, *English Friars and Antiquity*, p. 162.
[45] *The Metrical Chronicle of Robert of Gloucester*, ed. W.A. Wright, vol ii, RS, 1887, pp. 543–4.
[46] *Polychronicon Ranulphi Higden*, ed. C. Babington, vol ii, RS, 1869, pp. 158–61; *Fourteenth Century Verse and Prose*, ed. Sisam, pp. 148–9.
[47] On these works, see Bibbesworth, *Traité*, ed. Owen, pp. 9–18, and Rothwell in *Modern Language Review*, lxiii (1968), pp. 37–46.

to strengthen it. None is a comprehensive guide to the language, such as existed for Latin. The writings used by the aristocracy up to the late fourteenth century confirm the predominance of French among the nobility. Apart from Latin prayer-books and royal documents, the written material they handled was in French: Bibles, devotional treatises, works of fiction, personal letters and wills. We know of a few members of the aristocracy who themselves wrote books between the mid-thirteenth and mid-fourteenth centuries: Walter of Bibbesworth himself, Walter of Henley the writer on estate management, Sir Thomas Grey of Heton the chronicler, and the devotional author Henry duke of Lancaster. All produced their works in French.

The replacement of French by English as the preferred spoken and written language of the aristocracy took place gradually during the fourteenth century. The rate of this process can be roughly charted from literary records, but there must have been much variation from the higher aristocracy to the lower, and even from family to family. As early as the 1340s, Edward III had an English motto displayed on his bed, and carried a shield bearing two lines of English verse.[48] According to John Trevisa writing in 1387, French began to be disused in schools in about 1350 – a change of much importance.[49] It meant that the chaplains and clerks who subsequently served the aristocracy had little knowledge of the language, and that aristocratic boys who went to school after that date ceased likewise to be practised in it. In 1363 parliament, a forum dominated by the aristocracy, was opened by the chancellor in English, doubtless because it suited his auditors rather than himself.[50] In 1370 Chaucer addressed his poem *The Book of the Duchess* in English to John of Gaunt, and during the next thirty years wrote courtly literature in English, with a courtly audience much in mind. By 1387 Trevisa could observe that 'gentlemen hath now much left off teaching their children French', and that children in grammar schools knew no more French than their left heels.[51] He wrote this in a translation of Ranulf Higden's history of the world, which was one of several translations of scholarly Latin works commissioned by Thomas Lord Berkeley (d. 1415) to be made into English. Even a

---

[48] Juliet Vale, *Edward III and Chivalry*, Woodbridge, 1983.
[49] *Fourteenth Century Verse and Prose*, ed. Sisam, p. 149.
[50] *Rotuli Parliamentorum*, ed. Strachey, ii, 275.
[51] *Fourteenth Century Verse and Prose*, ed. Sisam, p. 149.

member of the baronage by 1387 found English more natural to read than French. By the 1390s writers of textbooks of French in England could no longer assume a strong background of spoken French, and we begin to see the production of dialogues in French in which the whole art of conversation was recreated for the student, rather than the vocabularies and simple grammars hitherto in use which had reinforced an existing conversational skill.[52] By the early fifteenth century the aristocracy had definitely ceased to speak the language at home among themselves. The teacher of French John Barton, who composed his grammar the *Donait françois* in about 1415, mentions several reasons why the 'good people' of England should learn it, but conversing to one another is not one of them. Rather, Barton identifies its purpose in England as a language for administration – writing letters and understanding the common law – and as a spoken language only for use abroad, when speaking to the 'good people' of France.[53] These two applications of French, literary at home and conversational overseas, continued to be relevant during the fifteenth century. True, the use of French for writing letters and documents was discontinued during the 1430s and 1440s,[54] but much romantic and religious literature, despite the achievements of Chaucer and his contemporaries, remained in French until the second half of the fifteenth century. A reader confined to English would have had difficulty in finding many romances, devotional books and histories to read until Caxton issued a wide range of translations in multiple copies during the 1470s and 1480s. Even after that the study of the common law kept alive Anglo-Norman of a kind, while political and cultural contacts with France at the level of king and court provided a continuing reason for learning the French of Paris. Several references to the teaching of French to noble children, or their use of it in adulthood, show that the language continued to be studied during the fifteenth century.

It is probable that all the kings of that century could speak French fluently. Henry VI was ordered to be taught 'languages' in 1428

52 Bibbesworth, *Traité*, ed. Owen, pp. 15–16.
53 E. Stengel, 'Die ältesten Anleitungsschriften zur Erlernung der französischen Sprache', *Zeitschrift für neufranzösische Sprache und Literatur*, i (1879), p. 25.
54 Helen Suggett, 'The Use of French in the Middle Ages', *TRHS*, 4th series, xxviii (1946), pp. 67, 70, 72, 79.

when he was seven,[55] and presumably spoke some French during his visit to France to be crowned in 1430. The French writer Commynes considered that Edward IV, whom he met in 1475, spoke 'quite good French',[56] and both Edward and Richard III owned books in the language.[57] Henry VII must have become fluent in it during his exile in Brittany, and he took care that his children should become so too, employing one native speaker of French, Giles D'Ewes, to teach them French and another, Bernard André, Latin.[58] Among the nobility of Edward IV's reign John Howard, later duke of Norfolk, spoke French on diplomatic business in France in 1475,[59] and Anthony Wydeville Lord Rivers translated from French *The Dicts and Sayings of the Philosophers*. The language was also learnt by women. Lady Margaret Beaufort owned books in French and was, like Rivers, a translator of them.[60] Her daughter-in-law Elizabeth of York probably knew the language too. When Katherine of Aragon was about to leave Spain in 1498 to marry Prince Arthur, the Spanish ambassador reported that Margaret and Elizabeth advised that she should learn French, since they did not understand Latin or Spanish.[61] French was known by some ladies even at a provincial level. Eleanor Hull (d. 1460), the daughter of a Somerset knight and the wife of a gentleman, translated a lengthy commentary on the seven penitential psalms from French into English in the middle of the fifteenth century.[62] Further to the north, Margaret Plumpton daughter of a Yorkshire esquire could speak French 'prettily' in 1463 when she was only 4.[63]

[55] *Proceedings of the Privy Council*, ed. Nicolas, iii, 296–8.
[56] Philippe de Commynes, *Memoirs*, trans. M.C.E. Jones, Harmondsworth, 1972, p. 258.
[57] Warner and Gilson, *British Museum: MSS in the Old Royal Collection*, entries indexed at iii, 138; H.D.L. Ward, *Catalogue of Romances . . . in the British Museum*, vol i, London, 1883, p. 358.
[58] On André, see *BRUO*, i, 33, and on Dewes, *Dictionary of National Biography*.
[59] Commynes, *Memoirs*, trans. Jones, pp. 260, 263.
[60] Fisher, *English Works*, ed. Mayor, i, 295.
[61] *Calendar of State Papers Spanish*, vol i: *1485–1509*, London, 1862, p. 156.
[62] Margaret Deanesly, *The Lollard Bible and other Medieval Bible Versions*, 2nd edn, Cambridge, 1966, p. 341. For her identity, see her will written in her own hand in *The Register of Thomas Bekynton, Bishop of Bath and Wells*, ed. Sir H.C. Maxwell-Lyte and M.C.B. Dawes, vol i, Somerset Record Soc., xlix (1934), pp. 352–3.
[63] *Plumpton Correspondence*, ed. Stapleton, p. 8.

Nunneries were traditionally centres of the speaking and teaching of French, hence Chaucer's remark about the provincial French of the abbey of Stratford-at-Bow near London,[64] and this tradition may have lingered long in certain places. As late as 1535 the king's commissioners visiting Lacock Abbey in Wiltshire reported that the rule of the house was written in a form of French 'like the French of the common law', and that the nuns could understand it very well.[65]

BELIEF

At the same early age that a child learnt language, the communication of adults, it was also introduced to adult codes of belief and behaviour: religious faith, morality and good manners. Indeed, the making of a child into a Christian began before it learnt to speak. It was christened, as we have seen, a day or two after its birth, and christening both made it a member of the Church subject to the Church's laws, and provided it with spiritual guardians and instructors in the persons of its godparents. The rite was in origin partly educational. Candidates for baptism in the early Christian Church, who were generally adults, received an examination or catechism of their belief immediately prior to receiving baptism itself. The catechism was retained in medieval times as the first part of the ceremony, and though its educational nature was by then virtually extinct (it was addressed to the godparents not to the child, and even to them in Latin), medieval priests seem often to have added an informal vernacular address to the formal part of the proceedings.[66] This charged the godparents to see that the child was taught the Apostles' Creed with its basic Christian beliefs, learnt the two basic medieval prayers (the Paternoster and the Ave Maria), and was brought for confirmation to the bishop in due course. Baptism might no longer be instructive, but some instruction was still expected to result from it.

The religious teaching of children, however, did not receive special emphasis in medieval times. Boys and girls, particularly those of the aristocracy, grew up in a society so permeated by clergy and religious activities that Christian belief and behaviour could

---

[64] Chaucer, *Works*, ed. Robinson, p. 18 (A 124–6).
[65] *LPFD, Henry VIII*, ix, p. 47 (no 160).
[66] *Manuale ad Vsum Sarisburiensis*, ed. Collins, pp. 32, 35–6, 37–8.

reasonably be expected to grow naturally, rather than needing to be planted and tended artificially. Thus Giles of Rome, though he gives a chapter to the religious education of children, does little more than elaborate the injunctions addressed by priests to godparents.[67] Kings and princes, he advises, should make their children learn the faith of Holy Church in youth, because faith cannot be proved by reason and is therefore appropriate to be learnt by children who are not swayed by considerations of reason. By 'faith' Giles meant merely 'a simple outline', consisting of the propositions stated in the Creed, and although in a later part of his book he mentions metaphysics and divinity as possible fields for the aristocracy to learn, he also regards them as highly technical subjects which are unlikely to be studied in practice.[68] The Church in medieval England gave little recognition to childhood as a separate state requiring special attention. Confirmation was a mere appendage of baptism, and was administered as soon as convenient afterwards, often when children were still only babies. There was little or no idea of 'coming of age' in religious terms, in the form of a first confession or first communion; there was no public instruction of children as such, no 'Sunday schools', or texts specifically devised for children's use. Most of the religious education of the young must have occurred informally. Parents, godparents and masters taught the Creed and the basic prayers, religious stories and the principles of morality. Chaplains and friars were at hand to reinforce and expand their teaching. Children were exposed to religious art, went into sacred buildings and watched their elders at their devotions. They learnt by experience what went on, and by example how they should behave.

The formal teaching of religious knowledge, in as far as it existed, was linked with the teaching of reading and Latin grammar which will be examined in the next chapter.[69] The alphabet itself was presented to medieval children in a religious framework, the letters being written out with a cross at the beginning and the word 'amen' at the end, the whole sequence being sometimes known as the 'Christ-cross row'.[70] As soon as children could recognize letters,

---

[67] *De Regimine Principum*, book ii, part ii, chapter 5 (ed. Molenaer, pp. 193–5).
[68] ibid., chapter 8 (ed. Molenaer, pp. 199–202).
[69] Below, p. 145–6.
[70] For a visual representation of the alphabet, see Orme, *English Schools in the Middle Ages*, p. 61.

they practised reading from religious texts: the primer, containing the Paternoster, Ave Maria, Creed and other common prayers, and liturgical books like the antiphonal and the psalter. Margaret Plumpton was learning the psalter as well as French in 1463,[71] and Henry Fitzroy 'mattins' (probably the mattins and hours of the Virgin Mary) in 1525 when he was 5 or 6.[72] In the case of boys, the learning of Latin grammar also involved religious material. An elementary exercise might take the form of studying and analysing the basic prayers in their Latin forms, as Gregory Cromwell is mentioned learning to translate the Paternoster and the Creed from Latin in about 1530.[73] Sentences for translation given out by medieval schoolmasters were often on religious topics: the times and seasons of the Church year, religious services, fasting and pilgrimages.[74] At a more advanced level the Latin poems read in schools included one on how to confess and others on the superiority of Christian ethics to the ways of the world.[75] We hear of one or two noble children possessing their own religious books in childhood, or being advised to read them. A primer was bought for Edward II in 1300 at a cost of £2 when he was 18,[76] and Edward IV wrote to his father the duke of York in his mid or late teens in the 1450s, asking for a 'portuous' or Latin breviary.[77] George Ashby, at about the same date, recommended that the young Prince Edward son of Henry VI should read the Bible to learn the virtuous deeds of the righteous and the downfall of the ungodly.[78] The books possessed by adult noblemen and women included a large proportion of religious works: Latin prayer books and vernacular lives of saints and devotional treatises. It is very likely that the taste for these works and the first experience of reading them were gained in childhood.

Medieval religion emphasized the need for belief to be expressed in terms of observances, and salvation to be won with the help of good works. Noble boys and girls were required to take part in doing

---

[71] *Plumpton Correspondence*, ed. Stapleton, p. 8.

[72] *LPFD, Henry VIII*, iv part iii, pp. 2593–4 (no 5806).

[73] ibid., v, p. 8 (no 18).

[74] See, for example, Orme in *Traditio*, xxxviii (1982), pp. 310–11.

[75] Orme, *English Schools in the Middle Ages*, pp. 102–5.

[76] *Liber Quotidianus Contrarotularis Garderobae*, London, Society of Antiquaries, 1787, p. 55.

[77] Ellis, *Original Letters*, i, 9–10.

[78] Ashby, *Poems*, ed. Bateson, pp. 17, 19.

these, just as their parents did. By the late fourteenth century and throughout the fifteenth, adult nobility were following regular daily routines of prayer, and boys and girls, as we have seen with regard to John Mowbray and Edward V, were expected to follow them too.[79] One got out of bed, said (or heard said) the mattins of Our Lady in one's chamber, attended mass in a nearby chapel, and said the vespers of Our Lady in the late afternoon before supper. Children were also present at all kinds of larger services in churches. Thus the daughters of Edward III, Isabella and Joan, aged about 7 and 8, went to high mass in the chapel of the Tower of London on 27 December 1340, St John's Day. They gave 6s as an offering and paid 40d to four Augustinian friars who sang at the mass in their presence. On Palm Sunday 1341, while they were staying with the nuns of Stratford-at-Bow, they gave 3s 4d to a Dominican friar who preached before them, and a week later they made Easter offerings at the high cross in the nunnery church.[80] Noble children, like the rest of the population, were frequent visitors at shrines. When Edward I was 13 in 1252, he went to St Albans where he offered vestments and money at the high altar of the abbey and at the altar of St Amphibalus.[81] In 1381–2 the 15-year-old Henry earl of Derby (later Henry IV), after barely escaping death in the Peasants' Revolt, visited St Albans too, as well as Kenilworth, Lincoln, Pontefract, Windsor and other religious houses, making offerings of money in each of them.[82] His grandson Henry VI, on arriving at Bury St Edmunds to spend Christmas in 1433 when he was 12, prayed dutifully at St Edmund's shrine there, and the local poet John Lydgate, who was a monk of the abbey, commemorated the visit by writing a Life of St Edmund in English verse for Henry's use. The manuscript of this contains a picture of the young king kneeling in prayer at the shrine.[83] In visiting shrines and churches and making them generous gifts, noble children were being trained for the

---

[79] Besides the ordinances for Mowbray and Edward V, see Landry, *The Book of the Knight of the Tower*, ed. Offord, pp. 14–17, and Caxton, *Book of Curtesye*, ed. Furnivall, pp. 4–5.

[80] PRO, E 101/389/11.

[81] Paris, *Chronica Majora*, ed. Luard, v, 320.

[82] PRO, DL 28/1/1 f. 4ᵛ.

[83] Dugdale, *Monasticon Anglicanum*, ed. Caley, iii, 113; Lydgate, 'St Edmund', in *Altenglische Legenden*, ed. C. Horstmann, Heilbronn, 1881, pp. 379–81; BL, Harley MS 2278, f 4ᵛ.

openhanded roles expected of them when they came to be adults. They were also brought up to give charity to the poor. The expenses of Isabella and Joan in 1340–1 include payments of 21*d* to the prisoners of Newgate and other poor people whom they met on their journey from London to King's Langley in Hertfordshire. Later, they handed out 7*d* 'in pennies' on the way from the Tower of London to Stratford, and gave 6*s* to twenty-four indigent folk at Stratford on Good Friday.[84] Holy Week was an especially popular time for acts of charity of this kind. On Maundy Thursday 1382 the young earl of Derby washed the feet of fifteen paupers at Hereford Castle (one for each year of his age),[85] and Henry VI made distributions of money to thirty-three (the age of Christ) on the same day in 1426, when he was only 4.[86]

We know little about the personal reactions of noble children to religion until the fifteenth century, and then only at second hand. No doubt young boys and girls amused themselves in their games by copying religious ceremonies and imitating the devotions of their elders. Sir Thomas Elyot describes how some of them, 'kneeling in their game before images and holding up their little white hands, do move their pretty mouths as [if] it were praying, others going and singing as it were in procession'.[87] There are one or two mentions of older children seeking guidance or comfort in their faith at times of doubt or fear. Bishop Fisher relates an anecdote of the childhood of Lady Margaret Beaufort which he had 'heard her tell many a time', concerning her betrothal in the early 1450s when she was about 12. She was the object of a proposal of marriage by the king's half-brother, Edmund Tudor, and she was evidently asked for her consent since she had a day by which to give an answer. Being doubtful what to say, she consulted an old gentlewoman who advised her to pray to St Nicholas bishop of Myra, the patron saint of maidens. She did so frequently, and with eventual success. On the night before her decision was required, she saw a vision of a man arrayed like a bishop who spoke to her the name of Edmund and told her to take him as her husband, which she did.[88] A generation later,

---

[84]   PRO, E 101/389/11.
[85]   PRO, DL 28/1/1 f 4ᵛ.
[86]   PRO, E 404/42/306.
[87]   *The Governor*, book i, chapter 4.
[88]   Fisher, *English Works*, ed. Mayor, i, 292–3.

The fifteenth century saw
an increase of educational
writing in England, with
laymen playing a larger
part.   10 (right)
Thomas Hoccleve
presenting his *Regement of
Princes* to Henry V.

11 (below)   The tomb of
Sir John Fortescue, who
wrote *De Laudibus Legum
Anglie* for Edward son of
Henry VI.

10

11

Noble boys received a formal training in reading and writing; girls a more informal one. The result (12, above), the will of Simon de Montfort written in a neat hand by his knightly son Henry in 1259.   13 (below)   Women like Margery Paston used male scribes to write their letters, only rarely adding a few words with their own hands.

13

DEVOTIONS AND DIVERSIONS

The young were trained in religious devotion from an early age.   14   The 12-year old Henry VI worshipping at the shrine of St Edmund, Bury, in 1433.   15   Music and dancing were standard noble accomplishments acquired in childhood. Here, noblemen and women dance to the music of drum and bagpipe.

17

ARMS AND ATHLETICS

Noble education provided for sport and military training, especially for boys.   16a
(top)   A boy on foot aims a lance at a quintain.   16b (centre)   He does the same
from a wooden 'horse' on wheels.   17 (bottom)   Hunting and archery both
became recognized as educational for children during the fifteenth century.

the pathetic life of Edward V after his deposition in 1483 was reported to Dominico Mancini by Edward's physician John Argentine, who was one of the last of his attendants to be allowed to visit him. Confined in the Tower, the 12-year-old victim of Richard III 'sought remission of his sins by daily confession and penance, because he believed that death was facing him' – a terror which few children, fortunately, were made to share.[89] Contrariwise, there must have been others like John Mowbray whose religious habits grew slack in adolescence through the acquisition of other interests and more tempting pleasures. The bishop of Rochester Thomas Brinton remarked in 1375 that many sons of the nobility, when they were children and under the care of a master, prayed regularly and had a conscience to refrain from vices. But when they achieved lordship in adulthood, they slept until terce (the middle of the morning) and scorned divine worship.[90] Despite the exposure of the medieval aristocracy to so many clergy and religious institutions compared with our own society, the fallen human nature of its members was no different from ours. Religious education by no means produced a uniform piety, and arrogance and slackness grew up alongside it like the tares of the parable among the planted wheat.

BEHAVIOUR

Belief, as the previous pages have shown, went a long way to forming behaviour. Religion included a code of ethics and a programme of good works. By being brought up as Christians, children were introduced to principles of self-discipline and good behaviour to others, ceremonial actions like fasting and charity, and the good manners appropriate to holy times and places. The influence of the Church upon behaviour was matched from another direction by that of the world. Lay society had its own conventions of how the individual should behave: how he should dress and keep himself clean, eat at table and bear himself in the company of other people. We know what the Christian code of ethics contained, and how it was taught, from the great corpus of medieval sermons, confessional books and pious treatises. But the Church, as we have noted, did not

[89] Mancini, *Usurpation of Richard III*, ed. Armstrong, pp. 92–3.
[90] *The Sermons of Thomas Brinton, Bishop of Rochester*, ed. Mary A. Devlin, vol i, London, Royal Historical Soc., Camden 3rd series, lxxxv (1954), p. 217.

develop special arrangements for the teaching of the young, and children went to the same confessions, heard the same sermons and read the same books as their elders. The history of the education of children in ethics, in consequence, is impossible to separate from the history of ethics and pastoral care as a whole. The teaching of manners to children, on the other hand, is a different matter. As early as the twelfth century it was a distinct process with its own written treatises specifically directed at the young, in which the rules of behaviour were recorded and explained. This was a precocious development compared with other areas of children's education. Reading and Latin grammar were formal studies with the physical skills all took longer than manners to achieve this status, and did not all do so until the sixteenth century.
and did not all do so until the sixteenth century.

References to how good men and women behave can be found in the literature of most societies. It is possible to reconstruct from the lettes of Cicero, for example, the Roman conventions of how a host should entertain his friends to a meal and how they should behave themselves on the occasion.[91] Latin possessed words like *urbanus* and *facetus* (the ancestors of our 'urbane' and 'facetious') to describe those who were civilized in their behaviour. The heroes of epic too, as we have often noticed, are shown observing conventions when they meet one another and talk together. When Beowulf arrives at the hall of King Hrothgar, the King's steward goes straight through the building to report the fact to the king, because that is the correct thing to do: 'he knew the "thew" [or custom] of the company'.[92] The consciousness of good manners among the Romans and the Anglo-Saxons, however, was not so highly developed that it generated writings of a didactic nature on the subject. Neither society produced etiquette books describing or teaching the code of manners which ought to be followed. The twelfth century, in contrast, was something of a new era in the history of manners. First, a new word came into use: *curialis* in Latin or *corteis* in French, first found in England towards the end of the eleventh century and

---

[91] Anna Bertha Miller, *Roman Etiquette of the Late Republic, as recorded in the correspondence of Cicero*, Lancaster, Pa., 1914, pp. 33–7.

[92] *Beowulf*, line 359. The word 'thew' continued to be used in the sense of good behaviour in later medieval literature in English.

meaning 'courtly' or 'courteous'.[93] The word derives itself from
curia or *cort*, the household of a king or a great magnate, and signifies
the coming of such places to be recognized models of good
behaviour, more consciously so than under the Anglo-Saxons. It
provided a comprehensive adjective, duly recorded in English as
'courteous', and eventually a new noun 'courtesy' which summed
up all the aspects of good behaviour associated with courts and those
who attended them. Secondly in the first half of the twelfth century,
a genre of didactic works began to be written in western Europe for
the first time, which taught the code of good manners in an explicit
way. Historians generally call such works 'courtesy books'.

The creation of a didactic genre may have owed something to
Roman literature, with which its authors were familiar and from
which they borrowed the concepts of *urbanitas* and *facetia*. The
main source of their inspiration, however, lay elsewhere. This can
be well illustrated from an anecdote of Robert Grosseteste (d. 1253),
the bishop of Lincoln so famous for good manners as well as for piety
and scholarship that, as we have seen, the nobility sent him their
sons to be educated in his household.[94] Contemporaries appear to
have been struck by the disparity between Grosseteste's humble
social origins and his courtly manners, a reaction which caused
stories about him to circulate after his death. In one version Henry
III and in another the earl of Gloucester asked the bishop how, with
his lowly parentage, he had acquired his fine behaviour. He replied,
'by reading the scriptures'! There, he said, he had read of famous
men who gave him models of prudence, modesty, liberality, chastity
and all the virtues. He had lived in spirit in the households of David
and Solomon, and they were greater kings than the king of
England.[95] The Old Testament, indeed, contains not only stories of
the deeds of famous men, but explicit accounts of how to behave,
notably in the 'wisdom literature' represented by the books of

93 *Curialis* is first found in England *c.*1080 (R.E. Latham, *Revised Medieval Latin
Word-List from British and Irish Sources*, 2nd edn, London, 1965, p. 126).
Corteis appears in *The Song of Roland* in French at about the same date.

94 Above pp. 56–7.

95 The story of Henry III is told by John Acton (d. 1349) in William Lyndwode,
Provinciale, Oxford, 1679, ii, 122, and that of the earl of Gloucester in *The
Lanercost Chronicle, 1201–1346*, ed. J. Stevenson, Edinburgh, Bannatyne Club,
1839, pp. 44–5.

Proverbs, Ecclesiastes and Ecclesiasticus. The contents of these books are mainly concerned with ethics and good principles, but they also include practical advice on drink, marriage, friendship and the avoidance of criminals and prostitutes. On manners in particular, Ecclesiasticus provides a detailed set of instructions on how to behave at banquets. The giver of a feast must see to the seating of the guests before he sits himself. Guests must take care when they speak, the old to avoid garrulousness and the young presumption. It is bad form to pursue debts or quarrels with one's fellow guests. When dinner appears, it is also improper to lick your lips or exclaim 'what a spread!' You should restrain your greed, not reaching out for every dish and jostling others as they help themselves, nor munching your food with an audible noise. The perfect guest takes little, leaves nothing and avoids being the last out of the house.⁹⁶ When we find that Grosseteste was himself the author of a poem on table etiquette containing exactly these kinds of advice, it is clear that the influence of the Bible described in the anecdotes was indeed a real one.

The earliest writers of courtesy books in medieval Europe were clerics, who wrote to spread good manners and personal habits among their fellow clergy. One of the first was Peter Alfonsi (d. 1140), whose *Disciplina Clericalis* has already been mentioned as a collection of stories and precepts with this motive.⁹⁷ Equally early was Hugh of St Victor's work, *De Institutione Noviciorum* (by 1141), written to instruct the novices of the abbey of Saint-Victor at Paris, and dealing with dress, speech, behaviour and eating habits among other matters.⁹⁸ The genre established by these authors proved to be extraordinarily popular.⁹⁹ The first known courtesy book to be written in England, the Latin poem *Liber Urbanus*, is thought to have been the work of Daniel of Beccles, a member of the household of Henry II, and to have been produced in about 1180.¹⁰⁰ Later poems of the same kind often adopted the title 'Urbanus' as well. The treatise called *Facetus*, which was probably written in France at

---

⁹⁶ Ecclesiasticus, chapters 31–2.
⁹⁷ Peter Alfonsi, *Disciplina Clericalis*, trans. Hermes, especially pp. 149–50.
⁹⁸ *Patrologia Latina*, ed. Migne, vol clxxvi, Paris, 1854, cols 925–52.
⁹⁹ On the genre as a whole, see Glixelli in *Romania*, xlvii (1921), pp. 1–40, and Gieben in *Vivarium*, v (1967) pp. 47–74.
¹⁰⁰ ibid., p. 51; Daniel of Beccles, *Urbanus Magnus*, ed. Smyly.

about the same time and also in Latin verse, was widely copied and read in England down to the early sixteenth century, so much so that the word 'Facet' passed into English as a general term for courtesy books of its kind.[101] In the thirteenth century, several other important treatises were written by Englishmen or circulated in England from elsewhere. John of Garland, the English grammarian and scholar, compiled his *Morale Scolarium* or instructions for the behaviour of scholars in 1241.[102] Bartholomew Glanville included a chapter on table-manners in *De Proprietatibus Rerum* at about the same date,[103] and Grosseteste's own contribution, the poem *Stans Puer ad Mensam*, 'the boy standing at the table', was written by 1253.[104] There are also two chapters of an academic nature on eating and drinking in Giles's *De Regimine Principum*.[105] All these works were in Latin, but by the mid-thirteenth century courtesy poems in French were being produced in England or reaching there from France. One, called *Urbain le Courtois*, occurs in variant forms in at least five manuscripts.[106] Advice on table-manners is also included in Walter of Bibbesworth's treatise on French[107] and Jean de Meun's *Roman de la Rose* (1269-78), which was read in England and later translated by Chaucer.[108] Finally, by the late fourteenth or early fifteenth centuries, courtesy poems begin to survive in English, some seventeen examples of which have been reprinted in modern editions.[109] All these are in the tradition of the earlier Latin and French versions, being generally translations or adaptations of them. The interest in handbooks of courtesy remained unabated

---

[101] *Der deutsch Facetus*, ed. Schroeder, pp. 14–28; *Le Facet en françoys*, ed. Morawski, pp. 3–19.

[102] John of Garland, *Morale Scolarium*, ed. Paetow, pp. 168–9, 174–5, 227–9, 243–6.

[103] *De Proprietatibus Rerum*, book vi, chapter 22 (ed. Seymour, i, 329–30).

[104] Printed by Gieben in *Vivarium*, v (1967), pp. 56–62; translated by Garton in *Lincolnshire Life*, May 1981, pp. 38–40.

[105] *De Regimine Principum*, book ii, part ii, chapters 11–12 (ed. Molenaer, pp. 208–12).

[106] Meyer in *Romania*, xxxii (1903), pp. 68–73. On the French poems in general, see Parsons in *Proceedings of the Modern Language Assoc. of America*, xliv (1929), pp. 383–455 and West, *Courtoisie in Anglo-Norman Literature*.

[107] Bibbesworth, *Traité*, ed. Owen, p. 136.

[108] Guillaume de Lorris and Jean de Meun, *Roman de la Rose*, lines 13,355–444.

[109] *Early English Meals and Manners*, ed. Furnivall; Caxton, *Book of Curtesye*, ed. Furnivall; *A Book of Precedence*, ed. Furnivall; *A Fifteenth-Century Courtesy Book*, ed. Chambers; *How the Wyse Man Taught Hys Sone*, ed. Fischer.

throughout the later Middle Ages, and continued among the writers and scholars of the Renaissance.

The genre of courtesy literature is thus a crowded one, and the relationship of the texts to one another is complicated, given the practice of translating and borrowing on the one hand and changing and adapting on the other. Some of the works, like those of Hugh of St Victor and John of Garland, are primarily aimed at clerics, others at the nobility, while others (by the fifteenth century) seem to envisage a readership of burgesses and yeomen as well as the aristocracy. Some specify their concern with children while others appear to be directed at adolescents, and their contents vary too, from *Facetus* which spends much time on ethics and morality to *Stans Puer ad Mensam* which is a thoroughly practical guide to table manners. No single work sums up the genre as a whole, but a typical example which covers several of the topics commonly dealt with (albeit a late work of the fifteenth century) is the English *Book of Courtesy*, composed by an unknown follower of John Lydgate after 1452 and printed by Caxton in 1477-8.[110] It is addressed to a boy and claims to be written in plain language suitable for the child's age. The poem begins with rising in the morning, proceeds through dress, going to church and meals, and ends with advice on recreations and reading. On getting out of bed, the boy is recommended to cross himself three times and say his prayers with the fellow-occupant of his chamber: the Paternoster, Ave Mary, Creed and the mattins of Our Lady. He should comb his hair, cleanse his ears and nose (but not by picking them), wash his hands, and clean and pare his nails if there is need. He should put on hood, gown, hose and shoes of a style accordant with his social status, avoiding foolish or effeminate clothes. When going out and about, he should walk soberly, restraining himself from throwing stones or sticks. On entering church he should asperse himself with holy water, kneel before the high cross on the rood screen, knock his breast (as a sign of penitence), give thanks to God, and repeat the three basic prayers. He should be demure and silent in church, and avoid the bad habits of those who make a 'clap' and 'jangle'. At table he should wait diligently on his master, for which other treatises (but not this one) supply directions on how to fill one's master's cup and carve his meat for him. When the boy is to be fed himself, he

---

[110] Caxton, *Book of Curtesye*, ed. Furnivall, pp. 1-53.

should wait to be seated and should observe a code of table-manners very similar in form to that of Ecclesiasticus: restraining himself from greed, observing cleanliness in eating and drinking, and avoiding unpleasant habits. His behaviour to others should be frank, yet modest; he should look men in the face without turning his eyes aside, behave humbly to superiors and cheerfully to equals. In speaking he should avoid prolixity, annoying others with what he says, or interrupting their own conversations. Lastly, he should enjoy himself in honest recreations: music, dancing and the reading of good authors. His reward will be that

> When men se a childe of suche governaunce,
> They seyn, 'gladde may this [child's] frendis be
> To have a sone soo manerly as he.'

There can be no doubt that manners of these kinds were consciously taught to young men, ever since Hugh of St Victor included the topic of etiquette in his instructions for novices. The *Facetus*, Grosseteste's *Stans Puer ad Mensam*, and other similar poems are frequently found in anthologies of school literature in the later Middle Ages and were evidently studied by boys in English grammar schools.[111] The vernacular courtesy books were doubtless known and used by the parents and masters of aristocratic boys, or given to them to read themselves. This is explicitly stated by the author of the 'Black Book of the Royal Household' in 1471–3, where he says that the master of the henchmen in charge of the noble boys there must show them 'the schools of urbanity and nurture of England' and oversee their behaviour at meals 'after the book of urbanity', which may refer to any one of the courtesy books from Daniel of Beccles onwards.[112] Indeed, the author likens courtesy, humorously at least, to an academic subject in which one should be trained as one is in a university, for he observes that the household knights who carve and serve the cup before the king himself should be 'well sped in taking of degree in the school of urbanity'.[113] The most notable absence from the courtesy books is a concern with women. True, Jean de Meun ventures on the subject in the *Roman*

---

[111] Thomson, *Catalogue of Middle English Grammatical Texts*, pp. 120, 143, 160, 213, 221, 247, 307 (*Stans Puer ad Mensam*); pp. 132–3, 160, 213, 221–2, 287, 306 (*Facetus*).

[112] Myers, *Household of Edward IV*, pp. 126–7.

[113] ibid., p. 106. Compare the use of the word 'facet' on p. 136.

de la Rose. He gives advice to them on dress, demeanour and table-etiquette of which the latter repeats exactly the precepts in the treatises for men. A woman should seat her guests properly and carve for them; she should avoid wetting her fingers in the sauce, dropping food as she conveys it to her mouth, or stuffing too much in. She should wipe her lips carefully before drinking, take small sips from her cup, and avoid getting drunk.[114] The advice, however, occurs in the context of a mocking and equivocal discussion in which Jean is as interested in satirizing the vanities and deceptions of women as he is in regulating their behaviour. There may be a deliberate ambiguity in his addressing to women the advice which was usually aimed at men.

The passage in the *Roman de la Rose* was used by Chaucer as the basis of his own description of the table manners of the Prioress:

> At mete wel ytaught was she with alle:
> She leet no morsel from hir lippes falle,
> Ne wette hir fyngres in hir sauce depe;
> Wel koude she carie a morsel and wel kepe
> That no drope ne fille upon hire brest.
> In curteisie was set full muchel hir lest.[115]

Here too, when we consider the juxtaposition of the Prioress's bad French and Chaucer's evident disapproval of her practice of giving the leftovers of her table to her dogs rather than to the poor, the satire of women seems to take precedence over their instruction. Not until the fifteenth century do we begin to find courtesy poems deliberately aimed at girls, and these – 'The Good Wife Would a Pilgrimage' and 'How the Good Wife Taught her Daughter' – seem to cater for an audience of wealthy town-dwellers rather than members of the aristocracy.[116] In practice there is no doubt that noble girls were brought up to use good manners in church and at table as boys were, as well as to observe conventions of speech, dress and demeanour appropriate to their own sex. Both the large *Book of the Knight of the Tower* and Chaucer's short description of Virginia in 'The Physician's Tale' consider the conduct of girls, and draw attention to desirabilities such as piety, modesty of dress and

---

[114]   Lorris and Meun, *Roman de la Rose*, lines 13, 283–570.
[115]   Chaucer, *Works*, ed. Robinson, p. 18 (A 127–41).
[116]   *A Book of Precedence*, ed. Furnivall, pp. 39–51; *The Good Wife Taught her Daughter*, ed. Mustanoja.

discretion in speech. The same ideal is stated by a witness of the provisional marriage ceremony of Henry VII's daughter Mary to Charles of Castile in 1508, where he praises

> the modesty and dignity with which she bore herself, the laudable gestures befitting so great a princess.... Her royal courtesy, her noble and truly paternal gravity (for one of her tender age) were apparent to all, such was the composure of her dress, her bearing and her good manners.[117]

But practice, in the case of women's education, so often outran theory. Manners, like most things that were learnt by girls, were acquired informally – orally and visually – from their mothers and mistresses, not written down and studied as by boys. In this respect the literature of manners, though it reveals the usual sexual difference of medieval education, is a very poor guide to the civilization of medieval women.

[117] '"The Spousells" of the Princess Mary', ed. J. Gairdner, *The Camden Miscellany IX*, Camden Soc., new series liii (1895), p. 19.

Five Letters and other arts

THE LITERACY OF MEN

When you thought of a knight or a lay nobleman in the Middle Ages, your first impression was of a fighter. Knighthood and chivalry meant skill at arms and then, perhaps, the code of behaviour which a knight should follow. Reading and writing, on the other hand, were associated primarily with the clergy. So closely indeed were they linked that the ability to read was often known as 'clergy' until the sixteenth century; 'the lettered' was equally often a synonym for churchmen, and someone employed to read or write accounts was, then as now, a 'clerk' even though he might actually be a layman. Stock characters and their attributes are powerful images, but they rarely express the whole truth, and certainly not here. Throughout the times with which we are dealing there were literate lay noblemen, just as there were worldly and warlike clerics. Almost as soon as the English Church was founded in the seventh century, it had recruited noble boys to be clerics and had trained them in the clerical skill of reading. The seventh century was not yet over before two of these boys, Sigebert of East Anglia in 631 and Aldfrith of Northumbria in 685, unexpectedly came to the throne, and Aldfrith who was definitely able to read Latin is the first clear English example of a literate layman.[1] Two centuries later King Alfred learnt to read in his youth, and when he grew up gathered the sons of his nobility into his household where, as we have seen, they were given instruction in letters.[2] The training of noble boys to read already had a long history by the time of the Norman Conquest, and although most of those involved were intended to become clerics, the process seems to have produced in men like Aldfrith, Alfred and the chronicle-writer Ethelweard at least a few lay noblemen who were also able to read.[3]

The history of noble literacy in early times is largely confined to the names of a few individuals, and it is hard to be sure how representative they were of the ranks to which they belonged. In the twelfth and thirteenth centuries, however, more general indications of the extent of literacy begin to survive. First, with regard to the kings of England, we encounter the famous maxim *rex illiteratus, asinus coronatus*, 'an illiterate king is a crowned ass'. This is referred to by William of Malmesbury in about 1125, and was subsequently quoted by several other writers of the twelfth century or later.[4] It seems to indicate for the first time an idea of obligation that kings at least should be able to read, and since we know that Henry I and Henry II were taught the skill in their youth[5] and that Henry II was urged to do the same for his own eldest son the Young King,[6] the obligation was evidently taken seriously by the Anglo-Norman royal family from the late eleventh century onwards. There seems no doubt that all the English kings from 1100 (except perhaps for Stephen) were able to read. The diffusion of literacy throughout the rest of the lay aristocracy appears to have taken longer. In the first half of the twelfth century, though writers refer to the literacy of actual knights and magnates, there is sometimes an implication that the knowledge was unusual in such people, and not yet true of their order as a whole. As late as the 1190s Tristan, in Beroul's version of

---

[1] Bede, *Ecclesiastical History*, book ii, chapter 15; book iii, chapter 18; book iv, chapter 26; *Life of St Cuthbert*, chapter 24.

[2] Asser, *Life of King Alfred*, ed. Stevenson, pp. 19–21, 60.

[3] For the latest discussion of this question, see Wormald in *TRHS*, 5th series xxvii (1977), pp. 95–114.

[4] Galbraith in *Proceedings of the British Academy* (1935), pp. 212–13; Jacques de Cessoles, *The Game of Chess*, trans. Caxton, ff bvi[v]–vii.

[5] Below, p. 148.

[6] *Patrologia Latina*, ed. Migne, vol ccvii, Paris, 1855, col 210.

the story, is unable to read or write himself though eminently civilized in other respects, and has to send and receive his letters through the medium of other people.[7] By the 1260s and 1270s, on the other hand, the works of the great friar-educationists in France proclaim the knowledge of letters to be a normal and essential skill which every nobleman should learn. Vincent and Giles say that the sons of 'gentle men' should be trained to read, as well as those of kings and princes, and the injunction is repeated as a matter of course in later works on noble education.[8] It seems likely that literacy spread from a few of the lay aristocracy to most of the order between about the middle of the twelfth century and the middle of the thirteenth.[9] Certainly, from the 1270s it was the orthodoxy in their case, just as it had already become for their rulers. The literacy of aristocratic women probably developed at much the same pace, but since its history has certain special features, we shall lay it aside for the present, to be examined in a later section.

The study of letters, from the ABC upwards, is one of the most formal and distinctive operations in the field of education, attracting disproportionate attention from writers and leaving more evidence of itself than other kinds of learning. The thirteenth-century educationists recommended that the study should begin in the second age of childhood, *pueritia*. Aristotle, as we have seen, wished boys to start their formal learning when they were 7,[10] and Bartholomew and Giles accordingly fixed on this age for beginning to learn to read, while Vincent opted for 6.[11] It is possible that the friar-educationists were being good Aristotelians in this respect rather than mirrors of their own times, and that boys in fact began to read when younger. The male *magistri* who attended the Young King and Prince William in the twelfth century, when they were only a year or so old, show that children were by no means secluded from male tuition until they were 7, and it may be that such tuition

---

[7] Beroul, *Tristan*, ed. Ewert, i, 72–3, 79; trans. Fedrick, pp. 100–1, 106.

[8] *De Eruditione Filiorum Nobilium*, ed. Steiner, p. 8; *De Regimine Principum*, book ii, part ii, chapter 7 (ed. Molenaer, pp. 197–9).

[9] On this process, see Clanchy, *From Memory to Written Record*, pp. 175–201, and Turner in *American Historical Review*, lxxx (1978), pp. 928–45.

[10] *Politics*, book vii, chapter 17.

[11] *De Proprietatibus Rerum*, book vi, chapter 5 (ed. Seymour, i, 300–1); *De Regimine Principum*, book ii, part ii, chapter 16 (ed. Molenaer, pp. 218–20); *Speculum Majus*, part iii, book xii, chapter 31.

extended to reading.[12] This was certainly the case in the fifteenth century. John Hardyng states in 1457 that the sons of lords are set to school to learn letters at the age of 4,[13] and this was paralleled in the 1470s by the two sons of Edward IV, the 'princes in the Tower'. Their schoolmaster, John Giles, was rewarded for teaching them in May 1476 when the elder boy Edward V was five and a half and his brother Richard two and three quarters. Since the reward was backdated to the previous Michaelmas, it seems likely that Edward enjoyed the master's services when he was 4, as Hardyng indicates.[14] When Sir Thomas Elyot came to discuss the question of a starting age in 1531, with the benefit of new knowledge about what the Greeks and the Romans had done in the matter, he too came down in favour of an early beginning of literary studies. He rejected the advice of certain classical educationists that boys should not be taught letters until they were 7, and opted for that of Quintilian that they should begin to learn them as soon as they could speak. In taking this view Elyot was not simply borrowing a new idea from Quintilian; he was also conforming to a tradition already well established in England.[15]

The study of letters was a lengthy task, if properly pursued. Medieval educationists, when they elucidated the matter, made it plain that they wished noble boys to be instructed to read Latin, not merely their mother-tongue of French or English, and the boys' curriculum consequently involved not only learning the alphabet and the pronunciation of familiar words but the grammar and vocabulary of a foreign language. Since we possess little evidence of what was taught to noble boys in households until the sixteenth century, we have to go to the contemporary grammar schools for the nearest model of what the teaching was.[16] Boys in schools began by learning the Latin alphabet from a form written down on a board or in a small pamphlet. Next, they practised how to recognize Latin words, pronounce them and sing them to the rules of plainsong. Liturgical books were used for this purpose, like the psalter and the antiphonal, in which the letters were written large and separately

[12] Above, p. 18.
[13] BL, Lansdowne MS 204, f. 12; Hardyng, *Chronicle*, ed. Ellis, pp. i–ii.
[14] *CPR 1467–77*, p. 592; *CCR 1476–85*, p. 1.
[15] *The Governor*, book i, chapter 5; Quintilian, *Institutio Oratoria*, I, i, 15–19.
[16] For a survey of the school curriculum, see Orme, *English Schools in the Middle Ages*, pp. 60–3, 87–115.

and therefore easy to read. From reading and song boys went on to be taught the forms and meanings of Latin words, in other words grammar and vocabulary. Textbooks and word-lists, both simple and sophisticated, were available for this purpose, and some boys had copies of their own. Henry V had eight 'books' of grammar in one volume bought for him in 1396–7,[17] and a 'Donatus' or elementary grammar was purchased for his brother John in 1398.[18] Once they had learnt some grammar, pupils in schools practised composing Latin prose and writing it out in a clear hand, beginning with simple sentences (making 'latins') and going on to 'dictamen' or the art of writing formal letters. The sons of the nobility were also taught good handwriting. Walter Map tells us of one of his relatives in the twelfth century, a young squire who 'could copy any set of letters',[19] and we still possess the will of Simon de Montfort which his knightly son Henry wrote for him in a neat hand in 1259.[20] Troilus indeed, in Chaucer's famous story, is counselled not to write his love-letters too carefully, but to bedew them with tears, as if the aristocracy were normally thought of as writing neatly, not badly.[21] Finally, pupils in schools read Latin poetry and learnt to compose verses themselves. The poem most often read was the *Distichs of Cato*, a third-century Latin collection of proverbs and moral observations, and it was this work that Benedict Burgh edited for the young nobleman William Bourchier in the 1440s. His version, like George Ashby's collection of prose maxims for Edward son of Henry VI, contains a Latin text and an English translation, and both works may have been meant for schoolroom use.[22]

The length of time that noble boys learnt reading, song and grammar varied, as did the level of attainment that they reached. As we have seen, the aristocracy generated a quota of learned men. Noble boys who were intended to become clerics or, later on, to study the common law learnt Latin for long periods during their childhood and adolescence. When they had exhausted the capabili-

[17] PRO, DL 28/1/4 f 2.
[18] ibid., DL 28/1/6 f 42.
[19] Map, *De Nugis Curialium*, trans. James, p. 155.
[20] C. Bémont, *Simon de Montfort*, trans. E.F. Jacob, Oxford, 1930, facsimile facing p. 278.
[21] Chaucer, *Works*, ed. Robinson, p. 412 (book ii, lines 1023–9). On aristocratic neatness, see also McFarlane, *Nobility of Later Medieval England*, pp. 45, 240–1.
[22] Burgh, *Cato*, ed. Jenkinson; Ashby, *Poems*, ed. Bateson.

ties of their household teachers, they left for the universities and the inns of court where some of them emerged with high honours. Their brothers, however, whose destiny was to inherit family property, be knighted or serve in a household did not need to study letters to such an advanced degree; how far did they attain? Vincent suggests that a noble boy who is going on to chivalric training should be taught for half a dozen years, from 6 till 12.[23] Giles extends the years by one, from 7 till 14.[24] We have some random references from the fourteenth century onwards to boys intended for knightly careers being educated at a known age. The ages tend to follow the plans of the educationists, by mostly falling below the age of fourteen. In principle a would-be knight could learn a great deal in six or seven years. At a town grammar school it was considered good to have mastered grammar in two or three years; three or four were usual and five or six were ample.[25] But these are estimates from institutions where boys were trained in grammar alone for several hours each day and for most of the year. In a great household, where education was less distinct from everyday life and consequently more varied and interrupted, the learning of Latin may have proceeded more slowly. In the case of the lay nobility, it is safer to measure their capabilities by studying the extent of literacy and learning which they displayed in adulthood. Individuals also varied in this respect, but it is possible to get a fairly clear picture of the average attainments of those who were literate, as early as the twelfth century and during each century afterwards.

There can be little doubt that the Anglo-Norman aristocracy in the first half of the twelfth century included laymen who could read, understand and even compose Latin writings.[26] The evidence comes from ecclesiastical writers – bishops and chroniclers – and though they talk of 'letters' and 'literature' without defining the language, it is most likely to have been Latin, the medium in which they themselves were writing, when little was written in French and what survived in English would hardly have been of interest. We do not know that William the Conqueror could read, and the literacy of

[23] *Speculum Majus*, part iii, book xii, chapter 31.

[24] *De Regimine Principum*, book ii, part ii, chapter 16 (ed. Molenaer, pp. 218–20).

[25] Orme, *English Schools in the Middle Ages*, pp. 133–4; *A Fifteenth Century School Book*, ed. Nelson, p. 21; Orme in *Renaissance Quarterly*, xxxiv (1981), pp. 26, 32.

[26] The following two paragraphs follow the work and arguments of Thompson, *Literacy of the Laity*, pp. 166–95.

his eldest sons Robert and William Rufus cannot be established, but their youngest brother Henry I was certainly able to do so. Orderic Vitalis says that when he reached the age for schooling his parents put him to study letters, and that he learnt 'the knowledge which is taught' (*doctrinali scientia*).[27] William of Malmesbury agrees that he went to the 'school of letters' and acquired a love of books which neither war nor business could destroy, though he never read much in public.[28] Henry II was taught first by a master from Saintes in France who was famous for versifying,[29] and then by Matthew at Bristol, where Roger the future bishop of Worcester learnt alongside him.[30] Peter of Blois was later to praise Henry's learning highly, to assert that he was 'very well up in letters' (*longe litteratior*), and to call his household a daily 'school' of conversation about literature and the discussion of questions.[31] Some of the earls of the mid-twelfth century were also literate in Latin. Robert earl of Gloucester, the illegitimate son of Henry I, was praised for his knowledge of letters by William of Malmesbury, Geoffrey of Monmouth and Walter Map.[32] William dedicated to him the fourth book of his *Gesta Regum Anglorum*, and said in doing so that Robert would be able to read the scheme of the whole work in the preface to the first book.[33] The brothers Waleran count of Meulan and Robert earl of Leicester were both commended by writers, the one as having been trained in philosophy and the other as 'erudite in letters'.[34] A fourth example, Brian FitzCount, was complimented by Gilbert Foliot abbot of Gloucester in 1143–4 for having personally compiled a 'book' or manifesto supporting Matilda's claims to the English throne.[35] There were also literate laymen of lesser standing.

[27] Orderic, *Ecclesiastical History*, ed. Chibnall, ii, 214–15; iv, 120–1.
[28] William of Malmesbury, *Gesta Regum Anglorum*, ed. Stubbs, ii, 467.
[29] Thompson, *Literacy of the Laity*, pp. 174, 190–1.
[30] *Materials for the History of Thomas Becket*, ed. Robertson, iii, 104.
[31] ibid., vii, 573.
[32] William of Malmesbury, *Gesta Regum Anglorum*, ed. Stubbs, ii, 355–6, 519, and *Historia Novella*, ed. K.R. Potter, London, 1955, p. 23; Geoffrey of Monmouth, *Historia Regum Britanniae*, ed. Griscom, pp. 86–7; Map, *De Nugis Curialium*, trans. James, p. 235.
[33] William of Malmesbury, *Gesta Regum Anglorum*, ed. Stubbs, ii, 355–6.
[34] Geoffrey of Monmouth, *Historia Regum Britanniae*, ed. Griscom, pp. 86–7; FitzNigel, *Course of the Exchequer*, ed. Johnson, p. 57.
[35] *The Letters and Charters of Gilbert Foliot*, ed. Z.N. Brooke and others, Cambridge, 1967, pp. 60–1.

One literate knight named Robert, 'a diligent hearer and lover of the scriptures', gave property to the abbey of St Albans in the late eleventh century.[36] Another 'literate and noble man' of Exeter diocese, who wished to break off his betrothal to become a priest, is mentioned between 1159 and 1181,[37] and Gerald of Wales informs us of a third: a literate knight who could compose Latin verses extempore, and did so after his death in a dream to a friend.[38] Even the lesser knighthood, it appears, had some Latinate representatives.

A change of literary attainments is apparent towards the end of the twelfth century. By that time there was emerging in France and England a large and growing body of literature in French, including both lives of the saints and devotional treatises, and also secular chansons de geste and romances. The literature in Latin now had a competing body of writings in French, closely related to the interests of the literate nobleman and easier for him to understand. A new situation consequently developed in which the nobility, though still initially trained to read Latin, were tempted to deviate into the reading of French books rather than go on to achieve perfection in Latin as some of their fathers had done.[39] By the reign of King John (1199–1216) a king could no longer be counted on to be fluent in Latin. Gerald of Wales presented John with his Latin history of the conquest of Ireland, but he assumed that the work would reach the king in French, by somebody translating it aloud extempore or making a permanent French translation in writing.[40] More generally, Gerald felt that Latin by John's reign no longer made its former impact. He himself, who wrote in Latin, had received less fame and advancement than his friend Walter Map, who went about preaching in the vernacular.[41] It is not too fanciful, perhaps, to link with this process the poor standing of the royal teachers of grammar after about 1200. Matthew, the master of Henry II who attested his pupil's charters and was later remembered for his learning, was succeeded by obscure men or part-time

---

[36] *Gesta Abbatum Monasterii Sancti Albani*, ed. Riley, i, 57.
[37] *Regesta Pontificum Romanorum*, ed. P. Jaffé, vol ii, Leipzig, 1888, p. 380 (no 13,905).
[38] Gerald of Wales, *Opera*, ed. Brewer & others, viii, 310.
[39] Thompson, *Literacy of the Laity*, p. 181.
[40] Gerald of Wales, *Opera*, ed. Brewer and others, v, 410.
[41] ibid., pp. 410–11.

teachers whose activities were not recorded. The title of 'master' to the English princes of the thirteenth and fourteenth centuries was held by a knight, not a scholar. Even mirrors of princes ceased to be written in England after 1216, and were imported from France instead. It was still possible to find a highly Latinate knight at the court of Henry III, but the man in question, Paulin Peivre or Piper, who wrote a life of St George in Latin verse and died in 1251, was clearly an unusual figure. Matthew Paris calls him 'a literate knight or a military cleric', as if he were a rare kind of hybrid, and he is the last lay nobleman in England known to have written a literary work in Latin until the fifteenth century.[42]

A good illustration of the limits of Latinity among the lay nobility in the thirteenth century is provided by the account of the topic in the 1270s by Giles of Rome, the most practical and influential of the great educationists.[43] Giles's ideal of the learning to be pursued by the children of kings, princes and other noblemen is a lofty one, no whit inferior to the ideals of the Renaissance. Noble boys should learn Latin because it is richer and more developed than other languages. Learning it accustoms one to learning in general; it teaches sense, reason and judgment, and having mastered it one can go on to all the other branches of knowledge which are written in Latin. Giles beckons the nobility to the whole range of contemporary knowledge: the seven liberal arts, the philosophies of metaphysics, economics, ethics and politics, and the higher studies of law, medicine and divinity. If the children of kings and princes learn these sciences, they will become demi-gods and much resemble God. Yet Giles reveals the goal only to make it appear doubtful whether anyone will ever reach it. If children are going to attend to the business of the world, he concedes, they will not have time to enquire into all the sciences. They should therefore concentrate on learning the faith and morality of Christianity. They should at least learn Latin, but if they cannot manage even that they should be taught good manners in French. Giles conveys the impression that, even at court with a good teacher, the odds were against a noble boy getting very far with his Latin. 'The sons of kings and princes', he

[42] Paris, *Chronica Majora*, ed. Luard, v, 242; J.C. Russell, *Dictionary of Writers of Thirteenth Century England*, London, 1936, pp. 94–5.
[43] *De Regimine Principum*, book ii, part ii, chapters 7–8 (ed. Molenaer, pp. 197–202).

believes, 'will not or cannot come to great perfection in knowledge.'
It was still a natural assumption when Christine of Pisa wrote her
Livre du Corps de Policie in France in 1404–7. A prince's master, says
Christine, should be readier and wiser in good manners than in
learning. For though in ancient times the children of princes were
taught by philosophers, 'princes be not so covetous nowadays to be
learned in science'. The son of a prince, she concludes, should know
the rules of grammar and understand Latin, but her use of optatives,
'if it please God' and 'I would it were so', shows that even this was
only to be hoped for, and could by no means be taken for granted.[44]

The evidence of Giles and Christine is confirmed in England by
what we know of the literature encountered by the lay aristocracy in
the thirteenth and fourteenth centuries. First, there is the field of
documents. A nobleman or a gentleman presided over a staff of
administrators who managed his property, and he might also hold a
public office as sheriff, escheator or tax-collector in his county. He
must often have needed to read a charter, a writ or a letter in Latin or
to scrutinize a set of Latin accounts. These documents, however,
followed standard forms, their nature must have been familiar, and
if the reader could not cope with them himself, then doubtless his
steward or chaplain or clerk assisted him in the matter. His last will,
if drawn up formally by a clerk, would also be in Latin. But when a
nobleman or gentleman wrote letters to his friends, or made his will
himself, he used French for preference. If he were an author like
Bibbesworth or Henley, he wrote in the same language. He could
manage predictable Latin at a pinch, but French was clearly what he
was fluent in. There were doubtless a few exceptional Latinists –
men well trained in the law like the royal judges and those originally
meant to be clerics who had studied at school or university. But most
of the aristocracy would have agreed with Sir John Cavendish, chief
justice of the king's bench, when he drew up his will in 1381. He
started to write it in Latin, but soon observed that 'whereas French
is better understood and more common and known to me and my
friends than Latin, I have caused all the rest of my will to be written
in French, so that my friends may understand it more easily'.[45]

Lists of the books belonging to kings and noblemen, which
survive in wills and inventories, point to the same conclusion. Most

---

[44] Christine of Pisa, *Livre du Corps de Policie*, ed. Bornstein, pp. 42–4.
[45] McFarlane, *Nobility of Later Medieval England*, p. 241.

titles are in French or (later on) English, whether they are religious and devotional manuals or narrative works to be read for pleasure. There are two categories of Latin books. First, there are frequent references to prayer-books, sometimes with mentions of ownership such as 'my psalter' and 'my missal' which show that the books were used for services. Henry VI is said to have knelt at mass with his book, quietly repeating the prayers, epistle and gospel along with the clergy,[46] and the Venetian writer on England in 1500 noted the custom of taking books of hours to church and reading them over 'verse by verse in a low voice, after the manner of churchmen'.[47] Church services, however, are like documents in form: regular and repetitive. It would not have been hard to find the relevant material with practice, and we cannot be sure that the prayers being read were grammatically understood: they may only have been meditated upon. Secondly, in the ownership of some kings and great noblemen there are scholarly works in Latin. Thomas duke of Gloucester, for example, had texts of theology, science and canon law in his library in 1397.[48] Yet here too we need not assume that men of such rank read Latin works of so high a standard by themselves. There were clerics around them who could translate for them extempore, as Gerald of Wales envisaged in the case of King John. The Knight of the Tower illustrates what might happen in his account of how he came to write his book.

> I went out of the garden and found in my way two priests and two clerks that I had, and told them that I would make a book as an exemplar for my daughters to learn to read. ... And then I made them to come and read before me the book of the Bible, the gests of the kings, the chronicles of France and of England and many other strange histories, and made them to read every book, and did do make of them this book.[49]

In such a way a man might 'write' a book from sources translated for him which he rearranged in his mind and then dictated to scribes, without necessarily even looking at a page or taking up a pen. The

---

[46] *Henry the Sixth*, ed. James, pp. 6, 28.
[47] *A Relation of England*, ed. Sneyd, p. 23.
[48] Viscount Dillon and W.H. St J. Hope in *Archaeological Journal*, liv (1897), pp. 300–3.
[49] Landry, *The Book of the Knight of the Tower*, ed. Offord, p. 13.

episode presents us with a paradox. The lay nobility were not good Latinists personally, but that does not mean that they were out of touch with Latin scholarship or learning. They shared in Latin indirectly through written translations and oral help from the clergy. So too, of course, did most of the rest of the lay population. Was there a rise in the level of personal Latinity in the fifteenth century? The Lancastrian royal family has often been praised for its interest in books, but it is not clear that any of its members were unusually expert in Latin. Henry IV is mentioned spending an afternoon in the library of Bardney Abbey in 1406 where the books, one assumes, were mainly in Latin,[50] but he had clergy with him, and his surviving letters are in French and English. The one Latin quotation which they contain, 'Nessescitas non habet legem', is not at all well spelt.[51] Henry V also wrote in French and English; he borrowed the works of St Gregory from Archbishop Arundel, but there is nothing to show that he read them alone or unaided.[52] The three political works which Hoccleve says that he knew were all available in French. Henry's younger brother Humphrey duke of Gloucester made a large collection of Latin books and patronized Latin authors, but we only know that he read French by himself.[53] He too is likely to have coped with advanced Latin through the help of Latin scholars. Henry VI was taught by an ex-schoolmaster, and in 1460 his peers referred to his interest in studying old writings,[54] but his personal Latinity does not appear to have exceeded the average. It is rather outside the royal family that a slight increase of noble attainments in Latin is to be found in Lancastrian times. First, there is the sending of the three noble heirs Holland, Hungerford and Tiptoft to study at Cambridge and Oxford between 1437 and 1443.[55] Holland and Hungerford were only 10 when they went there, and are unlikely to have studied to a high level, but Tiptoft was both older (13) and stayed for longer (at least two years). Indeed, he appears to have left only because of the death of his father and his own subjection to royal wardship, and he continued his studies later

---

[50] Leland, *Collectanea*, ed. Hearne, vi, 300–1.
[51] Kirby, *Henry IV*, pp. 161, 223.
[52] Kingsford, *Henry V*, pp. 14–15.
[53] Sammut, *Unfredo duca di Gloucester*, p. 215.
[54] Wolffe, *Henry VI*, p. 324.
[55] Above, p. 71.

in life, attending university in Italy, making a large collection of Latin books, and speaking Latin before the pope in 1460.[56] Tiptoft seems to display a new high level of personal Latinity, and he is joined in this respect by Peter Idley and Sir John Fortescue, both of whom grew up in Lancastrian England, though Fortescue at least wrote afterwards. Idley's *Instructions for his Son* were partly translated from Latin works, and Fortescue composed his *De Laudibus Legum Anglie* entirely in Latin. They are the first of their order clearly to demonstrate literary skill in the language since Paulin Peivre in the thirteenth century.

It is not clear what further progress was made in this respect by the Yorkist royal family and their subjects. Richard duke of York (d. 1460) was credited by John Hardyng with having good 'inspeccion' in Latin, meaning a good ability to study it, but was this merely flattery?[57] Richard's sons Edward IV and Edmund, in the two surviving letters which they wrote to him as schooolboys, addressed him in English not Latin, which suggests that there was no very self-conscious Latin culture within the family.[58] Sir John Fortescue, describing the Latin abilities of Edward son of Henry VI in the 1460s, did not rate them at the highest. Edward was 'sufficiently learned in grammar to be deservedly called a grammarian', but he had 'not completely acquired perfection'. His grammar was compared with his projected study of the law: he ought to know its elements and principles, but he had his professional servants to administer it for him.[59] Although Fortescue wrote *De Laudibus Legum Anglie* for the prince it was probably meant, like earlier Latin works addressed to kings, to be interpreted by its author or by other skilled Latinists. The Latinity of Edward V is difficult to define. He had a grammar master from the age of 4 until he was murdered at 12,[60] and he is the first prince of whom we know the number of hours that he studied, since in 1483 they were fixed at three.[61] This is not very many, but it may represent the reduction of a longer school regime as the prince entered the period of adolescence and greater physical activity. In 1482 Pietro Carmeliano addressed Latin verses

[56] *BRUO*, iii, 1877–9, with references.
[57] Hardyng, *Chronicle*, ed. Ellis, p. 23.
[58] Ellis, *Original Letters*, i, 9–10; Bentley, *Excerpta Historica*, pp. 8–9.
[59] Fortescue, *De Laudibus Legum Anglie*, ed. Chrimes, pp. 22–3.
[60] Above, p. 22.
[61] Orme in *BIHR*, lvii (1984).

to Edward,[62] and in the following year another Italian, Dominico Mancini, praised his erudition in letters. The prince, he said, could pronounce and understand any work in prose or verse which came into his hands, except by the most difficult authors.[63] Unfortunately, this assertion is not sufficiently clear about the language or the level. It is possible that Edward was a good Latinist, but the fact has not yet been established firmly enough.

It is with the bringing up of Prince Arthur and Henry VIII in the 1490s that we have the first undoubted evidence since the twelfth century that royal princes were being educated in Latin to a high level. Bernard André, who was one of Arthur's masters, tells us that when his pupil died in 1502 at the age of 16, he was familiar with no fewer than thirty-three ancient and modern authors in Latin, including Cicero, Homer, Livy, Ovid, Thucydides and Virgil. 'He had either committed them partly to memory or, with his own hands and eyes, had read them often and considered them.'[64] Henry, at about the same date, had Latin maxims collected for him by Skelton, significantly without the English translations which had been produced for Edward son of Henry VI.[65] In adult life his Latinity was well known, and in 1531 the Venetian ambassador noted that he knew grammar, philosophy and theology, and spoke and wrote five languages including Latin.[66] Ten years earlier in 1521, Henry published his Latin book against Luther: the *Assertio Septem Sacramentorum*. The work was a co-operative enterprise of a medieval kind, in which the king was assisted in gathering and arranging his material by scholars, as the Knight of the Tower had been.[67] The use of Latin, however, was notable and in the new style of Fortescue, not in the older tradition of noble writings in the vernacular. So although we can find a few forerunners of greater Latinity among the lay nobility in the fifteenth century, it is with Henry VII's arrangements for Arthur and Henry VIII that the higher standard was clearly established and became fashionable. The trend against Latin of about 1200 began to be reversed and, not inappropriately, the Latin master in the royal family achieved

[62] Warner and Gilson, *British Museum: MSS in the Old Royal Collection*, ii, 4.
[63] Mancini, *Usurpation of Richard III*, ed. Armstrong, pp. 92–3.
[64] *Memorials of King Henry VII*, ed. Gairdner, p. 43.
[65] Salter in *Speculum*, ix (1934), pp. 25–37.
[66] *Calendar of State Papers Venetian, 1527–83*, p. 293.
[67] On the authorship of the book, see Scarisbrick, *Henry VIII*, pp. 110–13.

greater prominence while the knightly master faded out. In the sixteenth century an increased Latinity was to spread widely through the English aristocracy, and in 1530 Sir Thomas Elyot could take it for granted that all noblemen should learn Latin to a high level. The goal was not a new one, for Giles of Rome had pointed it out, but there was now a much greater determination among both teachers and parents that it should be reached.

THE LITERACY OF WOMEN

The study of letters by noblewomen parallels that of men in many respects. Just as educationists presented the ideal of a nobleman who had mastered all the sciences, so there was at least a concept that a woman could do the same. Medieval Europe inherited traditions of learned ladies from the classical era, and invented new ones of its own. Among the saints, Katherine of Alexandria, a noble girl alleged to have flourished in the fourth century, had a special reputation for learning. Her basic 'vulgate' life, compiled in the mid-eleventh century and followed by later hagiographers, tells how her father set her to study the liberal arts. Assisted by the Holy Spirit, she made such progress in learning that men experienced in literary study could not confound her with questions and retired from her defeated.[68] Ladies of similar learning appear in romantic literature, as we have seen in *Guy of Warwick* and the Arthurian stories.[69] Melior, the heroine of the late twelfth-century romance *Partonopeu de Blois*, is the daughter of the emperor of Constantinople. Her father prepares her to govern the empire by hiring good masters from whom she learns not only reading but the seven liberal arts, medicine, divinity, astronomy and necromancy, so that by the time she is 15 she surpasses them all in her knowledge.[70] Nicholas Trivet's fourteenth-century *Life of Constance* portrays a similar figure, the daughter of another Roman emperor, who also learns the

[68] *Life of St Katherine*, ed. E. Einenchel, EETS, os, lxxx (1884), p. 8; Clemence of Barking, *Life of St Catherine*, ed. MacBain, p. 5; Bokenham, *Legendys of Hooly Wummen*, ed. Serjeantson, pp. 174–5; James de Voragine, *The Golden Legend*, trans. W. Caxton, 7 vols, London, 1900, vii, 1–4.

[69] Above, p. 000.

[70] *Partonopeu de Blois*, ed. Gildea, i, 186–8 (lines 4/575–628); for an English version, see *Partonope of Blois*, ed. A.T. Bödtker, EETS, es, cix (1912), pp. 224–5, 481–2.

seven arts and when grown up preaches Christianity to the Saracens, achieving many conversions.[71] In reading these works the medi. val nobility encountered the view that women could be schooleu in letters, and could reach as high or higher a standard of Latin scholarship as men themselves.

To be aware of an idea, however, is not necessarily to cherish it or put it into practice. The tendency of educational works, as opposed to romances, is to suggest that the learning of letters by women was a lower priority in noble society than that by men, and even encountered some hostility. True, Vincent of Beauvais in the *De Eruditione Filiorum Nobilium* champions the education of noble girls in reading and writing, including the study of holy scripture. The skills, he asserts, will make them better able to avoid harmful thoughts and fleshly temptations.[72] But Vincent's work was less widely read than that of Giles, and Giles, as we have seen, is curiously reticent about the schooling of women in letters. He talks instead of their need for seclusion, care in speaking and work with textiles, and only in the case of a woman of very high birth for whom textile work is inappropriate does he positively state that she should be made to learn a book or a science.[73] 'Do not choose a wife for her beauty or because she is lettered,' urges a French poem current in England in the fourteenth century, 'for such persons are often deceivers',[74] and it was an awareness of this prejudice that moved the Knight of the Tower to defend the teaching of reading to noble girls. Some people, he remarked, 'say that they would not that their wives nor also their daughters wist anything of clergy [i.e. the ability to read], or of writing'. He himself believed 'that as for writing, it is no force if a woman knows naught of it, but as for reading I say that good and profitable it is to all women'. The book which he wrote himself was intended not merely to give his daughters moral instruction but so that they themselves might 'learn to read'. Like Vincent he concluded that 'a woman that can read may better know the perils of the soul and her salvation than she that knows naught of it'.[75]

[71] *Origins and Analogues of some of Chaucer's Canterbury Tales*, ed. F.J. Furnivall and others, London, Chaucer Soc., 1872–88, pp. 2–4.
[72] *De Eruditione Filiorum Nobilium*, ed. Steiner, p. 176.
[73] *De Regimine Principum*, book ii, part ii, chapter 20 (ed. Molenaer, pp. 227–8).
[74] Meyer in *Romania*, xxxii (1903), p. 72.
[75] Landry, *The Book of the Knight of the Tower*, ed. Offord, pp. 13, 122.

In practice, the education of noble girls in letters certainly went on in medieval England, but as usual it was less formally organized than that of boys and has left few traces. The learned girls of fiction had male masters to teach them, and Matthew appears to have taught the sisters of Geoffrey of Anjou in France before he tutored Henry II.[76] We do not hear of other specialized masters of real noble girls in England, however, until the end of the fifteenth century, and if they were not taught by their brothers' masters, household chaplains or visiting clerics may have done the task. Felice in *Guy of Warwick* is instructed by Premonstratensian canons,[77] and Elizabeth de la Pole had a friar to give her some species of teaching when she was staying in Bruisyard Abbey in 1417.[78] Ladies, too – mothers, mistresses and nuns – may have given instruction in how to read; the teaching of the Virgin by St Anne was a popular subject in medieval art. What girls learnt and when seems to have resembled the early stages of the boys' curriculum. They began at an early age with the alphabet, and continued with reading practice from liturgical texts. Two 'books' of ABC were bought for 20*d* in 1397 for Blanche and Philippa the daughters of Henry IV, when they were 5 and 3 respectively,[79] and Margaret Plumpton was 4 in 1463 when she was complimented on having nearly learnt her psalter.[80] Girls therefore mastered Latin in the basic sense of pronouncing words correctly from a written text, and in the twelfth century some of them went on to study Latin grammar, but after 1200, as we shall see, they probably turned aside from Latin at an early stage, in favour of French and later on English. Some women also learnt to write, notwithstanding the Knight of the Tower's opinion that it was not necessary. Margaret Wake countess of Kent was accused in 1330 of having written a treasonable letter in her own hand,[81] and Chaucer in his characters of May and Criseyde portrays them personally writing their own love-letters.[82] That of May, like Margaret Wake's, was written for a surreptitious purpose, to

[76] Richardson in *EHR*, lxxiv (1959), pp. 193–7.
[77] *Gui de Warewic*, ed. Ewert, lines 63–8.
[78] BL, Egerton Roll, 8776 m 5.
[79] PRO, DL 28/1/6 f 36.
[80] *Plumpton Correspondence*, ed. Stapleton, p. 8.
[81] McFarlane, *Nobility of Later Medieval England*, p. 240.
[82] Chaucer, *Works*, ed. Robinson, pp. 122 (E 1995–2008), 476–7 (book v, 1589–1631).

communicate with a secret lover when a scribe, presumably, could not be trusted. Normally however, noble women who needed to write seem to have called in a literate male to act as their secretary. Professor Norman Davis has shown that the ladies of the Paston family dictated their letters to a variety of scribes. The 104 surviving letters of Margaret wife of John Paston I, for example, are in twenty-nine different hands, and normally she did not even sign them herself. Only rarely did a Paston lady add a personal signature or a few words of her own, and then in a halting unpractised hand.[83] Even in the well-educated family of Henry VII, Margaret Queen of Scots wrote to her father in 1506–7 using an intermediary, and only appended a few concluding lines in her own hand, notably badly spelt.[84] The evidence of handwriting is revealing of the nature of women's education. Noblemen often used secretaries too, but they were more likely to be capable of writing a neat hand when they had to, because of the hours of writing in which they were drilled as schoolboys. The inability of the Paston women or Queen Margaret to write well reinforces the impression of a more informal education in which, though reading was taught, the discipline of writing was never thoroughly imposed.

The changes in the nature of literary skills which we have seen in the case of men were paralleled among their wives and daughters. In the late eleventh and early twelfth centuries, such noblewomen as learnt to read did so in Latin, and a few gained a good understanding of the language. Saint Margaret of Scotland (d. 1093), one of the Old English royal family, devoted herself to the study of sacred writings and discussed hard questions with the learned men of her court.[85] Her contemporary Matilda, the wife of William the Conqueror, is said by Orderic Vitalis to have had a knowledge of letters,[86] and Matilda's daughter Adela, the mother of King Stephen, read both Latin poetry and prose. Indeed, one of her correspondents urged her to read Saint Augustine.[87] Saint Margaret's daughter Matilda, who married Henry I, could also read the language, for she commissioned a life of her mother in Latin which, its author says,

---

[83] *Paston Letters*, ed. Davis, i, pp. xxxvii–xxxviii.
[84] Ellis, *Original Letters*, i, 41–3.
[85] Thompson, *Literacy of the Laity*, pp. 170–1, 188.
[86] Orderic, *Ecclesiastical History*, ed. Chibnall, ii, 224–5.
[87] *Patrologia Latina*, ed. Migne, vol clxvi, Paris, 1894, col 1202; vol clxxi, Paris, 1893, col 146.

was intended for her to look at not merely to hear.[88] During the second half of the twelfth century, however, the interest of literate women like that of men turned from Latin to French. Marie of France, the French-born authoress who lived in England in about the 1160s, knew Latin but her most authentic works, the short stories or *Lais*, were written in French.[89] Clemence of Barking, who wrote a life of Saint Katherine in verse at the end of the century, also knew Latin but wrote in French.[90] After 1200 there is no sign that aristocratic women even knew Latin grammar personally. This is well shown by the records of the English nunneries, with their strongly aristocratic membership. Nuns read the Latin liturgy from service books and they knew the meanings of some individual words, but in general they had no grammatical understanding of the language.[91] Bishop Cantilupe, writing in Latin to the nuns of Limebrook in Herefordshire in about 1277, ordered his words to be interpreted to the nuns by their confessors in French or in English.[92] Bishop Stapledon, addressing the nuns of Canonsleigh and Polsloe in Devon in 1319, wrote to them in French. He laid down that they should use Latin at times and in places when silence was normally required, but not grammatically; if a candle were required during a service, they should simply say '*candela*'![93] Thomas Gascoigne translated *The Mirror of Our Lady* for the nuns of Syon in Middlesex in the mid-fifteenth century, because many of them, though they could sing and pronounce the services in honour of the Virgin, did not understand 'the meaning thereof'.[94] The abbess of Godstow in Berkshire likewise had the Latin register of her abbey's property translated into English in about 1460 for the same reason. 'Women of religion', she noted, 'in reading books of Latin are excused of great understanding where it is not their mother tongue.'[95]

The attainments of lay noblewomen in the later Middle Ages were evidently similar. They too had Latin prayer-books of their

[88]   Thompson, *Literacy of the Laity*, pp. 171, 188.
[89]   Fox, *Literary History of France: The Middle Ages*, pp. 167–71.
[90]   Clemence of Barking, *Life of St Catherine*, ed. MacBain, pp. xiii–xiv.
[91]   On this subject, see Power, *Medieval English Nunneries*, pp. 237–55.
[92]   ibid., p. 248.
[93]   ibid., pp. 248, 286.
[94]   ibid., pp. 253–4.
[95]   ibid., p. 253.

own, and references to 'my' missal or psalter occur in their wills as in those of their husbands. Prayer-books, however, could be meditated upon or simply chanted without grammatical understanding, as Osbern Bokenham describes in his life of Saint Elizabeth of Hungary:

> And thou she of lettrure no kunnyng had,
> Yet ful oftyn-tyme she wolde use
> To han a sauter opyn beforn hyr sprad,
> Wher-in she made hyr for to muse,
> And long yt was or she hyt wold refuse,
> As thow she had red even by and by.[96]

Two of the most devout ladies of the fifteenth century were the mothers of Edward IV and Henry VII: Cecily duchess of York and Lady Margaret Beaufort. John Hardyng believed that Cecily had 'little intellect' in Latin, and thought her better suited to read his history of England in English verse.[97] Lady Margaret said the office of Our Lady daily, but her confessor Bishop Fisher recalled that she often regretted not having given herself in youth to the understanding of Latin, in which she had only 'a little perceiving'.[98] When she wished fully to understand literature, Margaret turned to volumes in French and English, and so no doubt did other ladies of the later Middle Ages, most of whose non-liturgical books, like those of their husbands, were romances, French Bibles and devotional works. Women, like men, shared in the world of Latin culture through the intermediacy of their chaplains and friars, rather than directly and personally. The revival of personal Latin studies among women begins, as it does among men, at the very end of the fifteenth century. The first example in the nunneries seems to be one at Dartford Priory in Kent in 1481, when a nun of noble rank was permitted to have an instructor of grammar and the Latin tongue to teach her and the other gentlewomen of the house.[99] In the royal family, as we have already noticed, Mary the daughter of Henry VII had a schoolmaster of her own by 1514,[100] and Mary I the daughter

[96] Bokenham, *Legendys of Hooly Wummen*, ed. Serjeantson, p. 260.
[97] Hardyng, *Chronicle*, ed. Ellis, p. 23.
[98] John Fisher, *English Works*, ed. Mayor, pp. 292, 294–5.
[99] C.F.R. Palmer, 'Notes on the Priory of Dartford in Kent', *Archaeological Journal*, xxxix (1882), pp. 197–8.
[100] *LPFD, Henry VIII*, i part ii, p. 1162 (no 2656).

of Henry VIII likewise in 1523.[101] A growing number of highly Latinate noblewomen can be traced from this point onwards through the sixteenth century. Language and letters were by nature an area of education where noble women could achieve a parity with men. Girls did not have the stimulus of careers in the Church or lay administration which caused boys to be well trained in letters, but equally they were less distracted by physical training out of doors, and the relative seclusion of their lives should have provided the peace and concentration fruitful for intellectual development. The reality was somewhat different. In language indeed the sexes appear to have been fairly equal. Chaucer might mock the priory French of Stratford-at-Bow, but Walter Map, Gerald of Wales and William Langland were equally scathing about the bad French of men, and nobody seems to have thought that men in general spoke better French than women.[102] The inequality was centred in the study of letters. Educationists stressed literacy more for males than they did for females. More aristocratic boys appear to have followed formal curricula under specialized masters than did girls. Girls' education, though it encompassed the alphabet and 'song', failed between 1200 and 1500 to penetrate Latin grammar and consequently writing, which was taught alongside grammar. Aristocratic ladies were owners of books in French and later in English, and probably read them conscientiously, but their education gave them little preparation to write creatively. That a few of them succeeded in 'writing' books (sometimes, perhaps, by dictation) was a creditable achievement, given the adverse conditions. Marie of France and Clemence of Barking in the twelfth century were followed by Eleanor of Provence in the thirteenth, who probably wrote her verse romance *Blandin de Cornouailles* while she was queen of England in about 1240.[103] In the fifteenth century there are almost enough authoresses to speak of a revival, what with Eleanor Hull, Lady Margaret Beaufort and perhaps the compiler of the hunting poem 'Tristram' at a noble level,[104] and Julian of Norwich and Margery Kempe beneath the aristocracy. In the sphere of devotional writing, noble-

---

[101] *BRUO*, ii, 1148.
[102] Above, pp. 122; *Piers Plowman*, B, v, 236; xv, 365–9.
[103] M. Fauriel, *Histoire de la Poésie provençale*, 3 vols, Paris, 1846, iii, 92–5.
[104] Below, p. 195.

women held their own with noblemen, and it was not their fault that they were unfitted to write about politics, law or administration, to which males alone had freedom of entry.

MUSIC

The poet Thomas who composed the oldest surviving fragment of the Tristan story tells how the hero and his comrade Caerdin hid by a road in an oak tree to observe the passing by of King Mark and his household. It was a large company and took a long time to go past: footmen, grooms, laundresses and chambermaids, until at last there was a burst of song, and knights and ladies came in sight all singing 'beautiful tunes and pastourelles', 'delightful airs and songs'.[105] The episode reveals how much the skill in music was felt to be characteristic of noblemen and women, even in the middle of the twelfth century when Thomas was writing. It was a courtly activity *par excellence*: 'who will be so courtly [*cortois*] that he will sing to us?', as the countess of Joigni and her ladies are said to have asked in the presence of the young knight William Marshal in about the 1160s. William was extremely courtly, and he obliged them at once:

> The Marshal, who sang well,
> And who never boasted of anything,
> Began to sing a song
> With a simple voice and a sweet sound.[106]

The skill is ascribed to many other heroes and heroines of medieval literature. Gottfried von Strassburg's Tristan plays stringed instruments of all kinds from morning to night, and sings with excellence.[107] Horn surpasses everyone in the playing of instruments, also of every variety beneath the sky or known to man.[108] The Lady Fresne longs to sound lays on her harp,[109] and Felice, at least in the later versions of her story, is equally 'learned in music'.[110]

Music, of course, played a major part in English aristocratic life

---

[105] Thomas, *Le Roman de Tristan*, ed. Bédier, i, 334; Gottfried, *Tristan*, trans. Hatto, p. 322.
[106] *Histoire de Guillaume le Maréchal*, ed. Meyer, i, 126–7.
[107] *Tristan*, trans. Hatto, p. 69.
[108] *The Romance of Horn*, ed. Pope, i, 42; cf. *King Horn*, ed. Hall, pp. 14–15.
[109] Renaut, *Le Roman de Galerent*, ed. Boucherie, lines 3879–88.
[110] *The Romance of Guy of Warwick*, ed. Zupitza, p. 7.

throughout the Middle Ages. It was a social accomplishment of the nobility themselves, enabling them to sing and dance together for recreation as they did in the households of Mark and the countess of Joigni. It caused them to employ minstrels to play instruments for them, not only for pleasure but to help provide the splendid lifestyle required by aristocratic status. Ceremonial occasions in great households were accompanied with music. *Sir Gawain and the Green Knight*, a realistic evocation of such events, describes how at the Christmas feast in Arthur's court,

> the first cors come with crakkyng of trumpes,
> Wyth mony baner ful bryght that therebi henged;
> Nwe nakryn noyse with the noble pipes,
> Wylde werbles and wyght wakned lote,

which the poet's phrases show that he enjoyed; indeed, he believed that everyone did, for he added the affirmation 'that mony hert ful highe hef at her towches'.[111] In the real household of Edward IV, the 'Black Book' of 1471-3 informs us that the king retained thirteen minstrels for feast days, 'whereof some use trumpets, some shawms and small pipes, and some are string-men', to provide ceremonial music 'for the king and his household at meats and suppers'.[112] And along with this secular art there was religious music, and the employment by the aristocracy from at least the year 1300 of polyphonic choirs of boys, youths and men to add musical beauty to the services in their household chapels. Already in 1305 we find the countess of Hereford and Essex persuading her brother Edward II to send her a clerk from Windsor Castle to teach the children of her chapel,[113] and later on the chapel music of the earl of Northumberland (d. 1527) was evidently so renowned that after his death nineteen of his service-books were asked for and obtained by Cardinal Wolsey, to enhance the music of his own chapel.[114]

---

[111] 'The first course was served to the sounding of trumpets, with many bright banners hanging from them; new noises of drums and noble pipes wakened the echoes with wild, fierce notes, so that many hearts heaved high at their sounds' (*Sir Gawain and the Green Knight*, lines 116-20).

[112] Myers, *Household of Edward IV*, pp. 131-2.

[113] *Letters of Edward Prince of Wales, 1304-1305*, ed. Hilda Johnstone, Roxburghe Club, 1931, p. 133.

[114] Harrison, *Music in Medieval Britain*, p. 173. On household choirs in general, see ibid., pp. 17-26, 170-4.

The interest in hearing music was accompanied, among both sexes of the aristocracy, by a liking to produce it. Music-making was particularly suited to the more stationary and secluded lives of women, and seems to have been approved as well as tolerated as a suitable activity for them. Thus, turning again to Thomas we find him painting an appreciative picture of Queen Iseut in her chamber, making a 'sad lay of love'

> how my lord Guirun became enamoured and was slain for love of the lady whom he cherished above all, and how thereupon, one day, in treachery the Count gave his wife Guirun's heart to eat, and what grief the lady felt when she learned of the death of her friend. The Queen sings sweetly and suits her voice to her instrument. Her hands are fair, her lay is good, her voice sweet, and her tone low.[115]

Chaucer too portrays aristocratic female music-making in *Troilus and Criseyde*: a song composed by one noble lady of Troy is sung by a second to a group of others:

> Antigone the shene
> Gan on a Troian song to singen cleere,
> That it an heven was hire vois to here.
>
> . . .
>
> 'Now nece', quod Cryseyde,
> Who made this song now with so good entente?'
> Antygone answerde anoon and seyde,
> 'Madame, iwys, the goodlieste mayde
> Of gret estate in al the town of Troye,
> And let hire lif in moste honour and joye.'[116]

Later, as the personal records of the aristocracy increase, we can begin to identify the musical interests of real ladies. The accounts of Henry earl of Derby (later Henry IV) record the purchase of forty strings for the harp of his first wife, Mary Bohun, in 1387–8 when she was in her late teens.[117] In the family of Henry VII the elder daughter Margaret had a lute bought for her for 13s 4d in 1501, when

[115] Thomas, *Le Roman de Tristan*, ed. Bédier, i, 295; Gottfried, *Tristan*, trans. Hatto, p. 313.
[116] Chaucer, *Works*, ed. Robinson, pp. 410–11 (book ii, lines 824–82).
[117] PRO, DL 28/1/2 f 25ᵛ.

she was 12, and 10s' worth of lute-strings in the following year.[118] Her 9-year-old sister Mary had a lute of the same price in 1505, and made a good impression when she played it in public.[119] At the visit of Philip the Fair to Windsor Castle in 1506, she performed 'very well' on the lute and the clavichord and, said a contemporary observer, 'was of all folk .... greatly praised, that [despite] her youth, in everything she behaved herself so very well'.[120]

If singing and playing were female accomplishments, they were in no way seen as effeminate; on the contrary, we find them being practised by the strongest and heartiest of men. No one was more the warrior than William Marshal; he was waiting to take part in a tournament at Joigni when he sang to the countess and her ladies, and after the song he mounted his steed and went straight off to unhorse an opponent. Two centuries later, Froissart tells how Edward III whiled away the time in his ship before the naval battle off Winchelsea in 1350 by having his minstrels play a German dance which Sir John Chandos had told him about, and how he then made Chandos (one of the greatest fighters of the day) 'sing with his minstrels, and took great pleasure from it'.[121] Henry V the conqueror of France was an instrumentalist. Harp-strings were bought for him when he was 10 in 1397,[122] and the love of the harp stayed with him throughout all his other preoccupations, a new one which he had ordered in London being sent out to France for him in 1421, a year before his death.[123] When Henry VII's daughter Margaret married James IV of Scotland in 1503, her escort Sir Edward Stanley played on the clavichord at the celebrations and sang a ballade with two of his servants to the great delight of the king, who called up one of his own gentlemen and made them sing together.[124] Yet both King James and Stanley were soldiers, and they each fought at the battle of Flodden ten years later. So there is nothing new about the best-known union of music and military skill:

---

[118] Bentley, *Excerpta Historica*, p. 125; *Privy Purse Expenses of Elizabeth of York*, ed. Nicolas, p. 29.
[119] Bentley, *Excerpta Historica*, p. 133.
[120] BL, Cotton MS Vespasian C.xii, p. 284.
[121] Froissart, *Chroniques*, ed. de Lettenhove, v, 260, 267; *Chronicles*, trans. Brereton, p. 115.
[122] PRO, DL 28/1/6 f 36.
[123] Devon, *Issues of the Exchequer*, pp. 363, 367.
[124] Leland, *Collectanea*, ed. Hearne, iv, 284.

that of Henry VIII. He followed an ancient tradition in being a singer and player one moment, and an athlete and warrior the next.[125]

Music was therefore a manly skill as well as a womanly one, and as such attracted the notice of educational writers who were always more interested in the attributes of men than in those of women. In the *Politics*, music is identified as one of the four main subjects of boys' education, and Aristotle spent some time discussing it. He rejected its claim to importance on the grounds of promoting amusement or relaxation, since he did not believe that boys should be instructed to these ends, but he approved it because it had the power to form the character and to promote virtue.[126] The thirteenth-century educationists did not accord the skill so much respect. Giles of Rome omitted Aristotle's discussion of the topic, and gave it a much briefer treatment in the context of the seven liberal arts. He did not say much in its favour, seeing it primarily as a harmless pleasure, but he approved its being taught to children and specified those of kings and the aristocracy.[127] The arrangements for the education of Edward V in 1473 make it clear that music formed part of the upbringing of him and his companions. Mass was said every day in his household 'by note, with children', in other words with polyphonic accompaniment, and the noble boys who were with him were ordered specifically to be trained in music along with other 'exercises of humanity'.[128] The contemporary 'Black Book' of the royal household expected that the henchmen, too, would be taught by their master to harp, pipe and sing.[129] The teaching of music to children was doubtless done both by amateurs and by professionals. Bartholomew portrayed the nurse singing 'cradle songs' to her baby,[130] and parents, masters and household servants could easily have taught singing and even instrumental playing, like the master of the henchmen, as part of their general cultural expertise. In the greatest households, on the other hand, there were minstrels who could be called on to give professional instruction, and minstrels from elsewhere could probably be hired to teach for money, as the

[125] Hall, *Chronicle*, p. 515.
[126] *Politics*, book viii, chapters 3, 5–6.
[127] *De Regimine Principum*, book ii, part ii, chapter 8 (ed. Molenaer, pp. 199–202).
[128] Orme in *BIHR*, lvii (1984).
[129] Myers, *Household of Edward IV*, pp. 126–7.
[130] *De Proprietatibus Rerum*, book vi, chapter 4 (ed. Seymour, i, 299).

adult merchant George Cely paid for lessons on the harp and the lute from a harper of Calais in 1474–5.[131] The professional teacher of music to the nobility, however, like the tutors of Bianca in *The Taming of the Shrew*, is a sixteenth-century phenomenon rather than a medieval one. In the Middle Ages, when full-time musicians were fewer and so much aristocratic music-making, both by the nobility and their servants, was amateur, there was less of a distinction between the professional and the amateur or between the teacher and the player. The aristocracy seem to have involved themselves in a variety of musical activities. Good singing included the ability to perform songs of different kinds, as Gottfried's Tristan is credited with singing 'chansons', 'refloits' and 'estampies'.[132] Singing might be performed solo, as William Marshal is said to have done it, or in groups, and songs in several parts were popular by the end of the Middle Ages. Fortescue mentions the students of the inns of court learning to sing and exercise themselves 'in every kind of harmony' in the 1460s,[133] and the singing of Sir Edward Stanley and of Henry VIII was also done in parts or in unison with other singers. Frequently the singer accompanied himself or herself on an instrument, as Iseut is shown doing by Thomas, the harp being popular for this purpose from the twelfth century until the fifteenth. The aristocracy kept up with the evolution of instruments, and learnt to play the new and modified forms that were developed. One of the first mentions of the lute in English literature is its attribution by Chaucer to his aristocratic character Phoebus in 'The Manciple's Tale', together with other stringed instruments: the cithern and the psaltery.[134] The same is true of the development of keyed instruments, clavichords and clavicymbals, in the fifteenth century. The treasurer of York Minster bequeathed a clavicymbal and a lute to Thomas Gednay in 1432, apparently one of a number of gentlemen whom he was educating in his household,[135] and by the early sixteenth century Stanley and the Princess Mary were expert in this kind of playing, as we have seen. Men, at least, appear to have learnt wind instruments as well. Chaucer describes the Squire as

[131] Hanham in *Review of English Studies*, new series, vii (1956), pp. 270–4.
[132] Gottfried, *Tristan*, trans. Hatto, p. 71.
[133] Fortescue, *De Laudibus Legum Anglie*, ed. Chrimes, pp. 118–19.
[134] Chaucer, *Works*, ed. Robinson, pp. 225–6 (H 113–18, 267–8).
[135] *Testamenta Eboracensia*, ed. Raine, iii, 92.

'floytynge', which probably means on the flute, and a recorder was bought for Henry earl of Derby in 1387–8 at a cost of 3s 4d.[136] Henry VIII is mentioned performing on both.[137]

There was music composition, too, as well as performance. Chaucer says of the Squire, 'he koude songes make and wel endite',[138] and the attribution of the song in *Troilus and Criseyde* to a noble lady of Troy shows that a woman could be envisaged as a composer. The composition of lyrical verse was an accomplishment of some kings and noblemen from the twelfth century onwards, and since such verses were meant to be sung, they involved their authors with musical techniques, at least in matching words to existing tunes and possibly in the creation of new ones. Until the end of the Middle Ages, the aristocracy are unlikely to have had much expertise in written musical notation. Their music was kept in their memories and transmitted through performance, as we are told Sir John Chandos 'reported' the German dance tune which he had evidently heard and memorized elsewhere. In the fifteenth century, on the other hand, manuscript texts of musical works begin to survive which were used or composed by the aristocracy, revealing the beginnings of musical literacy among them. Like most such texts of the period, these are religious in character and confirm the interest of the nobility in sacred as well as in secular music. The early fifteenth-century 'Old Hall' manuscript contains two settings, one of the Gloria of the mass and the other of the Sanctus, attributed to 'Roy Henry'.[139] These are eligible to have been composed by Henry IV or Henry V, since both were instrumental players and Henry IV was described by a contemporary writer as 'sparkling in music'.[140] A later work of the century, a polyphonic setting of the Benedicamus by 'W. Haute, knyght', was written by one of the Kentish family of that name,[141] and in the musical family of Henry VII, Henry VIII was certainly musically literate and a composer. The historian Edward Hall describes his expertise at the beginning of his reign as including the making of songs and ballads, and the setting of 'two goodly masses, every of them [in] five parts, which were sung often-

---

[136] Chaucer, *Works*, ed. Robinson, p. 18 (A 91); PRO, DL 28/1/2 f 16ᵛ.
[137] Hall, *Chronicle*, p. 515.
[138] Chaucer, *Works*, ed. Robinson, p. 18 (A 95).
[139] Harrison, *Music in Medieval Britain*, pp. 220–1.
[140] ibid., p. 221.
[141] ibid., pp. 415–16.

times in his chapel and afterwards in diverse places'.[142] Men therefore were the earliest exponents of written music, which is hardly surprising. The performance of polyphonic religious music was a male preserve, and the study of its notation better accorded with the formal curriculum of men than the informal one of women. It remained for ladies to acquire a skill in musical literacy during the sixteenth century, and even then they did not break the domination in the sphere of writing music which men had already established.

DANCING

In the list of the Muses Euterpe the musician is immediately followed by Terpsichore the dancer. Among the aristocracy too the practice of dancing seems to have been as old and popular as music. When the countess of Joigni asked for a singer, it was because she wished to dance, and the sequel in which knights and ladies danced while William Marshal sang shows that the skill was already a social activity among noblemen and women by the middle of the twelfth century.[143] The early history of courtly dancing in England, however, is curiously obscure. Unlike music or chess it is not usually given as an attribute to heroes or heroines in twelfth- and thirteenth-century literature, which suggests that it did not at first possess much status in the eyes of those who wrote and read such works. Ecclesiastical writers did notice it, but generally with disapproval, associating the skill with irreligious and dissolute behaviour. Saint Augustine was credited with the remark that it was better to dig or plough on a Sunday than to dance,[144] and the fourteenth-century preacher John Bromyard declared that dancing was a parody of divine worship and a service of the Devil. The dances of the rich and noble, he added, with their love-songs and laughter were a mockery of the wretched starving poor.[145] Dancing, however, survived both the neglect and the disapproval of writers, and as time went on its

---

[142] Hall, *Chronicle*, p. 515. For the vocal compositions ascribed to Henry, see Trefusis, *Songs, Ballads and Instrumental Pieces composed by Henry the Eighth*, and for the secular vocal and instrumental ones, Stevens, *Music at the Court of Henry VIII*.

[143] *L'Histoire de Guillaume le Maréchal*, ed. Meyer, i, 126-8.

[144] Horman, *Vulgaria*, pp. 279-80; Elyot, *The Governor*, book i, chapter 19.

[145] John Bromyard, *Summa Predicantium*, Basel, c.1485, sub 'chorea'; Owst, *Literature and Pulpit*, p. 301; cf. pp. 12, 119, 154, 278, 383-4, 393-5, 481, 509.

status grew, for the later that we go the more we hear about it. Guillaume de Lorris describes at length the courtly dancing of men and women in the original part of the *Roman de la Rose*,[146] and by the late fourteenth century the skill is frequently mentioned by writers in a courtly context. In Chaucer it is an attribute of the Squire; it is done by knights and ladies at the court of Cambuskan in 'The Squire's Tale', and by the noblemen and women of Brittany in the tale of the Franklin.[147] In *Sir Gawain and the Green Knight* it is a favourite Christmas pastime of lords and ladies, both at the court of the king and in the household of Sir Bercilak in a remote corner of the kingdom.[148]

The interest of educationists in dancing resembled that of writers of fiction in developing slowly and late. Neither Bartholomew nor Giles mentions the skill by name, and it is not until the late fourteenth and fifteenth centuries that writers on education in England begin to take notice of dancing in order to show it their favour. One of the earliest is John Trevisa, who adds the observation in his translation of Bartholomew that children are skilful in learning 'carols', a word which in the Middle Ages means a song that was danced to.[149] Later on, John Harding couples music and dancing in 1457 as the typical activities of noble children when they are 10 or 12;[150] Fortescue describes dancing as one of the recreations of noble youths at the inns of court;[151] and the author of the 'Black Book' includes the skill as one of the subjects which ought to be taught to the noble boys of the royal household by the master of the henchmen.[152] These brief but approving references look forward to the first full exposition of dancing in an educational context, in Elyot's *The Governor* of 1530.[153] Trevisa's statement reminds us that children have been dancing since at least the fourteenth century and probably since time immemorial, but the first recorded examples of identifiable children doing so belong to the fifteenth, perhaps reflecting the

---

[146] Lorris and Meun, *Roman de la Rose*, lines 749–1292.
[147] Chaucer, *Works*, ed. Robinson, pp. 18 (A 96), 130–1, (F 276–87), 137 (F 900, 925–30).
[148] *Sir Gawain and the Green Knight*, lines 43, 47, 1026, 1655, 1886.
[149] Bartholomew, *On the Properties of Things*, ed. Seymour, i, 300.
[150] BL, Lansdowne MS 204, f. 12; Hardyng, *Chronicle*, ed. Ellis, pp. i–ii.
[151] Fortescue, *De Laudibus Legum Anglie*, ed. Chrimes, pp. 118–19.
[152] Myers, *Household of Edward IV*, pp. 126–7.
[153] *The Governor*, book i, chapters 18–25.

same increase of interest in the skill as do the educational references. The friar-poet Osbern Bokenham records how he was present in the household of Isabel Lady Bourchier countess of Eu on Twelfth Night 1446, and talked with her in her chamber 'whyl this ledyis foure sonys ying besy were wyth revel and wyth daunsyng'.[154] The countess had married in 1426, so her sons were all beneath the age of 19. Elizabeth of York the oldest daughter of Edward IV is mentioned dancing at two balls at Windsor Castle when she was 6 in 1472, once with her father and once with the 19-year-old duke of Buckingham, and her children, when she was queen, were also given to the skill.[155] When Arthur was married to Katherine of Aragon in 1501, we are told that his 10-year-old brother Henry took off his gown and danced in his jacket with their sister Margaret who was nearly 12, 'in so goodly and pleasant a manner that it was to the king and queen [a] great and singular pleasure'.[156] Henry remained a noted dancer in his adult life.[157]

Dancing was probably learnt as music was. The skill could be imparted to children informally by their elders or acquired by imitation, as children watched their elders while they danced. The earliest professional teachers of whom we hear were minstrels. George Cely learnt dancing from the harper of Calais with whom he studied the lute in 1474-5,[158] and the king's minstrels were paid 40s for teaching the 10-year-old son and heir of the earl of Rutland, Henry Manners, to dance in 1536.[159] The techniques of medieval dancing are hard to reconstruct because, although texts of dance music begin to survive in the thirteenth century, the recording of steps and gestures by means of notation was not developed until the fifteenth, and descriptions of dancing in medieval literature are lacking in precision. Dancing was slow to develop a generally recognized terminology, and most writers down to the end of the Middle Ages were content to use the two words 'dance' and 'carol' to comprehend all the varieties of dancing that went on. Yet that

---

[154] Bokenham, *Legendys of Hooly Wummen*, ed. Serjeantson, p. 138.
[155] C.L. Kingsford, *English Historical Literature in the Fifteenth Century*, Oxford 1913, pp. 386–7.
[156] Leland, *Collectanea*, ed. Hearne, v, 361–2; compare BL, Cotton MS Vespasian C. xii, pp. 283–4.
[157] Hall, *Chronicle*, p. 515.
[158] Hanham in *Review of English Studies*, new series, viii (1956), pp. 270–4.
[159] *HMC, MSS of the Duke of Rutland*, vol iv, 1905, p. 263.

varieties existed is quite certain. There were dances by couples or sets of couples as in Guillaume de Lorris's description, and dances by larger numbers joining hands chain-wise or in a ring. The dance could be confined to a single place or move, as the chain sort did, in an itinerary from one place to another. Steps varied too in how they were made and in what sequence, for Chaucer says of the parish clerk in 'The Miller's Tale', 'in twenty manere koude he trippe and dance',[160] and George Cely learnt various kinds of dances: six on one occasion, fourteen on another, and twenty on a third. At the level of the court there was a knowledge and probably an adoption of foreign dance tunes and techniques, like the German dance reported to Edward III by Sir John Chandos. The 13-year-old Richard II rewarded a Venetian dancing-master who played and danced before him in 1380,[161] and the 6-year-old Henry VI was entertained at Windsor by French players and dancers in 1428.[162] By the end of the fourteenth century, there are signs that a terminology of dancing was beginning to become established, and we start to find references to named dances in literature, though the terms are uncommon and rarely repeated. Chaucer talks of the 'love dance', the 'spring' and the 'ray' in *The House of Fame*,[163] while Gower describes the 'hove dance' (based on a German term for a courtly dance) and the 'newfoot', which looks like a fashion newly invented.[164] We hear of the 'morris dance' in 1458 and the 'hornpipe' in 1474, and other terms like 'round' and 'hay' occur in the early sixteenth century.[165]

The apparent growth of interest in dancing by English writers was paralleled more clearly and on a larger scale in Italy, where important developments took place in the literature of dancing during the fifteenth century. It was the Italian writers Domenico da Piacenza, Antonio Cornazano and Giovanni Ambrogio da Pesaro who wrote the first European treatises on dancing between about 1450 and 1470.[166] Their works identified principles of dancing:

[160] Chaucer, *Works*, ed. Robinson, p. 49 (A 3328–30).
[161] Devon, *Issues of the Exchequer*, p. 212.
[162] *Proceedings of the Privy Council*, ed. Nicolas, iii, 294.
[163] Chaucer, *Works*, ed. Robinson, p. 294 (lines 1235–6).
[164] Gower, *Complete Works*, ed. Macaulay, iii, 171.
[165] See *OED* under the words cited; for the 1474 use of 'hornpipe', see Hanham in *Review of English Studies*, new series, viii (1956), p. 271.
[166] On this and what follows, see Michel in *Medievalia et Humanistica* (1946), pp. 117–31.

rhythm, dynamics, care and memory; established a terminology to describe individual dances and their component movements; explained how steps and movements should be made, and developed a system of notation to record the sequence of each particular dance. The interest spread to France, and in about 1490 a short practical treatise in French entitled *The Art and Instruction of Dancing Well* was printed at Paris, presenting forty-eight dance melodies together with a notation, in the form of alphabetical letters, to describe the movements.[167] The earliest English treatise on dancing was a similar kind of work, *The Manner of Dancing Base Dances*, translated from French sources by Robert Coplande and published by him at London in 1522. This has no music, and confines itself to describing seven French dances, the kinds of steps they involve, and the sequence which has to be followed, again explained by means of a series of letters. The appearance of these treatises coincided with the popularity of a new kind of dance in Western Europe, the slow ceremonial 'base dance', and it was consequently this kind of dance which first came to be fully recorded in literature. There is no reason to suppose, however, that dancing changed its nature during the fifteenth century, or that the medieval dances were any less sophisticated than their Renaissance successors. The primary change appears to have been one of consciousness. An increased awareness of dancing led to the writing of treatises, and they in turn caused a terminology to become better established and methods of dancing to become more uniform. By 1530 Elyot could analyse dancing in detail and discuss its terminology, secure in the knowledge that his readers would understand and appreciate what he was writing.

OTHER SKILLS: THE VISUAL ARTS, MEDICINE AND INDOOR GAMES

The children of the nobility were born into a world of visual splendours, as well as those of sound and movement. Aristocratic life-styles emphasized display: the wearing of fine clothes, the use of gold and silver ornaments, and the decoration of rooms with beautiful fabrics and tapestries. Aesthetic tastes were formed as boys and girls grew up in these surroundings. Sometimes, in the

---

[167] *L'Art et Instruction de Bien Dancer*, ed. Rastell and Lequet.

wealthiest families, they were given their own expensive possessions, even while they were children. The registers of John of Gaunt in the 1370s and 1380s record his presents to his sons and daughters: a gold cup and a set of silver vessels for Henry, a collar of gold and a gold head-dress for Philippa, a fillet of three *balays* and twenty-eight pearls for Elizabeth.[168] The New-Year gifts of Henry VI in 1428, when he was 6, included a gold cup from his mother, another embellished with pearls and sapphires from the duke of Gloucester, and a rosary of coral beads and a brooch of gold from Sir Thomas Erpingham.[169] Aristocratic growing up certainly involved exposure to beautiful things.

Noble education, on the other hand, did not provide for formal lessons in art appreciation nor, in the case of boys, for any training in creative art except the writing of a good clear script. Aristotle had included drawing as part of a boy's curriculum, on practical and aesthetic grounds. It taught him to understand objects and avoid mistakes when buying and selling them, to judge the beauty of the human form, and properly to appreciate the work of artists.[170] In medieval Europe, however, the applied arts of drawing, painting, carving and metal-work were in the hands of craftsmen and artisans, and the involvement of the aristocracy in such activities, even as hobbies, would doubtless have been regarded by noblemen and commoners alike as a violation of the social order. So Giles of Rome quoted Aristotle to the extent that children should be taught to see, but he did not describe a curriculum for doing so, and was more interested in the negative policy of shielding children from works of art of a lascivious nature.[171] Other educationists were equally silent on the subject of creative art. Chaucer in consequence, when he says that the Squire could 'purtreye', is most unlikely to have meant that he could draw.[172] To 'purtreye' meant 'to represent something' in any sense, and Chaucer probably wished to say that the Squire could describe things well in speech or writing. Even in the fifteenth century, a nobleman able to paint like René of Anjou in France (d. 1480) is a rare figure and a harbinger of different attitudes to art

---

168 *John of Gaunt's Register, 1372–6,* ed. Armitage-Smith, i, 193–4; ii, 191, 281, 296; ibid., *1379–83,* ed. Lodge and Somerville, i, 110–11, 179, 231.
169 Rymer, *Foedera,* x, 387.
170 *Politics,* book viii, chapter 3.
171 *De Regimine Principum,* book ii, part ii, chapter 10 (ed. Molenaer, pp. 206–8).
172 Chaucer, *Works,* ed. Robinson, p. 18 (A 96).

which were developing with the Renaissance. The first recommendation by an English educationist that noble boys should be allowed to paint, carve or work in metal comes from the sixteenth century, and Elyot the writer in question was at pains to explain and defend what was clearly a new and potentially unpopular proposal.[173]

It was girls instead who practised creative art in the medieval system of education. While noble boys were separated in their tasks from artisans and craftsmen, noble girls were seen as having more in common with women throughout society, including their work of spinning, sewing and the making of textiles. As early as the 1150s John of Salisbury quoted approvingly the account by Suetonius of how Augustus had his daughters and grand-daughters taught to sew and to weave.[174] A century later Giles of Rome also considered sewing, spinning and working with silk to be the foremost occupations for noble women.[175] We find in reality the daughters of the English kings practising learning to work with textiles in their childhoods, and no doubt this went on in noble households too. Eighteen ounces of silk were bought for Joan, the 13-year-old daughter of Edward I in 1285–6, and silk, gold thread and a spindle 'for the embroidery work' of her younger sister Margaret.[176] Joan the daughter of Edward III had more than £2 spent on her behalf in 1340, when she was 7, on gold thread, silk and pearls 'delivered to her chamber, for diverse works which were going on there' and with which she may have been involved.[177] Certainly, in the fourteenth-century English *Romance of Emaré* the royal heroine is taught in childhood by her lady mistress 'gold and silk for to sew', and teaches the art to others when she grows up.[178] The making of textiles by noble girls was artistic in nature, more so than that by ordinary women, given the money and time available to buy costly materials and make them into intricate pieces of work. But it cannot be said that the educationists realized the artistic worth of such an occupation. The point of John of Salisbury's story was that Augustus wished his daughters never to be idle, and desired to

[173] *The Governor*, book i, chapter 8.
[174] John of Salisbury, *Policraticus*, ed. Webb, ii, 15.
[175] *De Regimine Principum*, book ii, part ii, chapter 20 (ed. Molenaer, pp. 227–8).
[176] Green, *Lives of the Princesses*, ii, 324–5, 365–6. I have not been able to locate the documents cited.
[177] ibid., iii, 241.
[178] *The Romance of Emaré*, ed. Edith Rickert, EETS, es, xcix (1908), pp. 2–3, 12.

provide them with a living in case they should ever grow poor. Giles of Rome's discussion of textile work comes in a chapter on idleness, and extols the labour for ethical reasons, not aesthetic ones. So too Langland, who advises

> Lovely ladyes with youre longe fyngres
> That ye han silk and sendal to sowe, whan tyme is,
> Chesibles for chapelleynes, cherches to honoure,[179]

is equally concerned with utility rather than art, and with pointing out a way for noble women to contribute to the good of the rest of society. In short, the failure to provide for the education of boys in creative art was matched by an equal conceptual failure regarding girls. Their textile occupations were seen in terms of work and charity, not in the making of beautiful things.

Medicine is also absent from the curriculum in educational works, apart from a casual mention of it by Giles of Rome among the higher studies which princes may, but are unlikely to, study. Romantic literature, however, so often ascribes a skill in medicine or surgery to noble ladies that they may well have learnt the art in practice. Marie of France in her *Lai des deux Amants* tells of the aunt of a princess who has studied for thirty years in the medical schools of Salerno, is learned in salves and drugs, herbs and roots, and able to make up prescriptions.[180] Melior's learning in the *Romance of Partonopeu* includes a similar knowledge of herbs, roots and spices and the ability to heal the sick.[181] In the story of *Yvain* by Chrétien of Troyes, its knightly hero is twice indebted to female medicine for his survival: once to a lady who cures him of madness with an ointment prepared by Morgan le Fay, and later when wounded to two maidens skilled in surgery and daughters of a lord.[182] Similar attributes occur in the English versions of these stories in the later Middle Ages.[183] When we have made due allowance for the 'science-fiction' which characterizes so many of the episodes in the romances, they leave a real possibility of the medical skill of noble women. Though hardly likely to be taught to children, the skill

---

[179] *Piers Plowman*, A, vii, 18–20; B, vi, 10–12; C, ix, 9–11.
[180] Marie de France, *Lais*, 'Lex Deux Amants', lines 103–8.
[181] *Partonopeu de Blois*, ed. Gildea, i, 187 (lines 4596–604).
[182] Chrétien de Troyes, *Yvain*, lines 2952–5, 4696–9; *Arthurian Romances*, trans. W.W. Comfort, London, 1975, pp. 218, 241.
[183] For examples, see Gardiner, *English Girlhood at School*, pp. 43–4.

could well have been learnt by girls from older women during adolescence. If so, it would enlarge our concept of the experience and abilities of women beyond the restricted view that we get from the educational writers.

When the aristocracy was not engaged in reading, dancing or song, its members took their indoor pleasures in the playing of chess, dice, 'tables' or backgammon and other board-games. Apart from dicing for stakes, which was noticed by medieval writers to be deprecated and discouraged, chess was the only one of these games which came to possess a significant role in noble education. The popularity of chess among the European aristocracy from the eleventh century onwards, together with the intellectual powers required to play it well, soon made it one of the fine accomplishments associated with ideal men and women.[184] Peter Alfonsi proclaimed it as one of the seven knightly skills,[185] and in twelfth- and thirteenth-century literature it is ascribed to Alexander the Great, Tristan, Renaut de Montauban and other heroes.[186] Women played it too. 'I wish', says Fresne in the *Roman de Galerent*, 'to mate somebody at chess',[187] and Huon of Bordeaux in the romance of that name plays chess with the daughter of Ivoryn. 'Lady,' said Huon, 'which kind of game will you play? Will you have it with moves or with dice' – for dice were often used to speed the play. The lady replied with a clear voice, 'Let it be with moves'.[188] The game was undoubtedly popular with children as well as with adults. The romance of *Boeve de Haumtone* says that well-taught children play chess,[189] and that of *Fulk Fitz-Warin* contains the fictitious account, already described, in which the young King John plays chess in a surly temper, and ends up hitting his opponent with the chessboard![190] In the fifteenth century we can actually find a romantic vignette in literature in which the daughter of a wealthy burgess is

184 On the medieval history of chess, see Murray, *History of Chess*, pp. 393–451.
185 Peter Alfonsi, *Disciplina Clericalis*, ed. Hermes, pp. 114–15.
186 Murray, *History of Chess*, p. 432; Gottfried, *Tristan*, trans. Hatto, p. 71; *Le Roman de Tristan en Prose*, ed. Curtis, i, 138; *The Four Sonnes of Aymon*, ed. Octavia Richardson, vol i, EETS, es, xliv (1884), p. 61.
187 Renaut, *Le Roman de Galerent*, ed. Boucherie, line 3885.
188 *Huon de Bordeaux*, ed. P. Ruelle, Brussels and Paris, 1960, p. 310 (lines 7537–9).
189 *Der Anglonormannische Boeve de Hantone*, ed. A. Stimming, Halle, 1899, pp. 104–5.
190 Above, p. 33.

taught to play chess by a king's son (in disguise, of course), with a comment to the effect that this was something that a gentlewoman should learn.[191]

In the late thirteenth century chess acquired an educational significance in addition to its social one, through the publication of commentaries on the game which used the pieces and their moves as a starting-point for discussing contemporary society. The chief such work, which is entirely devoted to the study and interpretation of chess, was the *Liber de Moribus Hominum* or *Liber de Ludo Scacchorum* by Jacques de Cessoles, a Dominican friar of Rheims who wrote it in the late thirteenth century or the early fourteenth.[192] The original Latin work was twice translated into French in the course of the following years, numerous manuscripts attest to its popularity, and in due course it reached England. Hoccleve credited Henry V with having read it, took material from it for his own *Regement of Princes*,[193] and Caxton translated it into English. It was the second volume that he published at Bruges in 1474, and was reissued by him at Westminster in about 1483 with illustrations.[194] Jacques's work surveys the orders of society embodied in the pieces: king, queen, 'alphyns' (counsellors and judges, now represented by the bishops), knights, rooks (interpreted as the king's executive officers), and the pawns who are made to represent various categories of common people. Drawing on the work of Giles of Rome, it reflects on the social duties of these orders and their responsibilities to one another, and like many post-thirteenth-century moral works it has one or two explicit references to the education of the young. Thus it advocates the teaching of letters, religion and the liberal arts to the sons of kings, and quotes Suetonius (perhaps through the medium of John of Salisbury) on Augustus's education of his sons in military skills and his daughters in those of textiles.[195]

By the late Middle Ages the playing of chess had thus become an educational game as well as a social exercise, and this remained the case in England down to the early sixteenth century. As late as 1523 the economist John Fitzherbert cited Jacques's work in his *Book of*

[191] *The Three King's Sons*, ed. F.J. Furnivall, EETS, es, lxvii (1895), p. 10.
[192] On the author, see Grente, *Dictionnaire des Lettres françaises*, i, 399–400.
[193] Hoccleve, *Works*, ed. Furnivall, iii, 77.
[194] Jacques de Cessoles, *The Game of Chess*, trans. Caxton.
[195] ibid., ff bvi^v–vii.

Husbandry, which was often reprinted till 1587, to prove that 'every man from the highest degree to the lowest is set and ordained to have labours and occupations'.[196] Sir Thomas Elyot also noticed the book in 1530, and praised it. Chess, he says, is a good exercise for sharpening the wit and quickening the memory, 'and is the more commendable and also commodious if the players have read the moralization of the chess and when they play do think upon it'.[197] These are appreciative references, but they are late glances back at a work whose popularity was by that time coming to an end. Caxton's translation was not reprinted after 1483, and Elyot admitted that by his time it was scarce because, he lamented, few men nowadays sought in their games for either virtue or wisdom.

[196] Fitzherbert, *The Boke of Husbandrye*, f 1v.
[197] *The Governor*, book i, chapter 26.

Six   Arms and athletics

Along with the artistic and the intellectual sides of noble life there was, from the cradle itself, the physical. Babies stretched and kicked; children learnt to walk, played games and ran about. Boys and girls moved with their households from one dwelling place to another in the ceaseless journeyings of aristocratic life, the younger no doubt in carriages or carts but the older on horseback. Since everyone of substance in the Middle Ages was a rider unless he or she was infirm, noble children were surrounded by horses and probably learnt to ride them at an early age. Eventually they acquired their own mounts. Henry the second son of Edward I was given a white palfrey in 1274 when he was 7.[1] Henry IV bought steeds for his 10-year-old son John in 1399–1400, and for John's brother Humphrey two years later when he was 12.[2] As they grew older, boys and also girls were introduced to hunting and bow-shooting, and at the highest level boys in their teens who were going to be knights exerted themselves in military skills: the wearing of armour, the use of arms and the management of war-horses.

From classical times educationists realized the importance of

[1] Johnstone in *BJRL*, vii (1922–3), pp. 397, 408.
[2] Wylie, *England in the Reign of Henry the Fourth*, iv, 219.

physical activity and sought to organize it. Aristotle, as we have seen, advised that young children should be encouraged to move about, play games and accustom themselves to the cold. When boys were older, gymnastic exercises should become a major part of their curriculum. Up to puberty these were to be of a gentle nature, since too much physical training injures bodily form and stunts the growth. Hard training should be reserved until three years after the end of boyhood, at about the age of 17.[3] The attitude of medieval writers towards physical education differed somewhat from this. Interest in pure gymnastic exercises declined, and was replaced by a preoccupation with military training for knighthood. This change is reflected in Giles of Rome's discussion of the subject. He reproduces the outlines of Aristotle's threefold scheme of movement for babies, light exercises for boys and strenuous training for adolescents. But he has little to say about boys, except that they should play at ball, and centres his treatment of physical education almost wholly on military training in adolescence. This begins at 14, earlier than Aristotle had recommended for strenuous exercises. It lasts for four years and involves learning the kind of riding and fighting required for a knightly career, before embarking on the career itself at 18.[4] The approach of Giles was followed by other writers of the later Middle Ages. They too had little or no interest in physical education for its own sake, or in the construction of a curriculum for boys beneath the age of 14. Instead, they concentrate like Giles on training of a military nature beginning at 14 or 16.[5] They also restrict themselves, as usual, to the training of boys. We shall see that in practice girls took part in physical activities, but educationists did not observe the fact and failed to mention it in their works.

MILITARY TRAINING

The aristocracy saw themselves and were seen by others as the military estate of society, charged with defending by force of arms

[3] *Politics*, book vii, chapter 17; book viii, chapter 4.
[4] *De Regimine Principum*, book ii, part ii, chapters 15–17 (ed. Molenaer, pp. 216–23); book iii, part iii, chapter 3 (ed. Molenaer, pp. 375–7).
[5] Christine of Pisa (*Book of Fayttes of Armes*, ed. Byles, p. 29) and Elyot (*The Governor*, book i, chapter 16) suggest a starting age of 14. The English translator of Vegetius (Oxford, Bodleian Library, MS Digby 233, f 184ᵛ) and Hardyng (*Chronicle*, ed. Ellis, pp. i–ii), prefer 16.

all those who prayed and those who worked. Though many of their members, even in the twelfth century, lived largely peaceable lives, they were all supposed to possess arms and armour and to know how to use them.[6] Knighthood was an obligation on the male aristocracy, sporadically enforced; their mark of status was the military shield or coat of arms, and they had themselves shown on their tombs in armour and with swords until the seventeenth century. It was this that caused medieval educationists, who wrote their works chiefly for the benefit of aristocratic males, to view physical education from such a military point of view. Since a large proportion of noble boys were intended to become fighters, their physical exercises were judged primarily by the extent to which they led to strength and skill in war. In the view of the writers, the care of boys from their earliest years should be arranged with warlike ends in mind. Even Aristotle had recommended the exposure of young children to the cold not simply to make them healthy but to harden them for military life, and Giles of Rome thought the same. Christine of Pisa urged the inculcation of a military mentality, as well as a strong physique. She quoted with approval classical anecdotes of the boy who went armed to battle, the boy who vowed to kill Sulla the tyrant as his master was leading him to school, and the boy who took a knife and held it at the throat of an old man who was threatening his father.[7] Nor was hers an unusual view; medieval writers criticized children for indolence, oaths and insubordination, but not for aggression. Christine saw it as part of the education of a boy, as soon as he had left the care of women, to be told by his master about knighthood and noble deeds, and this was probably often done.[8] 'Men', says a fourteenth-century sermon writer, 'setteth their children to learn gests [i.e. deeds] of battles',[9] and the rules for the education of Edward V, even when he was 3, laid down that he should be told about 'deeds of worship' along with other good matters.[10]

It followed that boys were encouraged to play with weapons at an early age, and special ones were purchased for their use. The sword of the future Henry V, then heir to the earldom of Derby, is mentioned in 1397 when he was 9, and that of his 11-year-old

[6]   On this subject, see M.R. Powicke, *Military Obligation in Medieval England*, Oxford, 1962.
[7]   Christine of Pisa, *Livre du Corps de Policie*, ed. Bornstein, pp. 120–2.
[8]   ibid., pp. 46–8.
[9]   Owst, *Literature and Pulpit*, p. 466.
[10]   Orme in *BIHR*, lvii (1984).

brother John was burnished for 4*d* in 1400–1.[11] Eight swords were got for Henry VI in about 1430 when he was 9, 'some greater and some smaller, for to learn the king to play in his tender age', and his master the earl of Warwick also had 'a little harness' or suit of armour made for him, decorated with gold.[12] Henry's military games bore singularly little fruit in adult life, but we hear of other boys who responded with enthusiasm to the warlike ethos about them. The life of William Marshal tells how, at the age of 5 or 6 in 1152, he was taken hostage by King Stephen to ensure the surrender of Newbury Castle by his father, John FitzGilbert. When John broke faith, Stephen threatened to kill the boy, to which John said defiantly that he had the anvil and hammers to forge better sons if he needed. William was accordingly led out to be hanged in public at Newbury by Stephen's forces, but as he was going along unconscious of his fate, he saw the earl of Arundel twirling a javelin and said, 'Sir! give me that arrow!' The kindly Stephen was so touched by this that he changed his mind, and led William back to his camp where they played 'knights', each holding a plantain and trying to knock off the head of the other's.[13] These childhood interests led to adult ones, for William had a brilliant military career when he grew up. They led in the same direction three hundred years later for Edward son of Henry VI. A 6-year-old when civil war broke out in 1460, he was only 7 in the following spring when his mother asked him what should be done with two prisoners after a battle, and received the determined answer, 'cut off their heads'![14] Six years later in France in 1467, the Milanese ambassador observed that 'though only 13 years of age', he 'talks of nothing but cutting off heads or making war, as if he had everything in his hands or was the god of battles'.[15] Fortescue, who attests to the prince's love of jousting and fierce horses at the same period,[16] was evidently worried by his corresponding lack of interest in law, and *De Laudibus Legum Anglie* was no doubt partly aimed at moderating a

[11]   Kingsford, *Henry V*, pp. 14–15; PRO, DL 28/4/1 f 14.
[12]   R. Pauli, *Geschichte von England*, vol v, Gotha, 1858, p. 263.
[13]   *L'Histoire de Guillaume le Maréchal*, ed. Meyer, i, 19–24. On the authenticity of the episode, see Painter, *William Marshal*, pp. 13–16.
[14]   Jean de Waurin, *Receuil des Chroniques*, ed. W. and E.L.C.P. Hardy, vol v, RS, 1891, p. 330.
[15]   *Calendar of State Papers Milan*, vol i, London, 1913, p. 19.
[16]   Fortescue, *De Laudibus Legum Anglie*, ed. Chrimes, pp. 2–3, 16–19.

character which had become too centred upon fighting and revenge. Prince Edward might have become a great English warrior king; instead, he was killed at the battle of Tewkesbury in 1471, still five months short of his eighteenth birthday.

The formal training of noble boys in military skills, when they were 14 or thereabouts, could be read about in a textbook, the standard medieval treatise on the art of war. This was the *Epitoma Rei Militaris* of Flavius Vegetius Renatus, a writer of the later Roman empire who dedicated it to the Christian emperor Theodosius I between AD 383 and 395.[17] Vegetius wished, in the evening of Roman power, to bring back into use the great military techniques of its mid-day strength. To this end he compiled an epitome or summary of earlier writings on war, and his work enjoyed an extraordinary long-term success. Not only did it supersede its sources and survive into the Middle Ages while they were lost, but it commended itself to the aristocracy of feudal Europe as a textbook relevant to them, despite its original concern with the rather different army of the Romans. The *Epitoma* is divided into five books: the first on the training of recruits, the second on army organization, the third on campaigning, the fourth on fortifications and sieges, and the fifth on naval warfare. Medieval texts, however, usually combined the last two books to make a set of four. The whole work was well known in medieval Europe, but the first book is the only part that need concern us here, since most of the educational material in the work is to be found in its account of how recruits should be trained.

The *Epitoma* was known to the nobility of western Europe by the middle of the twelfth century. Henry II's father Geoffrey of Anjou had a copy with him while he was besieging Montreuil-Bellay in 1151, and was reading it himself (no doubt to find out what it said about sieges) when he was interrupted by a visiting party of monks from Marmoutier Abbey and ended up discussing the work with them.[18] Geoffrey's copy was in Latin, but later on in the thirteenth century when noble literacy could no longer cope so well with Latin texts, a series of French translations began to be made for

---

[17] The standard Latin edition is that of Lang; there are post-medieval English translations by John Sadler (1572) and John Clarke (1767). For a survey of the work and its influence, see Wisman in *Le Moyen Age*, lxxxv (1979), pp. 13–31.

[18] *Chroniques des Comtes d'Anjou*, ed. L. Halphen and R. Poupardin, Paris, 1913, p. 218.

aristocratic use. The first which is known in relation to England was made into Anglo-Norman by a certain Master Richard for a 'Lord Edward' who was either Edward I before he became king in 1272, or his son Edward II before his accession in 1307.[19] This version now exists in only one manuscript, but other French texts of Vegetius reached England during the fourteenth and fifteenth centuries in the continental translations of Jean de Meun (1284) and Jean de Vignai (1326–50).[20] A copy of Vegetius in French was owned by Thomas duke of Gloucester in 1397,[21] a second was given by Sir Robert Roos (d. 1448) to Humphrey duke of Gloucester,[22] and a third belonged to Sir John Fastolf in about 1450.[23] Finally in the fifteenth century, Vegetius was translated from Latin into English. The first and more popular version was made into prose in 1408 at the command of Thomas Lord Berkeley, who had already commissioned translations of other technical works including Bartholomew and Giles of Rome.[24] Ten copies of this version are known, of which one belonged to Sir John Paston II (d. 1479) and another to Richard III or to his wife Anne Nevill.[25] The second translation was made into verse by a 'parson of Calais', probably in the late 1450s. The author presented it to Lord Beaumont, the chamberlain of Henry VI, to be given to the king, but it circulated less widely than the prose version, and survives today in only three copies.[26]

There can be no doubt from this evidence that Vegetius was familiar to the aristocracy of later medieval England. The poet

---

[19] Thorpe in *Scriptorium*, vi (1952), pp. 39–50; Legge in ibid., vii (1953), pp. 262–5.

[20] Vegetius, *L'Art de Chevalerie* trans. Meun, ed. Robert; Wisman in *Le Moyen Age*, lxxxv (1979), pp. 17–21.

[21] Viscount Dillon and W.H. St J. Hope in *Archaeological Journal*, liv (1897), p. 300.

[22] Sammut, *Unfredo duca di Gloucester*, p. 101.

[23] *HMC, Eighth Report on Historical MSS*, Appendix, part i, section 2, 268a.

[24] The translation has not yet been printed; it is discussed in John Trevisa, *Dialogus inter Militem et Clericum*, ed. A.J. Perry, EETS, os, clxvii (1925), pp. xciv–xcviii. I have used the text in Bodleian Library, MS Digby 233, ff 183–227. The conclusion of this and some other MSS identifies the translator by a rebus, ⌐toun, which seems to mean 'Longtoun' or 'Langtoun', since the sign ⌐ is the musical symbol 'long' – not, as has been suggested, a clef standing for 'Cleftoun'.

[25] BL, Lansdowne MS 285; Royal MS 18 A.xii.

[26] Vegetius, *Knyghthode and Bataile*, ed. Dyboski and Arend.

Hoccleve, reproving Sir John Oldcastle for his heretical opinions in 1415, urged him to read it rather than delve into holy scripture, and Hoccleve intended to translate the work for his patron Humphrey duke of Gloucester, but desisted, perhaps because of the existence of the Berkeley translation.[27] The contents of the *Epitoma* were also diffused through their incorporation in other influential treatises which circulated among the aristocracy and the clergy. Part or all of the educational material in book one appears in book six of the *Policraticus* by John of Salisbury, book two of the *Speculum Doctrinale* by Vincent of Beauvais, and part three of *De Regimine Principum* by Giles of Rome. It was also utilized by Christine of Pisa in her *Livre des fais d'armes et de chevalerie* (1408–9), which Caxton translated and published in England in 1489.[28] The use of Vegetius by the great friar-educationists shows that by the late thirteenth century it was not regarded simply as a work for adult knights to read but as an educational textbook for training young warriors. This is confirmed by the dedication of the Anglo-Norman translation to a young Lord Edward, and by an illustration in the work depicting Vegetius saying to a group of young men, 'come to me, sirs knights, who wish to have the honour of knighthood'.[29] Lord Berkeley's translator also regarded the work from an educational point of view. The concluding sentences of his version observe that it is both a 'great disport and dalliance' for elderly lords and warriors, and a 'great information and learning' for 'young lords and knights that be lusty, and love to hear and see and to use deeds of arms and chivalry'.[30]

The first book of the *Epitoma Rei Militaris* describes a strenuous course of exercises and techniques for soldiers to learn, the medieval translators generally rendering 'soldiers' as 'knights' and consequently aiming the advice at the aristocracy specifically. Training should begin at puberty. It should establish physical fitness, including the ability to run fast and jump well which are necessary to keep up with one's comrades and pursue the enemy. Swimming should also be learnt, lest floods and rivers cut the army off and make it vulnerable to attack. Trainee soldiers should be exercised in swords, spears and bows, using heavier models for training than

[27] Hoccleve, *Works*, ed. Furnivall, i, 14–15, 130.
[28] Christine of Pisa, *Book of Fayttes of Armes*, ed. Byles.
[29] Thorpe in *Scriptorium*, vi (1952), plates 13–14.
[30] Bodleian Library, MS Digby 233 f 227.

those employed in battle, in order to develop greater strength and longer endurance. For sword practice they should be pitted against targets made of a post six feet high and set in the ground. They should be given a wooden mace and a wickerwork shield, each twice the weight of a normal sword and shield, and learn to attack the target with agility, 'now leaping out, now leaping in'. They should vary their lunges to strike in turn at different parts of the target's 'body' – head, sides and thighs, and be advised that thrusts are better than strokes because they do more damage and expose one's body less. The trainees should also practise fighting one another with swords in lists or enclosures, and learn to cast spears, shoot with bows and sling stones. Finally, they should accustom themselves to wearing armour and carrying arms, by bearing heavy burdens on their marches. They should acquire dexterity with their arms and armour on, jumping on and off horses while armed and even while holding a naked sword. Most of the emphasis here is on the individual, but in a later chapter of book one Vegetius stresses the importance of keeping one's place in the ranks during marches and manoeuvres. Other parts of the treatise, which deal with discipline and the military hierarchy, also teach that the soldier must not act simply on his own but as an integral unit of the army as a whole.

The medieval readers of Vegetius did not adopt without question the whole of his system of training. The Berkeley translator observes that some Roman techniques came into being through 'feigned and false visions and dreams through illusion of devils, the which the Romans worshipped', though he admits that when the Romans were well instructed they were superior to pagans and to uninstructed Christian knights.[31] As we shall see, bow shooting was not a normal art of knights in war and nor was swimming. Other techniques of the book, however, came closer to those of medieval warfare and probably helped to shape the training of knights. We hear of youths in practice fighting against a target (the quintain), learning to ride in the style of war, and fighting each other in lists with swords on foot and lances on horseback. All these were similar techniques to those of Vegetius. The function of teaching boys in arms is likely to have been carried out by fathers, lords in the case of wards, and knightly masters. Fortescue's defence of wardship includes the assertion that a minor's lord will instruct him well in military matters, and we

[31] Ibid., f 187–ᵛ.

know that John Hastings earl of Pembroke was being supervised by his master when he was fatally wounded in 1389 at the age of 18.[32] The master of the henchmen was likewise charged to teach his noble pupils how 'to ride cleanly and surely, to draw them also to jousts' and 'to learn them [to] wear their harness'.[33] Trainee knights appear to have been required to do menial duties, at least symbolically, as they were made to do in hall: helping to look after their lord's or master's horse, and to put on his armour and equipment.[34] Boys also learnt together, and the tendency to gather them into great households in groups meant that each had companions with whom to practise. Fortescue describes the delight of Prince Edward 'in attacking and assaulting the young companions attending him, sometimes with a lance, sometimes with a sword, and sometimes with other weapons, in a warlike way and according to the rules of military discipline'.[35] Likewise the tutor of Thomas Cromwell's son Gregory in the 1530s praises the 'honest envy' between Gregory and his two gentlemen companions in 'playing at weapons'.[36] The accident to John Hastings took place during similar companionship. The earl, wishing to prove his horse before the next tournament, rode it against another young knight, Sir John St John, while the latter held out a lance at the order of the earl's master. Pembroke's horse shied at the lance and threw him against it, causing a mortal wound in the belly. The earl died in an hour and Sir John fled, fearing vengeance; later on, he was cleared of blame and awarded a royal pardon.[37]

Beyond the training sessions came the matches – the organized tournaments, which can be called both sporting fixtures in that they were competitive meetings, and educational classes because they gave further opportunities to learn and practise the techniques of war. The tournament of Blyth in Nottinghamshire in 1256 is a good example of one with an educational purpose: it was held for the

[32] Fortescue, *De Laudibus Legum Anglie*, ed. Chrimes, pp. 108–9; *The Westminster Chronicle, 1381–1394*, ed. L.C. Hector and Barbara F. Harvey, Oxford, 1982, pp. 408–11.
[33] Myers, *Household of Edward IV*, pp. 126–7.
[34] Lull, *Book of the Ordre of Chyvalry*, ed. Byles, p. 21.
[35] Fortescue, *De Laudibus Legum Anglie*, ed. Chrimes, pp. 2–3.
[36] Ellis, *Original Letters*, 3rd series, i, 342–3.
[37] *The Westminster Chronicle*, ed. Hector and Harvey, pp. 408–11; *CPR 1388–92*, p. 469.

benefit of the 17-year-old Edward I, and Matthew Paris observed that the prince attended it 'so that he might be instructed in military laws'.[38] *The Book of the Order of Chivalry* by Ramon Lull (d. 1316), translated by Caxton in 1483–5, recommends that apprentice knights should go with their masters to tournaments,[39] and no doubt those which were held in later medieval England attracted both trainee onlookers and young contestants. Tournaments went on being organized into the sixteenth century. In 1510 the young Henry VIII aged 19

> with two others with him challenged all comers to fight with them at the barriers with target and casting the spear of eight feet long; and that done, his grace with the said two aides to fight every one of them twelve strokes with two-handed swords, with and against all comers, none except being a gentleman. . . . The king behaved himself so well and delivered himself so valiantly by his hardy prowess and great strength that the praise and laud was given to his grace and his aides, notwithstanding that diverse valiant and strong persons had assailed him.[40]

In 1515 Henry arranged further exercises; Nicholas Carew and Francis Bryan, young gentlemen of the court, were chosen to be on one side and other young men against them, and they were provided with horses and armour by the king 'to encourage all youth to seek deeds of arms'.[41]

The culmination of training was war itself, but here little planning of time and place was possible. Wars are unpredictable, and although Giles of Rome believed that 18 was the right age to begin the career of chivalry, in practice there was much variation. Very young children, as we have seen, might get caught up in war by accident, and fairly young children could be taken along on campaign. John of Gaunt was only 10 when, in the ship of his eldest brother the Black Prince, he was present at the sea battle off Winchelsea in 1350.[42] By the mid-teens, boys were expected to take

[38] Paris, *Chronica Majora*, ed. Luard, v, 557.
[39] Lull, *Book of the Ordre of Chyvalry*, ed. Byles, p. 22.
[40] Hall, *Chronicle*, p. 515.
[41] ibid., p. 581.
[42] Froissart, *Chroniques*, ed. de Lettenhove, v, 258, 266; *Chronicles*, trans. Brereton, p. 114.

an active role in fighting. Edward II was 17 when, 'newly bearing arms', he led a squadron of troops in his father's campaign against the castle of Caerlaverock in Scotland in 1300. Edward III commanded his first expedition against Scotland in 1327 at the age of 14, his brother John of Eltham fought at the battle of Halidon Hill in 1333 when he was 17, and Edward's son the Black Prince was only 16 when he 'won his spurs' at Crecy in 1346. Disputes in the court of chivalry at the end of the fourteenth century, over the right to bear particular coats of arms, supply rough indications of the ages at which other members of the aristocracy began to bear arms and fight. The witnesses – knights and esquires – who gave evidence for the rival contestants were asked how long they had borne arms, or when they had first done so. Of ninety-four witnesses on behalf of Sir Richard Scrope in the case of Scrope v. Grosvenor (1386),[43] the youngest claim, that of Sir John Bromwich, was that he had borne arms at the age of 11 in 1342.[44] Plenty of others said they had done so in their mid-teens, and the largest group believed they had begun to bear arms when they were 20, which was perhaps a mere guess at a round number. Yet others had not seen war until their twenties, and since active fighters were only a minority of the English aristocracy by the thirteenth century, there must have been many not represented among the witnesses who never saw war at all.

HUNTING AND HAWKING

While fighting was undoubtedly the most prestigious physical activity, hunting came close behind it in importance. It was equally, if not more widely practised by the male aristocracy, and extended to women which the use of arms did not. Hunting, moreover, has included the young since ancient times, and children have learnt from it horsemanship, the management of weapons, knowledge of terrain, woodcraft and strategy – techniques which are very close to those of war. On these grounds hunting can be categorized as an educational institution, and was indeed viewed in this way by writers from the fifteenth century onwards. Hawking was equally popular as an aristocratic pastime, and frequently occupies a place

[43] *The Scrope and Grosvenor Controversy*, ed. N.H. Nicolas, 2 vols, London, 1832, i, 50–243.
[44] ibid., p. 205.

alongside hunting as a desirable accomplishment of heroes and heroines in literature. It had its own techniques in the care and training of birds, but it was generally regarded as a more leisurely and less demanding skill than hunting, and never achieved the same educational status. As Sir Thomas Elyot observed in 1530, it was 'a right delectable solace', giving a man 'good appetite to his supper' and withdrawing him from sports of a dishonest kind, but 'thereof cometh not so much utility (concerning exercise) as there doth of hunting'.[45]

The involvement of boys in hunting goes back to at least the ninth century. Asser informs us that Alfred in his youth 'unceasingly laboured in every art of hunting and not in vain, for no one could compare with him in his skill and good fortune'.[46] The literary heroes of the twelfth century onwards, Tristan, Horn and Guy of Warwick, are often praised for their knowledge of dogs and birds or wood and river, which they evidently gained in youth since they had it as young men. From the thirteenth century onwards there is plenty of evidence for hunting in childhood by historical figures. John Hardyng named fourteen as the appropriate age for the sport in 1457,[47] but records show that royal children, at least, were introduced to it at much younger ages. Alexander III of Scotland, the husband of Henry III's eldest daughter Margaret, was only 10 in 1251 when he was granted permission to pass through Galtres Forest in Yorkshire to hunt, and take whatever he killed.[48] Three years later Henry allowed his 9-year-old son Edmund of Lancaster to hunt in a similar fashion in Windsor Forest whenever he pleased.[49] Henry VIII's son Henry Fitzroy was even younger in 1525, a mere 6- or 7-year-old, when his servants were accused of enticing him away from his lessons to go out after hares and deer.[50] Throughout the later Middle Ages hunting was a favourite sport of royal princes. Richard II paid £25 to a London goldsmith in 1386, when he was 19, for a knife to be used in the woods and a hunting horn of gold, embellished with green tassels of silk.[51] Henry V, as we

[45]   *The Governor*, book i, chapter 18.
[46]   Asser, *Life of King Alfred*, ed. Stevenson, pp. 20, 59.
[47]   Hardyng, *Chronicle*, ed. Ellis, pp. i–ii.
[48]   BL, Lansdowne MS 204, f. 12; Hardyng, *Chronicle*, ed. Ellis, pp. i–ii.
[49]   *Close Rolls, 1253–4*, p. 91.
[50]   *LPFD, Henry VIII*, iv part iii, pp. 2593–4 (no 5806).
[51]   Devon, *Issues of the Exchequer*, p. 231.

shall see, had a hunting treatise translated for him while he was prince of Wales, and Henry VI went hunting hares and foxes when he was 12 and staying at Bury St Edmunds in the winter of 1433–4.[52] Even Edward V, in his short life of twelve years, is said by Domenico Mancini to have been devoted to horses and dogs while he lived at Ludlow Castle, in the happy days before he came to the throne and into the clutches of Richard duke of Gloucester.[53]

Nor was the lust for hunting merely a royal one; it spread throughout the aristocracy, right down to the children of the gentry. John Hopton, son of a Suffolk esquire, spent two days hunting deer with the vicar of Covehithe in 1463–4 when he was still a schoolboy,[54] and Cranmer's biographer tells how the archbishop's father encouraged him to hunt in Nottinghamshire round about the year 1500.[55] Gregory Cromwell, while he was being brought up in Essex in the early 1520s, was several times invited by the rector of Yeldham to hunt the fox, and once by the earl of Oxford who 'sent for me and my cousins, and made us good cheer, and let us see such game and pleasure as I never saw in my life'.[56] An Oxford schoolbook of about 1500 could take it for granted that boys would be moved by stories of hunting. 'Methinks it is a world to hunt the hare with greyhounds', runs one of its exercises, 'while the snow covereth the ground, for now she cannot lightly scape the dog's mouth.' 'This day . . . mine host and his neighbours went to the wood to kill the wild boar that men say is there. . . . I pray God prosper that they go about.'[57] As usual, we know little about girls. But literary sources frequently mention adult women who hunt, like Hyppolita and Emelye in Chaucer's 'Knight's Tale' and, as will appear, the treatises on hunting also imply their presence.[58] Women were certainly stationed to watch and to shoot at game with bows, and they may well have followed the chase on horseback, though their participation was probably less strenuous and adventurous than that of men.

A medieval hunt was much more than a headlong rush in pursuit

[52] Dugdale, *Monasticon Anglicanum*, ed. Caley, iii, 113.
[53] Mancini, *Usurpation of Richard III*, ed. Armstrong, pp. 70–1.
[54] C. Richmond, *John Hopton: a Fifteenth Century Suffolk Gentleman*, Cambridge, 1981, p. 133.
[55] Above, p. 41.
[56] Ellis, *Original Letters*, 3rd series, i, 339.
[57] *A Fifteenth Century School Book*, ed. Nelson, pp. 23–5.
[58] Below, pp. 195, 196–8.

of the uneatable. There was a skill in locating the beasts by means of their droppings, tracks and observed habits. Customs had to be followed about the seasons for hunting them and the weapons and dogs to be used. A system of horn-calls developed by which the hunters kept in touch with each other, and when the quarry was killed there were exact procedures for butchering the carcass and distributing the pieces. These matters were originally learnt through personal experience and from the oral instruction of older huntsmen, but in due course a literature of hunting appeared in which they could be read. Imaginative fiction was the first repository of hunting information, as it was in the case of education. There are references to it in romances as early as the twelfth century, notably in the stories of Tristan who was particularly praised by writers for his skill in the craft. Beroul's *Tristan* tells how he lived in the forest and took the game, how he trained his dog to hunt in silence and invented a new kind of bow for shooting deer by automatic means.[59] Gottfried von Strassburg declares that 'none ever learnt to track or hunt as well as he',[60] and by the fifteenth century he was credited with having personally introduced the terminology and the procedures of hunting currently in use. In Malory's words,

> he began good measure of blowing [horns] of beasts of venery and beasts of chase and all manner of vermin, and all the terms we have yet of hunting and hawking. And therefore the book of venery, of hawking and hunting is called 'the book of Sir Tristram's'.[61]

Narrative writers continued to feature hunting throughout the Middle Ages, and two middle-English poems of the late fourteenth century, *The Parlement of the Thre Ages* and *Sir Gawain and the Green Knight*, contain particularly full descriptions of how animals are hunted and disembowelled, in the context of moral or romantic stories.[62]

The first specialized treatises to appear on field-sports were those on hawking.[63] Handbooks in Latin attributed to a certain 'King

---

[59] Beroul, *Tristan*, ed. Ewert, i, 38–9, 48–9, 53; trans. Fedrick, pp. 76, 83–4, 87.
[60] Gottfried, *Tristan*, trans. Hatto, p. 69.
[61] Malory, *Works*, ed. Vinaver, i, 375.
[62] *The Parlement of the Thre Ages*, ed. Offord, lines 21–96; *Sir Gawain and the Green Knight*, lines 1133–1923 *passim*.
[63] On the specialized literature of hunting and hawking, see Hands, *English Hawking and Hunting*, pp. xxxiii–liv.

Dancus' and to William the Falconer appeared in Europe in the twelfth century, and were subsequently translated into French and English.[64] The earliest treatise on hunting, as far as England is concerned, was the *Art de Venerie* by William Twiti, huntsman to Edward II in the early fourteenth century. This was a short prose tract in French, later translated into English, containing random pieces of advice on the hare, the deer and the boar, such as how to refer to them technically, how to blow horn-calls and how to address the hounds while out in the field.[65] It is not a complete guide to the sport, and was evidently meant to supplement practical teaching and experience. A longer and more complex treatise on hunting, *Le Livre de Chasse*, was written in France by Gaston count of Foix in 1389–91 and translated into English by Edward duke of York as *The Master of Game*, between 1406 and 1413. This covers a wider range than Twiti's modest work, and in greater detail: the different kinds of beasts and their habits, how to track them, horn-calls, disembowelling, the care of hounds and the management of kennels.[66] A third book, written in English verse, also seems to date from the late fourteenth century or the early fifteenth, and claims to expound the techniques of hunting according to the precepts of Tristram. It is narrated by a lady and therefore presumably written by one, an unusual indication that women might possess or be thought to possess a detailed knowledge of hunting techniques and be able to pass them on to others. The first printed edition of this work, *The Book of St Albans* (1486), attributes it to a certain Dame Julian Barnes – a person who has aroused much speculation without ever having been convincingly identified.[67] Like Twiti's work, this 'Tristram' treatise presupposes a good practical knowledge of hunting and is mainly concerned to explain the complicated terminology of the sport: names of beasts, collective terms for them, the parts of an animal, and the proper words to be used when flaying and stripping the carcass.

The educational nature of hunting in early times can only be inferred, and the great thirteenth-century friars do not mention it in an educational context. By the fifteenth century, however, hunting

[64] ibid., pp. xxx–xxxii.
[65] Twiti, *La Vénerie*, ed. Tilander; Twiti, *The Art of Hunting*, ed. Danielson; Hands, *English Hawking and Hunting*, pp. xxxvi–xxxviii.
[66] Gaston, *Master of Game*, ed. Baillie-Grohman.
[67] Hands, *English Hawking and Hunting*, pp. xiv–xv, lv–lx, which also provides a facsimile of the work with notes.

began to be recognized as educational for children and to be featured in writings for or about them. Edward duke of York's translation of *The Master of Game* foreshadows this process, being written for Henry V while he was prince of Wales and therefore aimed at a young man still in his early twenties. The 'Tristram' poem in English directs itself more clearly to the young, since its lady narrator addresses it to her 'child', 'children', 'son' and 'sons' at different parts of the work. The first writer to mention hunting in the context of children's education seems to have been John Hardyng, in his description of how noble children were brought up in 1457. When boys reach 14, he declares,

> they shalle to felde i-sure,
> At hunte the dere and catch an hardynesse,
> For dere to hunte and sla[y] and se thaym blede,
> Ane hardyment gyffith to his corage,
> And also in his wytte he takyth hede
> Ymagynynge to take theym at avauntage.[68]

Hardyng saw hunting as the prelude to military training, the next and final part of his scheme of education, which began at 16. What evidently impressed him about the sport was its capacity to develop the mental qualities required for war: courage through the experience of killing and blood, and agility of mind from the need to plan the strategy of defeating an enemy. This view continued to be held in the early sixteenth century. 'Hunting', wrote William Horman in a translation exercise for the boys of Eton or Winchester, 'is a plain recording of [i.e. training for] war',[69] and Sir Thomas Elyot agreed in *The Governor*. If properly conducted, it is

> the very imitation of battle, for not only doth it show the courage and strength as well of the horse as of him that rideth . . . but also it increaseth in them both agility and quickness, also sleight and policy to find such passages and straits where they may prevent or entrap their enemies.

'By continuance therein', he concludes, hunters 'shall easily sustain travail in wars: hunger and thirst, cold and heat'.[70]

---

[68] BL, Lansdowne MS 204, f. 12; Hardyng, *Chronicle*, ed. Ellis, pp. i–ii.
[69] Horman, *Vulgaria*, p. 277.
[70] *The Governor*, book i, chapter 18.

There were critics of hunting in the Middle Ages as there are today, though their objections were different ones. Some moralists considered the sport mere vanity. 'Where are they who lived before us', asks one poet of the thirteenth century, 'who led hounds and carried hawks, and had the fields and woods?' He answers that they took their pleasure on earth, not in heaven; they lost their souls, and now they lie in hell where 'the fire it burneth ever'.[71] In the early sixteenth century satirists more than once contrasted the gentlemen of the day as they allegedly were (illiterate boorish hunters) with what they should have been (good scholars of Latin).[72] Quite apart from the inadequacy of this portrayal of gentlemen's knowledge of letters, which we have plenty of reasons for thinking was better than this, it can be questioned whether hunting was such a brutalizing exercise as the satirists portray it. It certainly dealt in blood and slaughter, and what many people would regard today as cruelty. At the same time it partook, as other activities did, of the medieval emphasis on order and decorum: the correct blowing of horn-signals and the proper disjointing of carcasses brought to the out-of-doors the indoor arts of ceremonial music and carving at the table. Medieval authors who came to the defence of hunting tried hard to justify it in civilized terms. Langland in the 1360s claimed it as part of the duty of knights to defend poor labourers, in this case by relieving them of wild animals that broke their hedges and devoured their food.[73] Gaston de Foix, with the threats of eternal perdition evidently in his mind, argued that hunting kept men busy and away from the idleness which was the breeding-ground of sin. 'He that fleeth the seven deadly sins, as we believe, he shall be saved; therefore a god hunter shall be saved.'[74] Most memorably of all, the author of *Sir Gawain and the Green Knight*, while not overtly adopting an apologetic position, manages to convey bettter than any writer the economic and emotional rewards which hunting could bring. Deer hunting is a getting of food in winter when food is scarce. Boar hunting is a physical challenge, a paramilitary combat with a powerful enemy who can kill you if you are weak or unskilful. Fox hunting is a battle of wits, a tortuous chase hither and thither,

[71] C. Brown, *English Lyrics of the XIIIth Century*, Oxford, 1932, pp. 85–7.
[72] E.g. Richard Pace, *De Fructu*, Basel, 1517, p. 15, translated in *Early English Meals and Manners*, ed. Furnivall, pp. xii–xiv; John Skelton, *Poetical Works*, ed. A. Dyce, London, 1843, i, 334–5.
[73] *Piers Plowman*, A, vii, 32–5; B, vi, 30–33; C, ix, 29–31.
[74] Gaston, *Master of Game*, ed. Baillie-Grohman, pp. 4–5.

and a parody of serious hunting in which the pursuers scream and jeer in a cathartic release of tensions. In all hunting there is the visual beauty of the woods, and the delight to the ear of the cries of hounds and horns as they echo around the rocks.[75] The Gawain-poet admits the lust for slaughter, but he points to so much else that the historian will be unwise rashly to accept the low opinions of the critics of hunting. As an activity for children, it could be educative of the mind and the imagination, as well as of bone and muscle, toughness and aggression.

ARCHERY

Another popular exercise of the medieval aristocracy, archery, was associated with hunting and recreation rather than war. Vegetius had recommended that Roman soldiers, both footmen and horsemen, should learn to shoot,[76] and the bow was regularly used in war by the aristocracies of the Viking and the Saracen worlds. In medieval England customs differed. A nobleman or gentleman might use a bow to kill an antagonist during a crime or a civil disturbance. Beroul's Tristan shot his enemy Godoïne through the window of Queen Yseut's bedroom,[77] and Robin Hood in one of his early sixteenth-century ballads offered a bow to Sir Richard at-the-Lee while they were being attacked by the sheriff of Nottingham.[78] As far as formal warfare was concerned, however, the English assigned the bow to the ordinary man-at-arms, not to the mounted knight or gentleman. It was the common soldiers who loosed the famous volleys of arrows at Crecy and Agincourt, and the bow seems never to have been a normal weapon of the English aristocracy in battle. When Lord Berkeley's translator came to the chapter of Vegetius in which the bow is mentioned, he noted that Cato recommended shooting in a book on knighthood, but he significantly failed to employ the word 'knight' elsewhere when he talked of the use of the bow in warfare.[79]

The bow was in fact a popular instrument of English noblemen and even women, but it was used for hunting or simply for shooting

[75] *Sir Gawain and the Green Knight*, lines 1133–1923 *passim*.
[76] *Epitoma Rei Militaris*, book i, chapter 15.
[77] Beroul, *Tristan*, ed. Ewert, i, 133; trans. Fedrick, p. 147.
[78] R.B. Dobson and J. Taylor, *Rymes of Robyn Hood*, London, 1976, p. 104.
[79] Bodleian Library, MS Digby 233, f 187ᵛ.

at targets as a pure skill in itself. Bows were already familiar knightly weapons for sporting purposes when William Rufus was accidentally killed by one while hunting in the New Forest in 1100. Beroul's Tristan is a skilful archer with a bow of laburnam wood, despatching deer in the forest, and Mark too handles a bow of the same material.[80] There is consequently nothing at all inappropriate in Chaucer's comic hero, Sir Thopas, being 'a good archer'; the accomplishment was perfectly respectable.[81] In aristocratic hunting the bow was particularly used for shooting on foot at a station, while deer were driven past by beaters. The king himself might shoot in such a way, and *The Master of Game* lays down that when he wishes to do so,

> the master forester ought to show [the master of game] the king's standing if the king would stand with his bow, and where all the remnant of the bows would stand. And the yeoman for the king's bows ought to be there to keep and make the king's standing, and remain there without noise till the king comes.[82]

What happened next is described in *Sir Gawain and the Green Knight*:

> The hindes were halden in with 'hay!' and 'war!'
> The does dryven with gret dyn to the depe slades.
> Ther myght mon se, as thay slypte, slentyng of arwes . . .
> What wylde so atwaped wyyes that schotten,
> Was al toraced and rent at the resayt.[83]

When they were not out hunting, noblemen and gentlemen might also shoot competitively at targets. The Knight of the Tower recalls an episode of this kind which he witnessed at the siege of Aiguillon in 1346, when the duke of Normandy came out to watch some knights amusing themselves by shooting at a mark. The duke

> demanded of one of the knights a bow and an arrow for to shoot. And soon after he had drawn his arrow, there were there

---

[80] Beroul, *Tristan*, ed. Ewert, i, 38–9; trans. Fedrick, pp. 76–7.
[81] Chaucer, *Works*, ed. Robinson, p. 164 (B² 1929).
[82] Gaston, *Master of Game*, ed. Baillie-Grohman, p. 189.
[83] 'The hinds were held in with cries of "hey!" and "ware!"; the does driven with great din to the deep slades. There might you see slanting of arrows as they were loosed. Whatever wild beast escaped the men who shot, was pushed down and killed at stations further on' (*Sir Gawain and the Green Knight*, lines 1158–68).

by him two or three that said, 'Certainly, my lord shooteth well'. 'Holy Mary!' said another, 'how he draweth right of measure.' 'Ha!' said the other, 'I would not be armed and that he had hit me.' And thus they began to praise him, but for to say truth it was nothing else but flattery, for he shot the worst of all others.[84]

Englishmen of the fifteenth century also enjoyed shooting at marks for wagers, not always more successfully than the duke of Normandy. The account books of Sir John Howard, first duke of Norfolk, record payments of 20*d* in 1443–4 'lost at shooting' and 8*d* 'for my master's losses at the pricks'.[85] Henry VII lost 13*s* 4*d* to Sir Edward Borough in 1492 'at butts, with his crossbow'.[86] Shooting at marks could be done on foot or on horseback. In the early sixteenth-century ballad, *A Gest of Robin Hood*, the king and Robin ride through the countryside loosing their shafts at chance targets or 'rovers' as they were called.[87] The prowess of this fictional king was imitated in reality by Henry VIII, who loved archery as all athletic sports. As a 19-year-old in 1510 he is said to have 'shot as strong and as great a length as any of his guard', and even when he was 40 he was still described as being an excellent shot.[88]

Ladies too could shoot. Readers and writers of fiction were used to classical stories of the archer goddess and the Amazons. The thirteenth-century French prose *Lancelot* contains an episode, perhaps inspired by such stories, in which a knight pursuing an enemy passes two damsels bathing in a spring, one of whom takes a bow and arrow and shoots him in the thigh to prevent his pursuit.[89] The Amazons were said to be still in existence in Asia in the fourteenth century by the author of *Mandeville's Travels*, still cutting off their right breasts in the interests of their skill, 'for they shoot well with bows',[90] and Chaucer describes Diana in 'The Knight's Tale', 'with bowe in honde, right as an hunteresse'.[91]

[84] Landry, *The Book of the Knight of the Tower*, ed. Offord, p. 104.
[85] *Manners and Household Expenses of England*, p. 248.
[86] Bentley, *Excerpta Historica*, p. 90.
[87] Dobson and Taylor, *Rymes of Robyn Hood*, p. 110.
[88] Hall, *Chronicle*, p. 515; *Calendar of State Papers Venetian, 1527–33*, London, 1871, p. 293.
[89] *The Vulgate Version of the Arthurian Romances*, ed. Sommer, v, 224–5.
[90] *Mandeville's Travels*, ed. M.C. Seymour, Oxford, 1967, pp. 113–14.
[91] Chaucer, *Works*, ed. Robinson, p. 40 (A 2347).

Unlike some fantasies of fiction, this one had its real-life counterparts. Edward duke of York, in an addition of his own to *The Master of Game*, advised the making of 'four lodges of green boughs at the tryst [i.e. station], to keep the king and queen and ladies and gentlewomen and also the greyhounds from the sun and bad weather'. The expectation that the queen would shoot and kill at her tryst is proved by further arrangements for the disposal of 'what the king slayeth with his bow, or the queen or my lord the prince'.[92] The duke may well have had in mind the English queen of the time, Joan of Navarre, the second wife of Henry IV. Margaret, the elder daughter of Henry VII, could certainly shoot and learnt to do so as a girl; in 1503 at the age of 14, while she was travelling northwards to marry James IV of Scotland, she was entertained by the earl of Northumberland at Alnwick and killed a buck in the park there with her bow.[93] Malory, in his fifteenth-century version of the prose *Lancelot*, enlarged considerably on his French source, turning the damsels at the fountain into a lady who lived in Windsor Forest and hunted daily with a female retinue, 'and they were all shooters and could well kill a deer at the stalk and at the tryst'. Lancelot is sleeping by a well when the lady comes by and looses a shaft at a hind, but it misses and smites the premier British knight instead, in the buttocks.

> When Sir Lancelot felt him so hurt he whirled up woodly [i.e. madly], and saw the lady that had smitten him. And when he knew she was a woman, he said thus:
> 'Lady, or damsel, whatsoever ye be, in an evil time bore ye this bow. The devil made you a shooter!'

Not a polite remark for a knight to make! The lady points out, reasonably enough, that she was intent on her sport and did not see him; she thought she had shot well, but her hand swerved. When Lancelot begins to wail 'ye have mischieved me', she leaves him in dudgeon or embarrassment and Lancelot has to pull out the arrow himself and get his wound dressed by the usual obliging hermit who lives nearby.[94] It is tempting to see this, the funniest yet least publicized episode in Lancelot's career as Malory's revenge on the

[92] Gaston, *Master of Game*, ed. Baillie-Grohman, pp. 190, 194, 196.
[93] Leland, *Collectionea*, ed. Hearne, iv, 278.
[94] Malory, *Works*, ed. Vinaver, iii, 1104–5.

egregious gigolo who ruined Arthurian literature. It is more likely, unfortunately, to be a sexist story, and to reflect the prejudices of contemporary males that a woman, when she shot, could not shoot straight.

The cultivation of archery by adults makes it likely that boys and some girls learnt the use of the bow for hunting or recreation throughout the medieval period. A succession of statutes and royal proclamations enjoining the use of bows can be traced back to the thirteenth century, but like other medieval literature they fail at first to mention children as such and were primarily directed at the lower orders rather than the nobility and gentry. Thus the Statute of Winchester of 1285, in ordering every male of the population to possess arms and armour, reserves bows and arrows for the poor whose goods are worth less than £6 13s 4d.[95] A proclamation of Edward III in 1365, complaining that archery is falling out of use, mentions that the nobility practise it for sport but seems mainly concerned with ordering the common people to shoot regularly at holidays, instead of playing games.[96] The Statute of Cambridge of 1388, re-enacted in 1410, specifically addressed itself to the possession of bows by labourers and artisans, and the practice of shooting by them on Sundays and festivals.[97] In the second half of the fifteenth century, however, with the effective end of the Hundred Years War and the loss of the English possessions in France, nostalgia grew up for the great exploits of the English with the long-bow at Crecy and Agincourt, coupled with a fear that the national weapon was falling into disuse. The rising popularity of Robin Hood in the fifteenth century, and the increasing romanticism with which his shooting exploits are treated in the surviving ballads, are a sign of this change in consciousness. From 1472–5 a series of parliamentary statutes began to be passed on the subject of shooting, a new one every five or ten years, deliberately recalling the past achievements of the English with the bow and emphasizing the value of shooting for national defence.[98] Some of the statutes were aimed at ensuring a good supply of bows, reasonably priced, and

[95] *Statutes of the Realm*, i, 97–8.
[96] Rymer, *Foedera*, vi, 468; there is an idiosyncratic translation in *CCR 1364–8*, pp. 181–2.
[97] *Statutes of the Realm*, ii, 57, 163; *Rotuli Parliamentorum*, ed. Strachey, iii, 643.
[98] ibid., vi, 156, 188, 223; *Statutes of the Realm*, ii, 432, 462–3, 472–3, 494, 521, 649–50.

others set out to enforce the practice of archery by the whole male population including the aristocracy, instead of football, quoits or cards which lacked an equivalent value.

The most important of these statutes was the one passed in 1512, early in Henry VIII's reign. It is the most comprehensive, enforcing the possession of bows and arrows and regular practice at shooting on all males under the age of sixty, with the sole exception of the clergy and the king's justices. It is also the first such legislation to adopt an educational position, by enjoining the teaching of shooting to children as opposed simply to its practice by people.

> Every man having a man child or men children in his house shall provide, ordain and have in his house for every man child being of the age of seven years and above, till he shall come to the age of seventeen years, a bow and two shafts to induce and learn them and bring them up in shooting, and shall deliver all the same bow and arrows to the same young men to use and occupy.

Boys, when they came to the age of 17, were to buy or be given a bow and four arrows for themselves.[99] The legislation was not necessarily very effective; in 1530 Sir Thomas Elyot complained that it was broken and not enforced, and in 1542 the authorities themselves admitted that the law had become ignored and re-enacted it.[100] The statute is significant in the history of education, however, as an early instance of intervention by the Crown and parliament in the educational sphere. The first statute to deal with an educational matter on a national scale had been that of Cambridge in 1388, repeated in 1406, which sought to provide a supply of agricultural workers by preventing the children of such workers being apprenticed to crafts in the towns.[101] The archery statute of 1512 is another early example, since it has the positive aim of promoting the universal compulsory education of males in this one respect. It came twenty years before the Reformation caused the Crown to begin to legislate for schools and universities, commencing in 1534.

There is no doubt about the deliberate training of noble boys to shoot throughout this last self-conscious era of the long-bow. 'In this art', wrote Caxton in 1489, 'Englishmen are learned from their

[99] ibid., iii, 2.
[100] *The Governor*, book i, chapter 27; *Statutes of the Realm*, iii, 837–41.
[101] ibid., ii, 57, 157–8.

young age', and the Italian Francisci noted the same a decade later: 'they are enthusiastically trained in it from their earliest youth'.[102] Low-quality staves for making children's bows are mentioned being sold in the fifteenth century for 10s or 13s 4d per hundred; in 1542 they were ordered to be sold at various prices from 6d to 1s each.[103] Edward and Richard, 'the princes in the Tower', were last seen alive out of doors there in the summer of 1483 'shooting and playing in the garden' when they were 12 and 10 respectively,[104] and Prince Arthur had an expensive bow bought for him when he was five and a half in 1493.[105] Henry VIII's abilities with the weapon have already been noted, and Henry's son Henry Fitzroy was duly provided with a bow at the age of 6 in 1525.[106] The Tudor educationist Roger Ascham has left us an affectionate picture of his early patron Sir Humphrey Wingfield, putting the statute into effect among the children of his household in the late 1520s,

> amongst whom I myself was one, for whom at term times he would bring down from London both bow and shafts. And when they should play he would go with them himself into the field, and he that shot fairest should have the best bow and shafts, and he that shot ill-favouredly should be mocked of his fellows till he shot better

– an indication of the orthodoxy that good bow-shooting had become.[107] It was due to Ascham that archery acquired its own written treatise in 1545, *Toxophilus* or 'the school of shooting', dedicated to Henry VIII. The work is in two parts, the first being a history of shooting and a commendation of its benefits, while the second discusses the equipment and techniques: the best kind of bow, bow-strings, arrows, the shooter's posture, the rules for loosing the bow, and guidance on how to shoot accurately. *Toxophilus* seems to be based on traditional usages, and in the

---

102   Christine of Pisa, *Book of Fayttes of Armes*, ed. Byles, p. 34; C.V. Malfatti, *Two Italian Accounts of Tudor England*, Barcelona, 1953, p. 36.
103   *Statutes of the Realm*, ii, 432; iii, 837–41.
104   *The Great Chronicle of London*, ed. A.H. Thomas and I.D. Thornley, London, 1938, p. 234.
105   Bentley, *Excerpta Historica*, p. 88.
106   *LPFD, Henry VIII*, iv part iii, pp. 2593–4 (no 5806).
107   Ascham, *English Works*, ed. Wright, p. 97.

absence of earlier treatises comes closest to informing us how shooting was done in the later Middle Ages.[108]

ATHLETICS AND BALL GAMES

A number of other games and exercises were popular with English males in general during medieval times, and with at least some of the nobility and gentry. We hear little of them, however, in writings for the aristocracy compared with arms training, hunting or archery. Medieval educationists and legislators, by viewing physical activities from a military standpoint, valued athletic pursuits only in so far as they made the athlete into a better soldier. If they did not they were ignored, and if they seemed to threaten his military training by seducing him into mere recreation they were attacked and forbidden. Running and jumping were both recommended by Vegetius as necessary to a warrior,[109] and William Worcester in his *Book of Noblesse* (1451–75) urged that the sons of princes should practise skipping, leaping and running like other military exercises, 'to make them hardy, deliver and well breathed'.[110] Elyot too praised running as one of four pursuits which are 'a laudable solace' or recreation, but also lead to hardness, strength and agility in war.[111] Running appears to have been practised as a competitive sport among ordinary people. William FitzStephen describes the youths of London running and leaping in summer in the late twelfth century,[112] and the Oxford schoolbook of about 1500 mentions organized games (apparently held near Oxford) in which competitive running and shooting took place for prizes.[113] It is quite possible that noble boys raced each other and practised running for its own sake, but we do not hear of such things.

Wrestling and stone- or bar-casting were also well-loved sports among the population at large.

> Atte stone castinges my lemman I ches,
> And atte wrastlinges sone I hym les

[108] ibid., pp. vii–119.
[109] *Epitoma Rei Militaris*, book i, chapter 9.
[110] Worcester, *Boke of Noblesse*, ed. Nichols, pp. 76–7.
[111] *The Governor*, book i, chapter 17.
[112] *Materials for the History of Thomas Becket*, ed. Robertson, iii, 11.
[113] *A Fifteenth Century School Book*, ed. Nelson, p. 27.

– so runs a thirteenth-century lyric, the song of a girl who watches the youths at sport and chooses the strongest thrower as her sweetheart, only to change her mind when he is soon put down in the wrestling.[114] Legislators had little time for stone-casting, and in the fourteenth century it was twice officially forbidden as being a distraction from archery.[115] Educationists ignored it until Elyot, and he though he mentions does not recommend it.[116] Nevertheless, medieval fiction features two noble heroes, Havelok and Florent, who join in the skill at plebeian competitions,[117] and Henry VIII is mentioned in 1510 as exercising himself at 'casting of the bar'; if he did, so perhaps did others.[118] Wrestling, though also popular with the commonalty, had a somewhat better reputation among writers. As early as the twelfth century the poet Thomas describes it as one of the skills of Tristan and as being played by the guests at his wedding with Yseut of the White Hands.[119] William Worcester approved it as having a military application,[120] and Elyot recommended it for the same purpose, especially between youths.[121] Henry VIII enjoyed this sport as well.[122] Chaucer says of Sir Thopas that he had no peer at wrestling, 'ther any ram shal stonde', and this has been taken by commentators to mean that wrestling was not an aristocratic pursuit.[123] The other evidence makes this unlikely, and Chaucer apparently means to satirize Thopas for entering plebeian wrestling competitions in which a live ram was the usual prize. This, in contrast, *was* an unknightly crossing of social barriers. The hero of another medieval story, Gamelyn the youngest son of a knight, engages in a wrestling competition for a prize ram, but he does so by

[114] 'I chose my lover at the stone-casting, but I soon gave him up at the wrestling' (R.H. Robbins, *Secular Lyrics of the XIVth and XVth Centuries*, 2nd edn, Oxford, 1955, p. xxxix).

[115] Rymer, *Foedera*, vi, 468; *Statutes of the Realm*, ii, 57.

[116] *The Governor*, book i, chapter 16.

[117] *The Lay of Havelok the Dane*, ed. W.W. Skeat and K. Sisam, 2nd edn, Oxford, 1915, pp. 37–9; *Octovian Imperator*, ed. Frances McSparran, Heidelberg, 1979, p. 76.

[118] Hall, *Chronicle*, p. 515.

[119] Thomas, *Le Roman de Tristan*, ed. Bédier, i, 278, 375; Gottfried, *Tristan*, trans. Hatto, pp. 306, 337.

[120] Worcester, *Boke of Noblesse*, ed. Nichols, pp. 76–7.

[121] *The Governor*, book i, chapter 17.

[122] Hall, *Chronicle*, p. 515.

[123] Chaucer, *Works*, ed. Robinson, pp. 164 (B^2 1930–1), 738.

accident and with the knightly motive of righting a wrong and avenging two other competitors who have suffered unjustly. His story throws some light on how the sport was practised. The match was supervised by two wardens and, in order to play, Gamelyn removed his shirt, hose and shoes which shows that he wrestled naked or in drawers. The contestants stood upright together (Elyot recommended clasping one hand behind your opponent's neck and the other on his arm), and 'cast turns', trying to shift one another by heaves of the body until one was thrown down.[124]

Swimming was also approved by writers, again for military reasons.[125] The evidence of *Beowulf*, whose hero is portrayed appreciatively for his swimming prowess, suggests that the skill was well esteemed as an attribute of warriors in Anglo-Saxon England.[126] After the Conquest, Vegetius's adjuration that every soldier should learn to swim during the summer was reproduced by John of Salisbury, Giles of Rome and Christine of Pisa, and the two fifteenth-century English translators of the *Epitoma* both interpreted the activity as being correct for 'knights'. Peter Alfonsi, too, included swimming among the seven knightly skills. In fact, these references are misleading. They reflect the medieval respect for Vegetius and the Romans, not what contemporaries were actually doing. The truth is that swimming fell out of fashion among the aristocracy after the Norman Conquest. It was not apparently felt to be compatible with medieval knightly techniques, and hardly ever appears in post-Conquest fiction as something that heroes do. On the contrary, Chrétien de Troyes in his *Lancelot*, the French prose *Tristan* and Malory's fifteenth-century translation of it all feature episodes in which knights who attempt to take to the water get into difficulties and are held up to ridicule. It was not therefore a military art in practice, but one or two of the medieval aristocracy are known to have swum in need or for pleasure, and it is possible that some boys mastered it, though never girls. A squire sent by Edward I to attend his sister Margaret queen of Scotland was drowned while swimming in the River Tay in 1273, and Edward II enjoyed frolics in the water and may have been able to swim. In 1315–16 he took a

---

[124] *The Complete Works of Geoffrey Chaucer*, ed. W.W. Skeat, vol iv, 2nd edn, Oxford, 1900, pp. 650–2.

[125] On what follows, see Orme, *Early British Swimming*, pp. 22–45.

[126] ibid., pp. 9–13.

holiday in the Fens and had a narrow escape from drowning 'while rowing about on various lakes' with men whom a contemporary chronicler called disapprovingly 'his silly company of swimmers'. Malory too was able to swim sufficiently to escape from Coleshill Castle in Warwickshire in 1451 by crossing the moat at night. The techniques of medieval swimming are probably enshrined with little change in the first English treatise on the subject, written by Everard Digby in 1587.[127] The extent to which it was practised, however, is doubtless summarized accurately by Elyot in 1530. It was, he tells us, little esteemed by that time, 'because there seemeth to be some peril in the learning thereof, and also it hath not been of long time much used, specially among noblemen'.[128]

Various kinds of ball- and other missile-games were popular in medieval society as a whole. William FitzStephen mentions communal games of football in London as early as the late twelfth century,[129] and the royal proclamation of 1365 categorized ball-games into those played with the foot, with the hand, and with sticks.[130] Quoits and 'kayles' (a form of skittles or ninepins) are both mentioned in 1388, and bowls and 'closh' (a game like croquet) by the middle of the fifteenth century.[131] The game of palm, in which the ball was hit with the hand as in fives, is referred to in France in 1404–7 and was known in England by 1440.[132] Closely allied to palm was tennis, which was also played at first with the hand, and occurs in a poem by Gower of about 1400.[133] The famous story of the French Dauphin sending tennis balls to Henry V in 1414, apparently in allusion to his youthful playfulness, is not known to have happened, but it was widely believed to be true in England within a year or two, and was frequently retold in writings.[134] In the sixteenth century tennis became a racquet game played in a special court, but during the Middle Ages it went on, as other ball-games usually did, in any suitable open space or by any available walls.

[127] ibid., pp. 86–8, 111–207.
[128] *The Governor*, book i, chapter 17.
[129] *Materials for the History of Thomas Becket*, ed. Robertson, iii, 9.
[130] Rymer, *Foedera*, vi, 468.
[131] *Statutes of the Realm*, ii, 57, 462–3, 569; *Middle English Dictionary*, ed. Kurath and Kuhn, sub 'boule', 'closh'.
[132] Christine of Pisa, *Livre du Corps de Policie*, ed. Bornstein, pp. 48–9; *OED* sub 'palm', II.6'.
[133] ibid., sub 'tennis'.
[134] Kingsford, *Henry V*, pp. x–xi, 113.

Educationists thought little of these games and rarely mentioned them. Giles of Rome merely suggested that boys might play at ball between 7 and 14, and Christine of Pisa likewise permitted them palm.[135] Legislators thought even less, and saw ball-games as foolish useless pursuits which tempted the populace from archery. The series of statutes and proclamations in favour of shooting from 1365 onwards prohibited the games, often by name, and by the early sixteenth century, bowls, closh, football, kayles, quoits and tennis had all been forbidden at one time or another. Not only were these orders probably ineffective among the people at large, they were not even observed by the aristocracy. If the Dauphin story is true, Henry V had a reputation as a tennis-player, and Sir John Howard appears to have been one in 1463.[136] Henry VII certainly played the game, and did so for money. In 1494 his expenses included £1 7s 8d for the cost of balls and loss of wagers; in 1499 he lost 8s, and in 1504 £2 was paid for him to play at 'cleke' at Burton-on-Trent – perhaps a kind of golf.[137] Henry VIII was also said to be 'a fine tennis player'.[138] There is consequently every reason to think that aristocratic boys, and indeed girls, played ball-games for pleasure, despite the strong encouragement to restrict themselves to those pursuits which would make a man a good fighter.

It will now be clear that the educational writers of the Middle Ages, with their concentration on men and on military training, fail to do justice to the range of physical exercises which were actually going on. In practice, the preoccupation with war by no means triumphed over the wish for recreation, and the pursuit of exercise was not confined to boys and men. Males did indeed monopolize the harder physical feats – arms, swimming, wrestling and stone-casting, but girls and women took part in riding, hunting, shooting and probably the less strenuous ball-games. The educationists and legislators, however, correctly remind us of the great influence of war on medieval sport. The three best-developed exercises of the Middle Ages were arms training, hunting and archery – all military or paramilitary activities. This was because the warlike ethic of the

---

[135] *De Regimine Principum*, book ii, part ii, chapter 15 (ed. Molenaer, pp. 218–20); Christine of Pisa, *Livre du Corps de Policie*, ed. Bornstein, pp. 48–9.
[136] *Manners and Household Expenses of England*, p. 221.
[137] Bentley, *Excerpta Historica*, pp. 98, 122, 131.
[138] *Calendar of State Papers Venetian, 1527–33*, p. 293.

aristocracy and the encouragement of the writers channelled aristocratic money (the main source of patronage for medieval sport) to these three pursuits. As a result the three attained high levels of development, which have hardly been improved on since. They acquired specialized equipment, widely accepted rules and terminologies, and in due course written treatises. The great athletic sports of today were correspondingly under-developed. They lacked equipment and treatises, had only local rules and terminologies, and fell well below modern standards in their techniques and achievements. It remains to point out that the physical exercises had other effects than physical ones. Those who pursued them improved their physiques, but they also had the opportunity to make mental and social gains. Arms training and hunting were capable of instilling courage and the sense of strategy, ceremoniousness and respect for rules. The treatises about them may even have tempted their devotees to read. The out-of-doors and the indoors are never mutually exclusive separate worlds, and both join hands in the indivisible unity of life and education.

Seven From 'Medieval' to 'Renaissance'

THE MIDDLE AGES: A RETROSPECT

The literary descriptions of medieval heroes, with their attributions of knowledge and accomplishments, were more than romantic ideals; they mirrored reality too. At best, a young nobleman or gentleman was well endowed by his education. A sociable upbringing with adults, boy companions and servants, often away from home, had taught him the behaviour appropriate to a wide range of people and circumstances. As occasion demanded he could be deferential, friendly, ceremonious and commanding. He spoke one language for preference out of French and English, but he knew something of the other and could use it at least a little when required. In an age which placed an emphasis on good public speaking, he was conscious of the need to speak clearly and effectively. He paid attention to his personal health and hygiene, and was careful of his table-manners. He was conventionally devout, going regularly to religious services, visiting shrines and giving charity to the poor. Religion provided him with a code of ethics as well, but this did not always prevail, for he had also been moulded by secular values from his earliest years, and religious teaching had to compete for his allegiance with the dictates of rank, privilege, wealth and power.

He was skilful in several techniques. He could read and

understand Latin, provided it was not very difficult, but he preferred to read French or (later on) English. He could write in one of the two latter languages, and oversee the letters and accounts of his servants. Indoors he was sociable with other men and women, and could dance, sing and sometimes play an instrument. He liked beautiful artefacts, though he had no skill in making them himself. Out of doors he rode well and knew how to hunt; he could shoot a little with a bow and had some expertise in wearing armour and using arms. His education pointed him in more than one direction. On the one hand it prepared him for the quiet domestic side of life: reading and writing, the administration of his private affairs, religious devotions and pious benefactions, the enjoyment of treasures of art. On the other, it trained him for more active and public roles: hard exercise in the hunting field, fighting and bloodshed in war, and the role of a civil governor in national or local affairs. It tried to instil in him self-discipline and respect for law, but it did not always succeed. The consciousness of his high birth and resources of men and money could make him jealous of his status and arrogant to others. The reading of princely mirrors might lead him to feel that little separated him from his sovereign in knowledge and achievements, and the chansons de geste which he read for amusement with their stories of blood-feuds between noble houses and rebellions of heroes against kings might stimulate him into similar exploits of his own.

The education of noble ladies emerges less clearly, for we see it too often through the eyes of men. Men concentrated on the aspects of ladies' education which they themselves preferred, and ignored the others. In the view of males, virtue meant more in a woman than accomplishments, and men wished for wives and daughters who were chaste in their morals, modest in their behaviour and reserved in their speech. In fact, a noble lady whether a married woman or a nun shared much of the knowledge and many of the accomplishments of her husband or brothers. She too had been brought up sociably and had learnt to behave deferentially to her betters and effectively to her servants. She probably spoke the same languages as her menfolk, and observed as they did personal hygiene, table manners and religious devotions. She too could sing, play on an instrument and dance. She could also take physical exercise, for she could ride, go hunting and shoot with a bow. She could assist in managing her household and the wider interests of her family. In one respect she was superior to a man, for her textile skills made her an applied artist which he was not. In others she was less fortunate, since her education was less formal than a man's and was acquired as part of life rather than separately from it. As far as religion, manners, music and dancing were concerned this made little difference, but in the sphere of literary capabilities it left her undeveloped. After the twelfth century she knew little Latin and was certainly less proficient in understanding it than the average nobleman. She could easily read French or English for her pleasure or edification, but she could only write these languages with difficulty. Her imagination in composing letters might be as good as a man's and her command of language as fluent, but she had to have recourse to a male scribe to put down her thoughts upon paper. In the physical sphere as well, social convention dictated that the exercise she took was light and limited compared with that of men.

It is possible to summarize the education of the medieval aristocracy to this extent because so many of its elements remained constant over long periods. The accomplishments of heroes like Horn and Tristan in twelfth-century literature reappear with little change in Chaucer's description of the Squire, and even in Edward Hall's account of the prowess of Henry VIII in 1510.[1] This does not mean, however, that there was a uniform and static 'medieval education' which did not change until it was abruptly transformed at the Renaissance. Many of the constant elements of education in the Middle Ages were those which are constant in all education, and have existed long before and since. Such elements, moreover, undergo variations of emphasis and application in every period, and this was also true in the Middle Ages. There were important changes during medieval times to the subjects of the curriculum, the ways in which subjects were taught and the attitudes of people towards them. Education in 1150 was by no means the same as it was in 1450. In the sphere of the curriculum there were obvious developments in the cultivation of language and literature. The study of Latin by the aristocracy in the early twelfth century changed by the thirteenth to a preference for reading French. In the fourteenth they abandoned French for English as their preferred language of speech, and by the fifteenth they were reading widely in English. After the 1490s they returned to the study of Latin at a high

---

[1] Above, pp. 83, 85; Hall, *Chronicle*, p. 515.

level. In the sphere of religion, though worship as such remained constant, the forms in which it was practised evolved throughout the Middle Ages, and education must have mirrored this. Children doubtless shared in the growing popularity of the mass, of the office of Our Lady, and of the recourse to friars for sermons and confessions. There were changes too in the cultivation of music and dancing. In music children had to keep pace with the development of polyphonic song, and in the fifteenth century adult noblemen (and hence perhaps some boys) began to be skilled in musical notation. Dancing probably underwent changes of fashion, and the seriousness with which it was regarded appears to have grown as time went on. In the sphere of physical education, though war-training was a constant element and Vegetius an enduring hand-book, the training of boys must have evolved along with changes in armour, arms and military organization. Even in hunting, the development of sophisticated techniques and the gradual disappearance of forests and the larger beasts of the chase made the sport somewhat different by the end of our period from what it had been at the outset.

There may have been fluctuations too in the comparative popularity of different parts of the curriculum. These are now hard to identify, because so few contemporary witnesses have left us an idea of their priorities and preferences. In the fifteenth century, however, when consciousness of education was better developed, something of the ebb and flow of educational policy becomes, perhaps, dimly visible. In the 1430s and 1440s there seems to have been a marked interest in grammatical learning among at least some of the court aristocracy. This appears in the sending of the three eldest sons to university – Holland, Hungerford and Tiptoft – and in the foundation of endowed grammar schools by Hungerford, Cromwell and Suffolk as well as by Henry VI himself.[2] It accords with a similar preoccupation within the Church, notably expressed in the view of William Bingham and his circle that the study of grammar in England was badly in decline, and in the promotion of grammar schools by them and by other clergy during the same period.[3] In the second half of the century, by contrast, there seems to have been a shift of emphasis in favour of military education

[2] Above, p. 71; Orme, *English Schools*, pp. 198, 202; Orme, *Education in the West of England*, pp. 142–3.
[3] Orme, *English Schools*, pp. 200, 212–13, 221–2.

among some writers who wrote for the aristocracy. No doubt the collapse of the English cause in France was a powerful influence in this respect. So we find Fortescue justifying wardship and household education because they taught skill at arms, not because they inculcated fluency in grammar.[4] His contemporary Worcester in the *Book of Noblesse* roundly attacked the preference of knights' and gentlemen's sons for the study of the common law, and urged them rather to be good men of arms in the tradition of Henry of Lancaster and the Black Prince.[5] Caxton too in his edition of Lull's *Order of Chivalry* (1484) bemoaned the lack of knightly practice in military techniques, and called on the king to have the book 'read unto other young lords, knights and gentlemen within this realm that the noble order of chivalry be hereafter better used and honoured than it hath been in late days'.[6] This view in turn gave way in the early sixteenth century to that of writers like Richard Pace and John Skelton that the aristocracy were too fond of physical pursuits and needed to be called back again to the study of grammar and good literature.[7]

Changes can also be seen in the institutions by which education was given. The aristocracy of the early twelfth century could only have recourse for training to households or religious houses, in other words to places concerned with other matters besides teaching. With the rise of schools in the twelfth century followed by the organization of universities in the thirteenth, new specialized openings appeared for those sons of the aristocracy who were going to be trained for clerical careers. A stream of noble youths set off for university to this end during the later Middle Ages, and here too there were changes, especially with regard to residence and discipline. The original habit of dwelling in private houses and chambers gradually turned into residence in colleges under creancers, and in the sphere of the schools the foundation of Winchester and Eton introduced collegiate facilities which aristocratic boys could use. The fifteenth century saw a similar widening of opportunities for noble boys destined for lay careers, with the organization of henchmen in some of the greatest households, the

---

[4] Fortescue, *De Laudibus Legum Anglie*, ed. Chrimes, pp. 108–11.
[5] Worcester, *Boke of Noblesse*, ed. Nichols, pp. 76–8.
[6] Lull, *Book of the Ordre of Chyvalry*, ed. Byles, pp. 121–5.
[7] *Early English Meals and Manners*, ed. Furnivall, pp. xii–xiv; John Skelton, *Poetical Works*, ed. A. Dyce, 2 vols, London, 1843, i, 334–5.

goings of some youths to the university towns to study for a year or two, and most notably the development of the inns of court. Even household education, by the end of the Middle Ages, was no longer what it had been in the twelfth century. Professional schoolmasters had begun to be hired to do the teaching, and the idea of a planned day of work, timed by the clock, was bringing greater organization to the lives of the boys they taught.

Thirdly, there was a change of consciousness, in that more and more activities of childhood came to be regarded as educational. One technique after another was made the subject of a textbook, and the earliest books which usually had no specific concern with children were often followed by others that did. In the early twelfth century reading, song and grammar were the only pursuits of childhood to be fully recognized as educational and to possess their own manuals aimed at children: the ABC and the various Latin grammars. During the twelfth century one or two princely mirrors and courtesy books began to concern themselves with young adults, notably those by Hugh of St Victor and Gerald of Wales, and during the thirteenth this concern reached downwards to children below the age of adolescence and even to infants. The great friar-educationists produced their detailed accounts of how young children should be reared and older boys brought up, establishing a literature of child-care and describing the whole field of boys' education for the very first time. Some treatises on individual topics were produced for children, too. Robert Grosseteste's *Stans Puer ad Mensam* directed the literature of etiquette at boys in particular, while Walter of Bibbesworth's treatise on French was written for an aristocratic lady to teach her children and included observations upon how they should be reared. In 1391 Chaucer extended the concept of educating children to the field of astronomical calculation, with his *Treatise on the Astrolabe*, and not long afterwards the writing of hunting treatises began to be directed at the young as well. The duke of York made *The Master of Game* for the young adult Henry V, and the 'Tristram' poem adopted the form of a lady instructing her son. By 1457 Hardyng was fully aware of the role of hunting in the education of boys, and he and one or two others were beginning at least to take notice of children's involvement in dancing. Fortescue in the 1460s gave the first account of the education of young men in the law, and in 1484 Caxton's publication of *The Book of the Knight of the Tower* made a work on the education of young noblewomen available in England for the first time.

This widening of what was considered to be educational can be seen in other areas of fifteenth-century life. We have already noticed the perception of the author of the 'Black Book of the Royal Household' that household training could be educational, not only for noble boys with masters but for boys engaged in menial tasks as well.[8] In the sphere of trade and craft, the word 'apprentice' with its implication of 'learning' had been current in English since at least 1300, and in French even earlier, but the fifteenth century appears to see an enlargement of the notion. Certainly, apprenticeship increasingly involved the learning of reading and writing as well as the craft itself.[9] The same can be seen in the case of wardship. Traditionally, this institution (as its name suggests) had been conceived as providing guardianship rather than education. Interest had centred on the administration of the ward's property, and though wards were also educated, the fact seems to have been very much taken for granted. The late fourteenth- or early fifteenth-century *Tale of Gamelyn*, once ascribed to Chaucer, is the classic story of the cheating of the younger brother by the elder brother in whose care he lies. The younger boy's complaints, however, are entirely economic and social in nature: his lands are being badly administered, and he himself is reduced to the status of a servant in his brother's household.[10] The first writer to regard wardship as an institution for teaching seems to be Fortescue in the 1460s, with his justification of it on the educational ground that the lord will 'instruct' and 'train' his ward well in good manners and military skills.[11] Later, this view came to prevail widely, and in the Elizabethan reworkings of the story of Gamelyn by Lodge and Shakespeare, the question of the young man's education becomes a topic of interest. Orlando's grievance in *As You Like It* is that his brother has 'trained me like a peasant' and undermined 'my gentility with my education'.[12]

Interest in people's past educations as well as their current ones also increased in the fifteenth century, after a long interval. Such an interest had first developed in the twelfth and the early thirteenth.

[8] Above, pp. 49–50.
[9] Orme, *English Schools*, p. 48.
[10] *The Complete Works of Geoffrey Chaucer*, ed. W.W. Skeat, 7 vols, Oxford, 1894–7, iv, 647.
[11] Fortescue, *De Laudibus Legum Anglie*, ed. Chrimes, pp. 108–11.
[12] *The Complete Works of Thomas Lodge*, 4 vols, Glasgow, Hunterian Club, 1883, i, 5; Shakespeare, *As You Like It*, I.i. *passim*.

We have noticed the mentions of childhood in the autobiography of Gerald of Wales, the *Life of William Marshal*,[13] and their fictional counterparts: the stories of heroes and heroines in romantic literature. In the thirteenth century, however, this interest declined. It remained as a motif in the romances, and the chronicler Matthew Paris has something to tell us about, for example, the growing up of Edward I, but references to one's own or other people's childhood and education become infrequent and are virtually absent for most of the fourteenth century. The *Life of the Black Prince* by the Chandos herald, for instance, reduces the account of the prince's bringing up to a mere list of virtues that he acquired, without any historical framework whatsoever.[14] In turn, with the growth of English literature in the second half of the century, a slow revival of interest in the childhoods of real people begins to take place. Langland, in the last version of *Piers Plowman* in the 1380s or 1390s, briefly mentions how his father and his friends sent him to school, and how he learnt there the meaning of holy scripture.[15] Lydgate enlarges on this in the early fifteenth century with a lengthy confession of his sins as a child: how he robbed orchards, came late to school and played with cherry-stones when he should have been in church, and gradually such reminiscences become more frequent.[16] Archbishop Rotherham in the statutes which he drew up for his college and school at Rotherham in 1483 made a point of recalling how he was born, brought up and schooled there,[17] and William Caxton two years later was moved to insert a prayer ino his history of *Charles the Great* for the souls of his parents, 'that in my youth set me to school'.[18] The growth of a similar consciousness among the nobility can be seen in the beginning of references to

13   Gerald of Wales, *Autobiography*, ed. Butler, pp. 35–8; *L'Histoire de Guillaume le Maréchal*, ed. Meyer, vol i.
14   *La Vie du Prince Noir by Chandos Herald*, ed. Diana B. Tyson, Tübingen, Beihefte zur Zeitschrift für Romanische Philologie, cxlvii (1975), pp. 50–1. Compare the autobiographical poem, 'Croys was maad al of need' of *c*.1400–30, prefixed to one MS of Bartholomew *On the Properties of Things*, ed. Seymour, i, 40.
15   Langland, *Piers Plowman*, C, vi, 35–7.
16   *The Minor Poems of John Lydgate*, ed. H.N. MacCracken, part i, EETS, es, cvii (1911), pp. 352–4.
17   A.F. Leach, *Early Yorkshire Schools*, Yorkshire Archaeological Soc., vol xxxii (1903), ii, 109–10, 150.
18   Caxton, *Prologues and Epilogues*, ed. Crotch, p. 96.

childhood on their tomb epitaphs. One of the earliest such examples, that of Edward Audley (d. about 1478), formerly at Eton College, mentions not only his father but his godfather, his learning grammar at Eton and his offices as one of the young companions of Edward V.[19] The epitaph of Thomas Howard, duke of Norfolk (d. 1524) had similar references to his education at grammar school and his household service as a young man to Edward IV.[20] These kinds of recall of childhood became very common in the sixteenth century, but they antedate the Renaissance and originate in the Middle Ages.

Education in medieval England, then, was by no means static, either in the case of the aristocracy or in general. Its best-known phase of development is that of the twelfth and thirteenth centuries with the growth of the secular schools and universities, the coming of the friars and the writings of the great mendicant scholars. The period between about 1350 and 1500, by comparison, is less remembered for its educational achievements. Yet in truth it possesses much significance in this respect, considering the variety of developments that were going on. Even those we have mentioned are by no means the whole of the story. In the schools new texts in English were being written, employing new methods of analysing and presenting Latin grammar, and the first Latin-and-English dictionaries were being produced.[21] Masters were writing new exercises *latinitates* and *vulgaria*, with an appeal to children and a portrayal of childhood scenes that make them into one of the earliest genres of English children's literature.[22] Endowed grammar schools began to be founded, with salaried masters and free schooling, making it easier for children to be taught and helping to raise the status and self-consciousness of schoolmasters.[23] In the universities, the number of endowed collegiate foundations also grew consider-

---

[19] Bodleian Library, MS Ashmole 1137 f 152ᵛ.
[20] J. Weever, *Ancient Funeral Monuments*, London, 1631, p. 834; London, 1767, p. 554.
[21] Thomson, *Middle English Grammatical Texts*, pp. 4–30; Orme, *English Schools*, pp. 95–8.
[22] ibid., pp. 98–100; Orme in *Profession, Vocation and Culture*, ed. Clough, pp. 236–7.
[23] Orme, *English Schools*, pp. 184–90, 194–207. On the improving economic status of schoolmasters, see Orme in *Profession, Vocation and Culture*, ed. Clough, pp. 222–3.

ably, providing more free places for scholars, more paid lecture-
ships, and eventually bringing fee-paying undergraduates into
collegiate life. The inns of court, as we have seen, added another
important educational facility to those of the schools and
universities.

Some historians of the fifteenth century have sought to trace
cultural changes to influences from outside England, notably Italian
humanism. Certainly, aristocratic and school education in England
owed a great deal to continental Europe, though the primary
influence was still that of the thirteenth-century French grammarians, encyclopaedists and mirror writers; the new ideas from
Italy did not begin to penetrate the schools until the 1480s. At the
same time, the English themselves deserve some credit for their
educational achievements. Lords of households, founders of schools
and colleges, lawyers at the inns and practising schoolmasters were
probably not in general responding consciously to ideas from abroad
in their educational work. More likely, they were stimulated chiefly
by one another and by local conditions, and they were certainly
inspired by English traditions as well as by foreign ideas. To the
friars of Clare in the fifteenth century, Giles of Rome had written his
great treatise for an Englishman.[24] To many English schoolmasters
John Leland of Oxford was 'the flower of grammarians' and the
model upon whose work they based their own.[25] To Worcester and
Caxton it was the knights of Edward III who provided the standard
at which young men should aim, and to Fortescue it was the law and
government of England in which he wanted the young Prince
Edward to be trained. Cultural and educational changes did not
have to come to England from outside, for fifteenth-century
Englishmen were capable of developing their own ideas and
enterprises, no less than we ourselves.

'MEDIEVAL' AND 'RENAISSANCE'

One major question remains which is worth consideration, and this
is the relationship of education in the Middle Ages to the education
of the next era: the Tudor period or the 'English Renaissance'. How
does education compare in its nature and quality between the two

[24] Above, p. 97.
[25] Thomson, *Middle English Grammatical Texts*, p. 8.

eras, and was there a transmission of medieval ideas and institutions into the sixteenth century? No serious writer today will be likely to say as Dr Johnson could do in 1747, that the sixteenth century saw the triumph of Learning 'o'er her barbarous foes': in other words, over a previous era of absolute cultural darkness.[26] The researches of the last two hundred years into medieval history have established beyond doubt that the Middle Ages possessed civilized ideas and institutions, including the practice of education. The study of university history and the discovery, by Leach and others, of schools with modern features as early as the twelfth century, have brought to notice two major institutions which originated in the Middle Ages and continued throughout the sixteenth century, thereby establishing links between the two eras. A present-day student of Tudor education will therefore be aware that the subject possesses a previous history, and that he must not be surprised to find the origins of Tudor institutions in earlier centuries. At the same time, he will still be likely to feel that sixteenth-century education possesses, to a significant extent, characteristics that are new, and that the century is a new era rather than a mere continuation of the past, or a continuation with only modest changes.

The current view of the relationship between medieval and Tudor or Renaissance education has been established by two classic studies of educational history: Professor Kenneth Charlton's *Education in Renaissance England*, published in 1965, and Mrs Joan Simon's *Education and Society in Tudor England*, which came out in the following year. Although each wrote independently of the other and had somewhat different horizons, both authors came to largely similar conclusions about the question. Both embark on a discussion of the Middle Ages as an essential preliminary to the sixteenth century, not simply to point a contrast but to discover origins, and both devote their opening chapters to this task. Both pay tribute to the educational institutions of the Middle Ages: knightly education, apprenticeship, schools, universities and the inns, and both identify the fifteenth century in particular as a time of educational activity. Both recognize the survival of medieval forms of education into the sixteenth century. They note that institutions such as the endowed schools and university colleges go on being founded in a clear line of development from the later Middle Ages. They find some

[26] Samuel Johnson, 'Prologue at the Opening of the Theatre in Drury Lane', 1747.

continuity in the sphere of educational literature. Mrs Simon points out that Lily's *Carmen de Moribus* (*c.*1520), for example, on the rules of conduct for schoolboys, belongs to a genre of courtesy poems which went back several centuries,[27] while Tudor works on the education of princes and gentlemen, as Charlton observes, derived at least in part from the medieval genre of the mirrors of princes.[28] Mrs Simon traces the views of Richard Pace in 1517: that the sons of the rich would not learn and were overtaken by the sons of the poor who did, to the writings of Robert Holcote in the early fourteenth century,[29] and Charlton likewise finds Chaucer anticipating the humanist view that nobility arises from personal virtue rather than ancestry and riches.[30] Tradition as well as change, concludes Charlton, formed the fabric of sixteenth-century education, and Mrs Simon perceives 'the survival of medieval institutions, no less than methods of teaching' as stretching ahead even further and on to our very own times.[31]

Both writers, however, come down decisively in favour of the sixteenth century as a new era of education. Its innovations were greater and more significant than what it inherited, and differed in quality from what had gone before. 'Educational developments in the sixteenth century', says Mrs Simon, 'broke away from the pattern prevailing in earlier years. . .; there began to emerge a system of education in the modern sense.'[32] Professor Charlton agrees: 'Renaissance views about the nature of man and of the child and therefore about their education differed radically from those of their medieval ancestors.'[33] The two authors see new developments in most aspects of education. Among sixteenth-century writers in general, there was a greater awareness of the subject and a greater emphasis upon its importance. Among educationists in particular, there was a new interest in the individual human being, alike in his psychology, intelligence, physique and recreation. More concern was felt to harness education to the needs of the individual's adult life and those of the society in which he would live. In the

[27] Simon, *Education and Society*, p. 79.
[28] Charlton, *Education in Renaissance England*, p. 81.
[29] Simon, *Education and Society*, p. 100 and n.
[30] Charlton, *Education in Renaissance England*, p. 77.
[31] ibid., p. x; Simon, *Education and Society*, p. 4.
[32] ibid.
[33] Charlton, *Education in Renaissance England*, p. x.

institutional field there was, despite the disturbances of the Reformation, a large increase in the number of recorded schools of all kinds and endowed grammar schools especially. There was a new involvement of the Crown in endowing schools and controlling what they taught. In the school curriculum, medieval texts were replaced by the classical authors of Greece and Rome, and Catholic religious teaching by that of Protestantism. Outside the schools, there was an increasing sophistication of what Professor Charlton terms 'informal education': the learning of a trade, commercial subjects such as mathematics, modern languages and the sending of young noblemen on educational tours overseas.

The researches of the last twenty years have amply justified this view of the relevance of medieval education to the Tudor period. The present volume, it is hoped, will have made clearer the creation of a genre of educational literature in the twelfth and thirteenth centuries which was ancestral to that of the Renaissance. In the history of school endowments, the period between 1264 and 1450 has been confirmed as the formative age of the typical free grammar school, which went on being founded throughout the sixteenth and seventeenth centuries.[34] In the sphere of the teaching of grammar, many of the methods which used to be credited as innovations to Stanbridge and Whittinton in early-Tudor times can now be traced back to at least John Leland in 1400, and perhaps even earlier.[35] The more that we learn about medieval education, however, the less the extent to which Renaissance ideas and practices can be called new. This is true of the three areas that have just been mentioned, and of others. Thus the Tudor recognition of childhood as a special phase of life with its own psychology, behaviour and literature had long been anticipated by the thirteenth-century descriptions of childhood by Bartholomew Glanville and Walter of Bibbesworth, and by the growth of a literature for children in the schoolbooks of the fifteenth century. The great friar-educationists, as we have noticed, anticipated many of the perceptions of their humanist successors. They too were interested in the individual's psychology and the adaptation of teaching to his special needs and capabilities. They too wished noblemen to be learned and well-mannered as well as effective in war, and they too had a wide concept of education, in

---

[34] Orme, *English Schools*, pp. 184–90, 194–207.
[35] Thomson, *Middle English Grammatical Texts*, pp. 4–47.

which a boy's whole faculties should be developed for all eventualities of public and private life. The diffusion of copies of Giles of Rome among the aristocracy, and his imitation by later writers whose works also had a circulation, show that these views did not remain confined to theorists. They were beginning to find a readership among the nobility as well, a long time before the Renaissance.

ELYOT AND VIVES: A STUDY IN OLD AND NEW

The mixture of medieval and non-medieval elements in English Renaissance education is worth illustrating in detail, and can easily be done by taking two major writings of the sixteenth century: *The Governor* by Sir Thomas Elyot on the bringing up of noblemen, and its counterpart for ladies, *The Instruction of a Christian Woman* by Juan Luis Vives. *The Governor* was probably written in 1530 and published in 1531, still early on in the century and only nine years after the appearance of so 'medieval' a work as the English translation of Christine of Pisa's *Livre du Corps de Policie*.[36] It was nevertheless much more than a transitional work, to be soon overtaken by others more up to date. By Tudor standards it was a 'best seller', achieving eight editions between 1531 and 1580, more than any other contemporary treatise on the education of aristocratic men.[37] It was frequently quoted by other Tudor writers, was one of the volumes acquired in the 1570s by the tutors of James I, and after it had ceased to be printed was drawn on freely by Henry Peacham for his *Compleat Gentleman* of 1622 which carried its influence up to the Civil War.[38] There can be no doubt that the work in general was characteristic of English culture for most of the mid and late sixteenth century, and that its educational section, which occupies the first of its three books, reflected and moulded the ideas of many nobility and gentry during that period.

There was nothing new about a member of the lay aristocracy writing a book about education in 1531, when we remember

[36] A.W. Pollard and G.R. Redgrave, *A Short Title Catalogue of Books Printed in England*, London, 1926; 2nd edn, vol ii, London, 1976, no 7270.

[37] For the editions, see ibid., nos 7635–42.

[38] D.T. Starnes, 'Notes on Elyot's *The Governor*', *Review of English Studies*, iii (1927), pp. 37–46, and 'Elyot's "Governour" and Peacham's "Compleat Gentleman"', *Modern Language Review*, xxii (1927), pp. 319–22.

Geoffroy de la Tour-Landry and Christine of Pisa in France, or Bibbesworth, Idley and Fortescue in England. Nor was *The Governor* an entirely new kind of book. Historians of educational literature have realized for some time that it has features in common with the princely mirrors of the Middle Ages,[39] and in truth it can fairly be said to belong to their genre. As a survey of the ethics and activities proper to the male aristocracy, illustrated by stories of famous kings and noblemen chiefly from classical times, it has many counterparts among the medieval mirrors, from those of John of Salisbury and Gerald of Wales to those of Hoccleve and Lydgate. By giving a section to how the young should be taught, it follows the practice instituted by Giles of Rome and followed by many French mirror-writers of the later Middle Ages, as well as by Fortescue in England. It is true that earlier mirrors had primarily concerned themselves with kings, whereas Elyot directed his treatise at the 'governors' or aristocracy who ruled society beneath the king. But this alteration was a shift of emphasis, rather than a radical change. The aristocracy, as we have seen, had read the 'kingly' mirrors. Giles of Rome had recognized this fact by extending his remarks on several occasions to include the nobility and their children; he had seen the education of kings and noblemen as basically similar and had rarely sought to distinguish between them.[40] Elyot belonged to this tradition. He regarded princely mirrors as suitable reading for the nobility, and wished Erasmus's *Institution of a Christian Prince*, the latest example of the genre, to be familiar to gentlemen 'at all times and in every age'.[41] He also saw the 'education and virtue in manners' of the aristocracy as something 'which they have in common with princes',[42] and the historical examples in his book feature kings and noblemen indiscriminately. In short, he did not start but completed the orientation of the mirror towards the aristocracy, and did not change but preserved the unity of their education with that of kings.

There was more originality in Elyot's material than in his form. Born in about 1490, he had been educated and had educated himself

---

[39] Lehmberg, *Sir Thomas Elyot*, pp. 73–4; Charlton, *Education in Renaissance England*, p. 81.

[40] E.g. *De Regimine Principum*, book ii, part ii, chapter 18 (ed. Molenaer, pp. 223–5).

[41] *The Governor*, book i, chapter 11.

[42] ibid., chapter 3.

in the rediscovered Latin and Greek classical authors of the Renaissance. It is not always clear which ones he had studied himself and which he knew only from summaries by other educational writers of his day, for he had read Erasmus and possibly also the works of Castiglione and Patrizi.[43] He was certainly familiar at first hand with Quintilian's *Institutio Oratoria*, which had not been known in medieval England, and made more use of the works of Cicero than his predecessors had done.[44] He knew at least by name a wide range of Greek and Latin authors and their works: poets, philosophers, orators, historians, geographers and scientists. Most of these were new to England, but a few had long been familiar: Aristotle, Aulus Gellius, Vegetius and Galen (though Galen had not been used by educationists), and Elyot also drew on other 'medieval' sources including the Bible, St Augustine and Jacques de Cessoles. His chapter on archery too is close in spirit to the late fifteenth- and early sixteenth-century legislation on that subject.[45] There is therefore a minority of traditional sources in his work, and although it is not clear that he used Giles of Rome or Christine of Pisa, both of whose works were still available in England in his day, there are certainly general correspondences between his work and theirs. These reflect in part the fact that they all shared common sources, and partly, as we shall now attempt to argue that they belonged to a common educational tradition and not to separate ones.

The justifications for this argument can be found in all three major aspects of Elyot's plan for education: the personnel in charge of it, the policies they are to follow and the subjects they should teach. The personnel and their duties are still the same as those of the later Middle Ages. When the child is born, a suitable nurse is appointed to feed it, and another woman 'of approved virtue, discretion and gravity' to make sure that the child is not exposed to any improper deeds or words – an office comparable with that of the medieval 'mistress of the nursery'.[46] Like Giles repeating Aristotle,

---

[43] Lehmberg, *Sir Thomas Elyot*, pp. 74–82.
[44] Lehmberg (ibid., p. 75) suggests that Plutarch's *Moralia* essay on 'The Education of Children' was a major influence, but Elyot does not mention Plutarch by name in the educational section of *The Governor*, and the resemblances seem general rather than specific. May not Elyot have only got to know Plutarch after 1530, through his travels on the continent?
[45] *The Governor*, book i, chapter 27.
[46] ibid., chapter 4.

Elyot uses Quintilian to argue that a boy should be cared for by women until he is 7, and then be entrusted to a 'tutor', a man of 'ancient and worshipful' status.[47] The tutor is simply the knightly master of the Middle Ages, the word 'tutor' like 'governor' which Elyot also employs[48] having superseded 'master' in this sense. Like these knightly predecessors, Elyot's tutor is to have general over-sight of his pupil's upbringing: behaviour, music and physical training being specially mentioned as part of his concern.[49] Only for literary studies is the boy assigned to a separate 'master' of Latin and Greek, like the sons of kings and the royal henchmen in the fifteenth century, and just as their masters had begun to be or to be styled 'schoolmasters', so Elyot uses this title as well, even when he means a teacher of grammar in a private household.[50] Here as elsewhere Elyot reveals himself as an idealist rather than a realist, who took as his model the best arrangements in society rather than the average ones, for the employment of both tutor and schoolmaster had been characteristic of the very highest nobility, and is less often recorded lower down.

Elyot is also traditional in seeing the household as the main sphere of a boy's education, though he allows that the child may go to school as well.[51] He assumes that a Tudor boy, like a medieval one, will be given companions, and warns as earlier theorists had done against their leading him astray.[52] Like Vincent and Giles he urges the tutor to study the nature of his pupil, discover his inclinations and give him advice accordingly.[53] In their vein too he wishes the master to avoid cruelty in his discipline, and urges him rather to rule through praise and the sense of shame.[54] His plan of the boy's curriculum accords with tradition in the division of childhood into ages and the choice of pursuits for each age: nursery life and the beginnings of literary study until 7, further literary study from 7 to 14, and physical training from 14 to 21.[55] He differs here from earlier writers chiefly in stressing that the last of these ages should also be a time for

[47] ibid., chapter 6.
[48] ibid., chapter 9.
[49] ibid., chapters 6–7, 16.
[50] ibid., chapters 9, 13.
[51] ibid., chapter 13.
[52] ibid., chapter 4.
[53] ibid., chapter 6.
[54] ibid., chapter 9.
[55] ibid., chapters 5–6, 10–11, 16.

literary study at a high level,[56] for Vincent and Giles, though they had advocated such study, had not so emphatically linked it with the period of the late teens. Elyot also shares with his medieval precursors a limitation of view when it comes to defining the subjects of the curriculum. His procedure here is a logical one, beginning with literary study, proceeding to a call for higher literary standards and concluding with a survey of physical exercises, but he does not deal with everything that noble children learnt. He has nothing to say about basic religious teaching, he mentions French only in passing,[57] and although he makes occasional references to good manners he does not group them together. In consequence his account still falls short of completeness.

It is in the literary part of the curriculum that there is, at first sight, the greatest break with the past. First, Elyot wishes a child to learn not only Latin but Greek; secondly he prescribes a course of authors in each language, most of whom had not been read by the medieval nobility, and thirdly, as has been stated, he expected the study of these authors to go on through adolescence and to reach a high level.[58] From 7 (or earlier) until 14 he lays down that boys shall study grammar, simple prose and poetry. From 14 until 21 they are to master logic, rhetoric, history and geography, each from a list of Greek and Latin texts, and he also hints at the learning of music, geometry and astronomy, though he does not mention textbooks for these.[59] Finally, boys at the age of 17 are to study moral and political philosophy, including the works of Plato, Aristotle, Cicero and the Bible, particularly the 'wisdom literature' and the New Testament. His plan is truly ambitious. He wishes a child to speak Latin and Greek from its earliest years and to have, if possible, nurses and female servants who are speakers of Latin.[60] His ideal of a good schoolmaster is also extremely high, for he quotes Quintilian to the effect that such a man should be an adept in poetry, rhetoric, music, astronomy and philosophy, and considers even the university graduates of his day to be lacking in these respects. Well might he say 'how few grammarians after this description be in this realm'![61]

---

[56] ibid., chapter 11.
[57] ibid., chapter 10.
[58] ibid., chapters 5, 10–11.
[59] ibid., chapters 7–8.
[60] ibid., chapter 5.
[61] ibid., chapter 15.

His range of authors, too, is wide and includes recherché and technical works. Yet the more we consider his scheme, the more we are put in mind of the thirteenth century. Grammar, logic, rhetoric and so on – these are the subjects of the medieval university curriculum which Giles of Rome had recommended to kings and princes as the path to becoming demigods and images of God.[62] Elyot's horizon is not significantly wider or further off than that of Giles had been. He does, however, reflect the new determination among both scholars and the aristocracy to reach that horizon, which led the latter from the 1490s onwards to study Latin to a higher level, rather than turning aside early on to the reading of French or English.

As well as describing literary studies, Elyot attended to what we nowadays think of as artistic pursuits: music and painting, which he placed as a kind of prologue to the literary curriculum, and dancing which he included with physical education. As far as music is concerned, his handling of the topic is of little rather than great originality. Music, as we have seen, had long been learnt by noble children and had featured in medieval literature – not, in truth, to any great extent in Giles of Rome but in romantic fiction and in fifteenth-century educational schemes like those of Hardyng and the author of the 'Black Book'. Elyot extends the treatment of music to a chapter, but his respect for the art is a limited one.[63] Where children are concerned he regards it primarily as a recreation rather than a subject of learning, which the tutor should gloss with comparisons between musical and political harmony to give the subject value. As a pleasure for adults, it must be practised moderately and in private, lest the performer disparage his rank by imitating common musical players. The interest of Elyot in dancing was greater. This too had long been practised by young people and mentioned by fifteenth-century curricular writers, but Elyot was the first to give it expanded treatment in an educational context. His expansion was indeed a notable one, for he accords it seven of his twenty-four educational chapters, an idiosyncratic proportion.[64] In doing so he reflects the process which began in Italy and spread to

---

[62] *De Regimine Principum*, book ii, part ii, chapter 8 (ed. Molenaer, pp. 199–202), and see above, p. 150.

[63] *The Governor*, book i, chapter 7.

[64] ibid., chapters 19–25.

France and England by which dancing became reduced for the first time to rules and directions in literary form. He is conscious of the novelty of writing about dancing, and spends a chapter defending it against charges of ungodliness. In the end, however, his attitude resembles that towards music. Its educational value is not inherent but must be implanted by considering the steps as symbols of the virtues: prudence, industry, modesty, circumspection and so on. This was itself a medieval approach, which had been followed by Jacques de Cessoles with regard to chess in a book familiar to Elyot and approved of by him.[65] Most original of all, in the artistic sphere, is his chapter on painting and carving,[66] for although the thirteenth-century educationists must have read Aristotle's endorsement of these arts, they had failed to adopt it themselves. Elyot's view of painting and carving is that they partly serve as a recreation in private, for as with music he is fearful of a nobleman confusing himself with a common artisan. But he also sees them as having practical and intellectual applications. They develop a visual sense in travelling about or in reading, they assist with the understanding of maps and charts, and they help reveal the nature of fortresses and armies in war-time. All this was new, and had not been conceived of by medieval writers to a like extent.

Elyot devoted five chapters to physical activities of an outdoor kind, besides what he wrote about dancing.[67] Here too we find him mingling old and new. He follows the medieval tradition in giving the care of physical education to the knightly tutor, and in concentrating his attention as Giles had done on youths of 14 upwards, with only casual mentions of younger boys.[68] Most of the skills he discusses had been practised by the medieval aristocracy or mentioned in Vegetius and his derivatives, and Elyot's role is that of a consolidator, surveying all the Vegetian activities and adding to them hawking, hunting, wrestling, dancing and one or two games such as tennis and bowls. He resembles Giles in seeing physical training as concerned to a major degree with the creation of fighting men, and in discussing individual exercises in terms of their military application. Thus wrestling is 'profitable in wars', the examples of runners are warriors, swimming is valuable 'in extreme danger of

---

[65] ibid., chapter 26.
[66] ibid., chapter 8.
[67] ibid., chapters 16–18, 26–7.
[68] ibid., chapter 16.

wars', hunting is 'the very imitation of battle' and bows and arrows are 'the most excellent artillery for wars'. Even literary and artistic studies are partly valued by Elyot, as they had been by Christine of Pisa, because they help to make the pupil a more knowledgeable and courageous soldier.[69] On the other hand he has little to say by medieval standards about arms training, which he merely commends in one sentence,[70] and he is more conscious than his predecessors of the value of physical exercises for health and recreation. His introductory chapter on the subject quotes Galen on the importance of exercise for health,[71] and he frequently mentions recreation when dealing with individual sports. Running is 'both a good exercise and a laudable solace'; swimming cleanses the body and refreshes after other labours; hunting (as practised by the ancient Persians) promoted health and is both 'solace and pastime', while archery exercises the body and gives pleasure when it is used to kill game. Health and enjoyment must always have been among the motives of those who took exercise or organized it, but Elyot gave more recognition to these motives than previous writers on education had done.

The Governor, unlike the works of Vincent and Giles, contains no section on women, but it was not the author's intention to neglect them, for he says at one point that he means to compile another book 'only for ladies'.[72] It was more natural to plan a separate work about women in 1531 than it had been in the thirteenth century, for not only had *The Book of the Knight of the Tower* reached England in the interval but a second independent work on the subject had followed it more recently, from the pen of the Spanish scholar Juan Luis Vives. Vives wrote his *De Institutione Foeminae Christianae* in Latin at Bruges in 1523 and published it at Antwerp in the following year with a definite English orientation, including a dedication to Queen Katherine of Aragon and complimentary references to the family of Sir Thomas More.[73] More was an advocate of women's education, and in 1524 an English version of Erasmus's *Devout Treatise on the Paternoster* was published at London, made from the Latin by

[69] ibid., chapters 8, 10.
[70] ibid., chapter 17.
[71] ibid., chapter 16.
[72] ibid., book ii, chapter 7.
[73] There is an abridged English translation of the work in Watson, *Vives and Women*, pp. 29–136.

More's daughter Margaret Roper and bearing a preface in praise of the education of women by Richard Hyrde, a scholar of More's circle.[74] Later, Hyrde translated Vives's book into English as well, and this was published in about 1529 as *The Instruction of a Christian Woman*.[75] There were thus two recent precedents for works about women or by them, and Elyot's own contribution to the subject, *The Defence of Good Women* (written between 1531 and 1538, but not published until 1545) added a third example to the genre.[76] Of the works concerned, that of Vives was the most ambitious and also the most influential. Hyrde's preface to Erasmus contains only half a dozen pages, and Elyot's book, though longer, is still basically a short treatise of a literary not a scholastic nature. It takes the form of a dialogue between Caninius who attacks the education of women, Candidus who defends it, and Queen Zenobia who exemplifies the education in practice. Vives's work, on the other hand, is a treatise of medium length in three books, and provides a systematic account of all three stages of women's life: girlhood, marriage and widowhood. Moreover, whereas the works by Erasmus and Elyot were only published once, the Vives translation came out at least nine times in England between about 1529 and 1592, and must have been a major influence on the education of Tudor women, enjoying a similar pre-eminence to that of *The Governor* in the case of men.[77]

Vives believed he was handling female education in a new way. Earlier writers, he claimed, who for him were either classical like Plato and Aristotle or early Christian such as Cyprian and Augustine, 'appear rather to exhort and counsel [women] into some kind of living, than to instruct and teach them'. He by contrast proposed to avoid exhortations and to concentrate on 'rules of living'.[78] It may be doubted, however, whether there is quite so clear a distinction between the hortatory style of Vives's predecessors and his own instructive one; certainly the medieval educationists whom Vives does not mention – Vincent, Giles and the Knight of the Tower – had given instructions for women as well as mere exhortations. Vives was original in English terms in writing a

---

[74]   The preface is printed in ibid., pp. 162–73.
[75]   Wrongly dated 1540 by Watson.
[76]   Printed in Watson, *Vives and Women*, pp. 211–39.
[77]   For the editions of these works, see Pollard and Redgrave, *Short Title Catalogue of Books, 1475–1640*, nos 7658, 10477, 24856–63.
[78]   Watson, *Vives and Women*, pp. 32–3.

systematic treatise on women's education, for the Knight's book hardly comes into that category, but his format of birth and childhood, the study of letters, precepts for behaviour and advice about marriage, is in the tradition of Vincent and Giles and is chiefly new in applying to girls what had long been written for boys. Both Vives and Elyot are also new in the classical authors on whom they draw for female material: Xenophon and Plato, Plotinus and Plutarch, and the usual wide range of Greek and Latin literary works, and they have one or two opprobrious things to say about the authors hitherto popular in England. Vives attacks the romantic literature of the Middle Ages – *Ipomedon, Partenopeu de Blois* and *Guy of Warwick*[79] – while Elyot censures Aristotle for his assertion that women are imperfect by nature. Aristotle, says one of Elyot's characters, spoke 'spitefully . . . of cankered malice, whereunto he was of his own nature disposed', and was personally dissolute in his manner of living.[80] Elyot was not necessarily doing more than presenting alternative views of Aristotle at this point, but he was certainly moving away from the general endorsement of Aristotle's ideas on women by the great thirteenth-century writers.

Vives, Hyrde and Elyot are most strikingly original in their view that women (like men in *The Governor*) should be trained in literary studies to a high level. Medieval writers were not altogether blind to such a possibility, for they featured a few highly learned women in saints' lives and romances, but the women concerned were portrayed as exceptional people, and no attempt was made to encourage modern women to imitate them in this respect. Vincent and the Knight both asserted that ladies should learn to read, but this in practice meant French, and Latin only in order to follow a prayer-book. The sixteenth-century writers in comparison present famous women of learning as models for contemporary women to follow, and urge the latter to study the classical languages and literature to a far higher standard than before. They praise the learned women of antiquity, like Diotima and Aspasia whom Socrates was not ashamed to attend for instruction,[81] and point to the well-instructed ladies of the present day: Queen Katherine and her sister Joan, Mary Tudor duchess of Suffolk and the children of

[79] ibid., p. 59.
[80] ibid., pp. 223–4.
[81] ibid., pp. 231–2.

Sir Thomas More.[82] They suggest the study of authors both Latin and Greek, and Vives in a separate treatise *De Ratione Studii Puerilis* sets out a list of the works they ought to read.[83] He also proposes distinctly, for the first time, that women should learn to write.[84] He and his fellow writers, however, see the outcome of female learning as solely personal or domestic: greater virtue, a better understanding of religion, and an improved ability to teach one's own children.[85] Vives rules out any teaching by women in public schools, and although Elyot relates how Zenobia's learning helped her to govern her kingdom after her husband's death, he does not seem to argue that learned women should have a greater role in English public life.[86]

Elsewhere in these authors' discussions of women's education, moreover, it is tradition that dominates and not originality. Like medieval writers, those of the sixteenth century have a limited interest in women's skills compared with the skills of men. Hyrde's Erasmus preface has nothing to say on the subject apart from literary studies, and though Elyot touches on one or two of the practical skills of Zenobia – her love of hunting and her work in rebuilding fortresses – his primary interest is likewise confined to literary training. Vives, the most ambitious writer in scope, is the most clearly limited, for although his account of girls' education covers sixteen chapters, the only skills he recommends apart from Latin and Greek are how 'to handle wool and flax' as Vincent and Giles had done before him, together with one addition: the learning of cookery.[87] Apart from a brief reference to play for small girls, he makes no mention of physical training, says nothing of music, and gives a chapter to dancing only in order to rule it out completely. What with his attacks on ladies reading romances and attending tournaments, he enlarges the freedom of women to study only to cut it down in other spheres. Rather than extending the range of their accomplishments, Vives and Elyot prefer to concentrate, as medieval writers had done, on women's characters. In Vives, the two chapters on the rearing of girls and the three on their training are

[82]   ibid., pp. 53, 170.
[83]   ibid., pp. 62–3, 144–5, 165, 232–3.
[84]   ibid., p. 55.
[85]   ibid., pp. 55, 165, 236.
[86]   ibid., pp. 55, 236–8.
[87]   ibid., pp. 43, 46.

well outnumbered by the ten which discuss the importance of virginity, keeping oneself chaste, seclusion, modesty in dress and behaviour, the love of God and submissiveness to parents in taking a husband. Elyot too lays stress on the virtues desirable in women: justice, fortitude, temperance, moderation and circumspection, especially the latter three. His Zenobia sums up her studies as having taught her to be circumspect in her behaviour and obedient to her spouse, disagreeing with him only on matters of potential dishonour or loss, and even then merely through offering him good counsel. She seldom leaves her house, dreads infamy more than the loss of her liberty, and fears going even to suppers and banquets lest social intercourse give rise to suspicion.[88] We are still in the world of Chaucer's Virginia, in which women are praised for their virtue and reclusiveness, rather than their skills and outgoingness.

CONCLUSION

A detailed study of this kind makes clear that sixteenth-century education inherited a great deal from the Middle Ages. The inheritance was widely distributed. As Elyot and Vives demonstrate, many Tudor ideas about children and how they should be taught were medieval ones, and the literature in which they were expressed: mirrors, technical treatises, school exercises and romances, were medieval genres. The main institutions of education: the family, apprenticeship, the great household, schools, universities and the inns of court had all existed in the Middle Ages and, in some cases, had been created then. The professional Tudor schoolmaster had emerged in the twelfth century and consolidated his position during the fifteenth; the techniques of Tudor grammar bore the marks of the medieval grammarians, and the time-tabled Tudor day was the invention of Lancastrian and Yorkist organizers. The new university colleges and endowed schools of the sixteenth century followed a pattern developed in the later Middle Ages, and since so many older foundations survived the upheavals of the Reformation, it followed that Tudor youths often studied, ate and slept in the same surroundings, under similar regimes, as their medieval predecessors. The schoolboys of Elizabethan Exeter, for example, still had their lessons in a schoolhouse bequeathed to them

---

[88] ibid., pp. 233–6.

in 1344, and the line of their fee-earning masters, appointed by the local archdeacon, went back to the early thirteenth century and possibly before.[89]

There is equally no doubt that the Tudor period saw changes and innovations in education. The medieval inheritance was partly remodelled and added to, and in part discarded or destroyed. The advent of humanism into the schools in about the 1490s modified the kind of Latin that was taught there and replaced most of the texts of the Middle Ages with the authors of classical Rome. The Reformation had a major effect upon education. Negatively, it brought about the disappearance of most of the schools of the monasteries and altered the status of the chantry schools. Positively, it led to greater intervention by the Crown and the Church authorities. The religious teaching of children became, for the first time, a definite charge on the clergy, and a course of teaching (the catechism) was made an essential preliminary to confirmation. Schoolmasters began to be told what to teach and were subjected to a system of licensing. The crown became involved in refounding cathedral schools and administering those of the former chantries. In the universities, new visitations were held, the study of canon law was suppressed, and scholars were expelled for religious or political nonconformity. More endowed schools were founded than in the fifteenth century, and several of a larger size than had hitherto been seen except at Winchester and Eton. Classes became more highly organized into systems of six or seven forms, and schoolmasters became more conscious of their vocation. Treatises were written by Ascham, Brinsley, Coote and others to expound their qualifications and duties, greatly enlarging the chapters on these matters that had appeared in the Middle Ages. Outside the schools other kinds of learning acquired a more formal organization, notably the teaching of foreign languages, fencing, dancing and secular music. In the sphere of physical education, the motives of health and recreation were given more prominence, and the first treatises were written on archery, riding and swimming.

It is when making a value judgment between medieval and Renaissance education that difficulties arise. In the first place, our knowledge of how people were brought up in the past is incomplete. We do not know enough about the ideas and methods of parents in dealing with children, masters with apprentices, and even school-masters and university tutors with their pupils. There is a danger of judging the medieval centuries as a time of simplicity and stability in education, and indeed in other matters, because we are unable to see the complexities which existed and fully to measure their sophistication. It is true that absolute comparisons can be made in some respects. There is no doubt that more free schooling was to be had in the late fifteenth century than in the fourteenth, and still more in the late sixteenth. There were probably more schools of a formal kind in Tudor England than there had been before, though the figures are distorted by the better survival of records and the more frequent mentions of schools within them. But the judgment of progress which might reasonably be made from this evidence will be modified if we take into account the smaller population and resources of the earlier centuries. It will be weakened still further if we consider that school education is only part of education as a whole, that there were fewer schools in medieval England because there was less need of them, and that a less schooled society may still develop its members well in other respects. It may be that medieval people, though less highly trained in specialized ways than their successors, had the advantages which come from non-specialization: width of experience and adaptability. The judgment that education at a particular time was better by nature, or that more people than before were better educated, must always be in large measure a subjective one, for we are likely to disagree about what is necessary, valuable or significant in education.

There is nothing improper in praising the educational innovations and developments of the Tudor age. The adjective 'Renaissance' is equally proper to describe the special characteristics of that age. An impropriety only occurs when the originality of the sixteenth century is magnified at the expense of the medieval contribution to education, or so as to deny its relevance to modern times. For medieval education is the ancestor, and not the antithesis, of our own. Viewing the history of English education over the last thousand years, one major unifying process can be found in the increasing separation of education from the rest of life. This separation has grown both in people's perception of education and in how they have sought to organize it. Mentally, it has involved an increasing distinction between childhood and manhood, and the recognition of more and more activities as being educational.

Practically, it has led to the creation of more and more officers, treatises and institutions to teach them. The history of this process stretches far back into the Middle Ages, and indeed beyond. To summarize what has been said, the medieval centuries possessed or developed the schools of song, grammar and commercial subjects, the system of apprenticeship, the university and the inns of court. In the sphere of treatises it had the grammar, the formulary of administrative practices, the university textbooks and the specialized treatises on kingship, war and hunting. It also developed, by the thirteenth century, the treatise on education in general. Socially, it involved several kinds of people as controllers or managers of education: the various kinds of clergy, the aristocracy and (in the fifteenth century) municipal authorities and merchant guilds. The history of education since 1500 has been, in one sense, simply the widening of this basis. With regard to childhood, more and more literature has been devoted to children and more legislation to safeguarding their needs. More and more activities have been recognized as educational, textbooks written to teach them, specialized institutions developed to house them, and people admitted to learn them. In our share in this process, our affirmation of many of the principles of medieval education and our preservation of many of its institutions, we ourselves are linked with the Middle Ages and build on what they made.

Bibliography

Aristotle, *The Politics*, trans. Jowett, B., Oxford, 1905.
L'Art et Instruction de Bien Dancer, ed. Rastell, R., and Lequet, A.E., New York and Wakefield, 1971.
Ascham, Roger, *English Works*, ed. Wright, W.A., Cambridge, 1904.
Ashby George, *George Ashby's Poems*, ed. Bateson, Mary, EETS es, lxxvi (1899).
Asser, *Asser's Life of King Alfred*, ed. Stevenson, W.H., Oxford, 1959.
Bartholomew Glanville, *De Proprietatibus Rerum*, Cologne, c.1472, and other early editions.
Bartholomew Glanville, *On the Properties of Things. John Trevisa's Translation of Bartholomaeus Anglicus* De Proprietatibus Rerum, ed. Seymour, M.C., and others, 2 vols, Oxford, 1975.
Bartlett, R., *Gerald of Wales*, Oxford, 1982.
Bentley, S., *Excerpta Historica*, London, 1831.
Beowulf, ed. Wrenn, C.L., and Bolton, W.F., 3rd edn, London, 1973; ed. and trans. Swanton, M., Manchester and New York, 1978.
Beroul, *The Romance of Tristran*, ed. Ewert, A., 2 vols, Oxford, 1939–70.
Beroul, *The Romance of Tristan*, trans. Fedrick, A.S., Harmondsworth, 1970.
Bibbesworth, Walter of, *Le Traité de Walter de Bibbesworth sur la langue française*, ed. Owen, Annie, Paris, 1929.
Boethius, Pseudo-, *De Disciplina Scolarium*, ed. Weijers, O., London and Köln, 1976.

Bokenham, Osbern, *Legendys of Hooly Wummen*, ed. Serjeantson, Mary S., EETS, os. ccvi (1938).
A Booke of Precedence, ed. Furnivall, F.J., EETS, es, viii (1869).
Boyle, L.E., 'William of Pagula and the *Speculum Regis Edwardi III*', *Mediaeval Studies*, xxxii (1970), pp. 329–36.
Broekhoff, J., 'Chivalric education in the Middle Ages', *A History of Sport and Physical Education to 1900 (Selected Topics)*, ed. Zeigler, E.F., Champagne, Ill., 1973, pp. 225–33.
Bruce, Mary Louise, *The Making of Henry VIII*, London, 1977.
Calendar of Close Rolls, 1272–1509, 47 vols, London, 1892–1963.
Calendar of Inquisitions Post Mortem, 1216–, 16 vols, in progress, London, 1904–74.
Calendar of Patent Rolls, 1216–1509, 57 vols, London, 1891–1916.
Cary, G., *The Medieval Alexander*, ed. Ross, D.J.A., Cambridge, 1956.
'Cato, Dionysius', *Parvus Cato, Magnus Cato translated by Benet Burgh*, London, *c.*1481; ed. Jenkinson, F., Cambridge, 1906.
Caxton, William, *Caxton's Book of Curtesye in Three Versions*, ed. Furnivall, F.J., EETS, os, iii (1868).
Caxton, William, *The Prologues and Epilogues of William Caxton*, ed. Crotch, W.J.B., EETS, es, clxxvi (1928).
Cessoles, Jacques de, *The Game of Chess*, trans. Caxton, W., Bruges, *c.*1475; London, *c.*1483; facsimile ed. Blake, N., London, 1976.
Charlton, K., *Education in Renaissance England*, London, 1965.
Chaucer, Geoffrey, *The Works of Geoffrey Chaucer*, ed. Robinson, F.N., 2nd edn, London, 1957.
Child-Marriages and Divorces . . . Chester Depositions, 1561–6, ed. Furnivall, F.J., EETS, os, cviii (1897).
Chrimes, S.B., *Henry VII*, London, 1972.
Christine of Pisa, *The Book of Fayttes of Armes and of Chyualrye*, trans. Caxton, W., ed. Byles, A.T.P., EETS, os, clxxxix (1932).
Christine of Pisa, *The Middle English Translation of Christine de Pisan's 'Livre du Corps de Policie'*, ed. Bornstein, Diane, Heidelberg, 1977.
Clanchy, M.T., *From Memory to Written Record: England, 1066–1307*, London, 1979.
Clemence of Barking, *The Life of St Catherine*, ed. MacBain, W., Oxford, Anglo-Norman Text Soc., xviii (1964).
Close Rolls, 1227–1272, 15 vols, London, 1902–75.
Cockayne, G.E., *The Complete Peerage*, ed. Gibbs, V., and others, 13 vols in 14, London, 1910–59.
A Collection of Ordinances and Regulations for the Government of the Royal Household, London, Soc. of Antiquaries, 1790.
D'Abernon, Peter, *Le Secré de Secrez by Pierre d'Abernun of Fetcham*, ed. Beckerlegge, O.A., Oxford, Anglo-Norman Text Soc., v (1944).

Daniel of Beccles, *Urbanus Magnus Danielis Becclesiensis*, ed. Smyly, J.G., Dublin, 1939.

David, C.W., *Robert Curthose, Duke of Normandy*, Cambridge, Mass., 1920.

Devon, F., *Issues of the Exchequer*, London, 1837.

Dictionary of National Biography, ed. Stephen, L., and Lee, S., 22 vols, London, 1885–1901.

Dillon, Viscount, and Hope, W.H. St J., 'Inventory of Goods and Chattels belonging to Thomas duke of Gloucester', *Archaeological Journal*, liv (1897), pp. 275–308.

Dugdale, Sir W., *Monasticon Anglicanum*, ed. Caley, J., and others, 6 vols in 8, London, 1817–30.

Early English Meals and Manners, ed. Furnivall, F.J., EETS, os, xxxii (1868; revised edn, 1894).

Ellis, Sir H., *Original Letters Illustrative of English History*, 3 vols, London, 1824: 2nd series, 4 vols, London, 1827; 3rd series, 4 vols, London, 1846.

Elyot, Sir T., *The Boke named the Gouernour*, London, 1531.

Emden, A.B., *A Biographical Register of the University of Cambridge to 1500*, Cambridge, 1963.

Emden, A.B., *A Biographical Register of the University of Oxford to AD 1500*, 3 vols, Oxford, 1957–9.

Emden, A.B., *A Biographical Register of the University of Oxford AD 1501 to 1540*, Oxford, 1974.

Epistolae Academicae Oxon, ed. Anstey, H., 2 vols, Oxford, Oxford Historical Soc., xxxv–xxxvi (1898).

Erasmus, *The Education of a Christian Prince*, ed. Born, L.K., New York, 1936.

Der deutsche Facetus, ed. Schroeder, C., Berlin, 1911.

Le Facet en Françoys, ed. Morawski, J., Poznan, 1923.

A Fifteenth-Century Courtesy Book, ed. Chambers, R.W., EETS, os, cxlviii (1914).

A Fifteenth Century School Book, ed. Nelson, W., Oxford, 1956.

Fisher, John, *The English Works of John Fisher*, ed. Mayor, J.E.B., part i, EETS, es, xxvii (1876).

Fitzherbert, John, *The Boke of Husbandrye*, London, c.1523.

FitzNigel, Richard, *The Course of the Exchequer*, ed. Johnson, C., London, 1950.

Fortescue, Sir J., *De Laudibus Legum Anglie*, ed. Chrimes, S.B., Cambridge, 1942.

Fourteenth Century Verse and Prose, ed. Sisam, K., Cambridge, 1921, reprinted 1955.

Fox, J., *A Literary History of France: The Middle Ages*, London and New York, 1974.

Froissart, Jean, *Chroniques*, ed. de Lettenhove, Kervyn, 25 vols, Brussels, 1867–77.

Froissart, Jean, *Chronicles*, trans. Brereton, G., Harmondsworth, 1968.

Gabriel, A.L., *The Educational Ideas of Vincent of Beauvais*, 2nd edn, Notre Dame, Indiana, 1962.

Galbraith, V.H., 'The literacy of the medieval English kings', *Proceedings of the British Academy*, xxi (1935), pp. 201–38.

Gardiner, Dorothy, *English Girlhood at School*, London, 1929.

Garton, C., 'Bishop Grosseteste and table manners', *Lincolnshire Life*, May 1981, pp. 38–40.

Gaston de Foix, *The Master of Game*, trans. Edward duke of York, ed. Grohman, W.A. and F. Baillie-, London, 1909.

Genet, J.-Ph., *Four English Political Tracts of the Later Middle Ages*, London, Royal Historical Soc., Camden 4th series, xviii (1977).

Geoffrey of Monmouth, *The Historia Regum Britanniae*, ed. Griscom, A., London and New York, 1929.

Gerald of Wales, *The Autobiography of Giraldus Cambrensis*, trans. Butler, H.E., London, 1937.

Gerald of Wales, *Opera*, ed. Brewer, J.S., and others, 8 vols, London, RS, 1861–91.

Gesta Abbatum Monasterii Sancti Albani, ed. Riley, H.T., 3 vols, London, RS, 1867–9.

Gieben, S., 'Robert Grosseteste and medieval courtesy-books', *Vivarium*, v (1967), pp. 47–74.

Giles of Rome, *De Regimine Principum*, Augsburg, 1473, and other early editions.

Giles of Rome, *Li Livres du Gouvernement des Rois*, trans. Gauchy, Henri de, ed. Molenaer, S.P., New York and London, 1899.

Glixelli, S., 'Les Contenances de table', *Romania*, xlvii (1921), pp. 1–40.

The Good Wife Taught her Daughter [and two similar poems], ed. Mustanoja, T.-F., Helsinki, Annales Academiae Scientiarum Fennicae, series B, vol lxi part ii (1948).

Gottfried von Strassburg, *Tristan, with the surviving fragments of the Tristran of Thomas*, trans. Hatto, A.T., revised ed., Harmondsworth, 1967.

Gower, John, *The Complete Works of John Gower*, ed. Macaulay, G.C., 4 vols, Oxford, 1899–1902.

Green, Mary A.E., *Lives of the Princesses of England from the Norman Conquest*, 6 vols, London, 1849–55, reprinted 1957.

Green, R.F., *Poets and Princepleasers: Literature and the English Court in the late Middle Ages*, Toronto, 1980.

Grente, G., *Dictionnaire des Lettres françaises*: vol i, *Le Moyen Age*, ed. Bossuat, R., and others, Paris, 1964.

Gui de Warewic, ed. Ewert, A., 2 vols, Paris, 1932–3.

The Romance of Guy of Warwick, ed. Zupitza, J., 5 vols, EETS, es, xxv, xxvi, xlii, xlix, lix (1875–91).

Hall, Edward, *Hall's Chronicle containing the History of England*, [ed. Ellis, H.,] London, 1809.

Hands, Rachel, *English Hawking and Hunting in* 'The Boke of St Albans', London, 1975.

Hanham, Alison, 'The musical studies of a fifteenth-century wool merchant', *Review of English Studies*, new series, vii (1956), pp. 270–4.

Hardyng, John, *The Chronicle of John Hardyng*, ed. Ellis, H., London, 1812.

Harrison, F.Ll., *Music in Medieval Britain*, 2nd edn, London, 1963.

Henry the Sixth: a Reprint of John Blacman's Memoir, ed. James, M.R., Cambridge, 1919.

L'Histoire de Guillaume le Maréchal, ed. Meyer, P., 3 vols, Paris, Société de l'Histoire de France, 1891–1901.

Hoccleve, Thomas, *Hoccleve's Works*, ed. Furnivall, F.J., and Gollancz, I., 3 vols, EETS, es, lxi, lxxii, lxxiii (1892–7).

Holdsworth, Sir W., *A History of English Law*, 3rd edn, 16 vols + index, London, 1922–66.

[Hooker, John.] *The Life and Times of Sir Peter Carew, Knight*, ed. Maclean, J., London, 1857.

Horman, William, *Vulgaria*, London, 1519.

The Romance of Horn, ed. Pope, Mildred K., 2 vols, Oxford, Anglo-Norman Text Soc., ix–x (1955–64).

King Horn, a Middle English Romance, ed. Hall, J., Oxford, 1901.

How the Wyse Man Taught Hys Sone, In drei Texten herausgegeben, ed. Fischer, R., Erlangen, Erlanger Beiträge zur Englischen Philologie, ii (1884).

Hue de Rotelande, *Hue de Rotelande's Ipomedon*, ed. Kölbing, E., and Koschwitz, E., Breslau, 1889.

Hue de Rotelande, *Ipomedon in drei englischen Bearbeitungen*, ed. Kölbing, E., Breslau, 1889.

Hugh of St Victor, *The Didascalicon*, trans. Taylor, J., New York and London, 1961.

Idley, Peter, *Peter Idley's Instructions to his Son*, ed. D'Evelyn, Charlotte, Boston and London, Modern Language Assoc. of America, Monograph Series, vi (1935).

Ives, E.W., 'The common lawyers', *Profession, Vocation and Culture in Later Medieval England*, ed. Clough, C.H., Liverpool, 1982, pp. 181–217.

Ives, E.W., 'The common lawyers in pre-Reformation England', *TRHS*, 5th series, xviii (1968), pp. 145–73.

John of Garland, *Morale Scolarium of John of Garland*, ed. Paetow, L.J., Berkeley, Calif., Memoirs of the Univ. of California, iv no ii (1927).

John of Gaunt's Register [1372–6], ed. Smith, S. Armitage-, 2 vols, London, Royal Historical Soc., Camden 3rd series, xx–xxi (1911).

John of Gaunt's Register, 1379–1383, ed. Lodge, Eleanor C., and Somerville, R., 2 vols, London, Royal Historical Soc., Camden 3rd series, lvi–lvii (1937).

John of Salisbury, *Ioannis Saresberiensis Episcopi Carnotensis Policraticus*, ed. Webb, C.C.J., 2 vols, Oxford, 1909.

Johnstone, Hilda, *Edward of Caernarvon, 1284–1307*, Manchester, 1946.

Johnstone, Hilda, 'The wardrobe and household of Henry, son of Edward I', *BJRL*, vii (1922–3), pp. 384–420.

Jones, J.W., 'Observations on the origin of the division of man's life into stages', *Archaeologia*, xxxv (1853), pp. 167–89.

Ker, N.R., *Medieval Manuscripts in British Libraries*, Oxford, 1969–, in progress.

Kingsford, C.L., 'The first version of Hardyng's Chronicle', *EHR*, xxvii (1912), pp. 462–82, 740–53.

Kingsford, C.L., *Henry V*, 2nd edn, London, 1923.

Kirby, J.L., *Henry IV of England*, London, 1970.

Kirby, T.F., *Annals of Winchester College*, London and Winchester, 1892.

Knowles, D., *The Monastic Order in England, 940–1216*, 2nd edn, Cambridge, 1963.

Knowles, D., *The Religious Orders in England*, 3 vols, Cambridge, 1948–59.

Landry, Geoffroy de la Tour-, *The Book of the Knight of the Tower*, trans. Caxton, W., ed. Offord, M.Y., EETS, ss, ii (1971).

Langland, William, *The Vision of William concerning Piers Plowman*, ed. Skeat, W.W., 2 vols, Oxford, 1886.

Lefevre, Y., 'De l'usage du français en Grande-Bretagne à la fin du XIIe siècle', *Etudes de Langue et de Littérature du Moyen Age offertes à Félix Lecoy*, Paris, 1973, pp. 301–5.

Legge, M. Dominica, *Anglo-Norman Literature and its Background*, Oxford, 1963.

Legge, M. Dominica, 'The Lord Edward's Vegetius', *Scriptorium*, vii (1953), pp. 262–5.

Lehmberg, S.E., *Sir Thomas Elyot, Tudor Humanist*, Austin, Texas, 1960.

Leland, John, *J. Lelandi antiquari de rebus Britannicis Collectanea*, ed. Hearne, T., 6 vols, 2nd edn, London, 1770.

Letters and Papers, Foreign and Domestic, Henry VIII, ed. Brewer, J.S., and others, 21 vols + addenda, London, 1864–1932.

Liber Regie Capelle, ed. Ullmann, W., Cambridge, Henry Bradshaw Soc., xcii (1961).

Lorris, Guillaume de, and Meun, Jean de, *Le Roman de la Rose*, ed. Lecoy, F., 3 vols, Paris, 1965–70.

Lorris, Guillaume de, and Meun, Jean de, *The Romance of the Rose*, trans. Dahlberg, C., Princeton, NJ, 1971.

Lull, Ramon, *The Book of the Ordre of Chyualry*, trans. Caxton, W., ed. Byles, A.T.P., EETS, os, clxviii (1926).

Lydgate, John, *Falls of Princes*, ed. Bergen, H., 4 vols, EETS, es, cxxi–cxxiv (1924–7).

Lydgate, John, and Burgh, Benedict, *Lydgate and Burgh's Secrees of Old Philosoffres*, ed. Steele, R., EETS, es, lxvi (1894).

McFarlane, K.B., *The Nobility of Later Medieval England*, Oxford, 1973.

Malory, Sir T., *The Works of Sir Thomas Malory*, ed. Vinaver, E., 2nd edn, 3 vols, Oxford, 1967.

Mancini, Domenico, *The Usurpation of Richard III*, ed. Armstrong, C.A.J., 2nd edn, Oxford, 1969.

The Manner of Dancing Base Dances, London, 1522.

Manners and Household Expenses of England, [ed. Turner, T.H.,] London, Roxburghe Club, 1841.

Manuale ad Vsum . . . Sarisburiensis, ed. Collins, A. Jefferies, Cambridge, Henry Bradshaw Soc., xci (1960).

Map, Walter, *De Nugis Curialium*, trans. James, M.R., London, Cymmrodorion Record Series, ix (1923).

Materials for a History of the Reign of Henry VII, ed. Campbell, W., 2 vols, London, RS, 1873–7.

Materials for the History of Thomas Becket, ed. Robertson, J.C., 7 vols, London, RS, 1875–85.

Meyer, P., 'Les Manuscrits français de Cambridge: III', *Romania*, xxxii (1903), pp. 18–120.

Michel, A., 'The earliest dance manuals', *Medievalia et Humanistica* (1946), pp. 117–31.

Middle English Dictionary, ed. Kurath, H., and Kuhn, S.M., Ann Arbor, Mich. and London, 1954–, in progress.

Murray, H.J.R., *A History of Chess*, Oxford, 1913.

Myers, A.R., *The Household of Edward IV*, Manchester, 1959.

Nichols, J.G., *Literary Remains of King Edward the Sixth*, 2 vols, London, Roxburghe Club, 1857.

Niles, P., 'Baptism and the naming of children in late medieval England', *Medieval Prosopography*, iii (1982), pp. 95–107.

Orderic Vitalis, *The Ecclesiastical History of Orderic Vitalis*, ed. Chibnall, Marjorie, 6 vols, Oxford, 1969–80.

Orme, Nicholas, 'Chaucer and education', *The Chaucer Review*, xvi (1981), pp. 38–59.

Orme, Nicholas, *Early British Swimming, 55BC–AD1719, with the first swimming treatise in English, 1595*, Exeter, 1983.

Orme, Nicholas, 'An early-Tudor Oxford schoolbook', *Renaissance Quarterly*, xxxiv (1981), pp. 11–39.

Orme, Nicholas, 'The education of the courtier', *English Court Culture in the Later Middle Ages*, ed. Scattergood, V.J., and Sherborne, J.W., London, 1983, pp. 63–85.

Orme, Nicholas, 'The education of Edward V', *BIHR*, lvii (1984).

Orme, Nicholas, *Education in the West of England, 1066–1548*, Exeter, 1976.

Orme, Nicholas, 'English schoolmasters, 1100–1500', *Medieval Prosopography*, ed. Bulst, N., and Genet, J.-Ph., Kalamazoo, Mich., 1984, forthcoming.

Orme, Nicholas, *English Schools in the Middle Ages*, London, 1973.

Orme, Nicholas, 'A grammatical miscellany of 1427–65 from Bristol and Wiltshire', *Traditio*, xxxviii (1982), pp. 301–26.

Orme, Nicholas, 'Langland and education', *History of Education*, xi (1982), pp. 251–66.

Orme, Nicholas, 'Schoolmasters, 1307–1509', *Profession, Vocation and Culture in Later Medieval England*, ed. Clough, C.H., Liverpool, 1982, pp. 218–41.

Owst, G.R., *Literature and Pulpit in Medieval England*, 2nd edn, Oxford, 1961.

Oxford English Dictionary, ed. Murray, J.A.H., and others, 12 vols + supplement, Oxford, 1933.

Painter, S., *William Marshal*, Baltimore, Maryld., 1933.

Paris, Matthew, *Chronica Majora*, ed. Luard, H.R., 7 vols, London, RS, 1872–84.

The Parlement of the Thre Ages, ed. Offord, M.Y., London, EETS, os, ccxlvi (1959).

Parsons, H. Rosamond, 'Anglo-Norman books of courtesy and nurture', *Proceedings of the Modern Language Assoc. of America*, xliv (1929), pp. 383–455.

Partonopeu de Blois, ed. Gildea, J., 2 vols, Villanova, Pa., 1967–8.

Paston Letters and Papers of the Fifteenth Century, ed. Davis, N., 2 vols, Oxford, 1971–6.

Patrologia Cursus Completus: Series Latina, ed. Migne, J.P., 221 vols, Paris, 1844–64.

Peter Alfonsi, *Petri Alfonsi Disciplina Clericalis*, ed. Hilka, A. and Söderhjelm, W., 3 vols, Helsingfors, 1911–22.

Peter Alfonsi, *The Disciplina Clericalis of Petrus Alfonsi*, trans, Hermes, E., Söderhjelm, W., 3 vols, Helsingfors, 1911–22.

Plumpton Correspondence, ed. Stapleton, T., London, Camden Soc., iv (1839).

Pollock, Sir F., and Maitland, F.W., *The History of English Law before the time of Edward I*, 2nd edn, 2 vols, Cambridge, 1898.

Power, Eileen, *Medieval English Nunneries, c.1275 to 1535*, Cambridge, 1922.

Powicke, F.M., and Fryde, E.B., *Handbook of British Chronology*, 2nd edn, London, 1961.

Privy Purse Expenses of Elizabeth of York, ed. Nicolas, N.H., London, 1830.

Proceedings and Ordinances of the Privy Council of England, ed. Nicolas, N.H., 7 vols, London, Record Commission, 1834–7.

The Regulations and Establishment of the Household of Henry Algernon Percy, [ed. Percy, T.,] London, 1770.

A Relation . . . of the Island of England. . . , 1500, ed. Sneyd, Charlotte A., London, Camden Soc., xxxvii (1847).

Renaut, *Le Roman de Galerent, Comte de Bretagne*, ed. Boucherie, A., Montpellier, 1888.

Richardson, H.G., 'Letters of the Oxford Dictatores', *Formularies which Bear on the History of Oxford*, vol ii, ed. Salter, H.E., and others, Oxford, Oxford Historical Soc., new series, v (1942), pp. 329–450.

Rosenthal, J.T., 'Aristocratic Cultural Patronage and Book Bequests, 1350–1500', *BJRL*, lxiv (1981–2), pp. 522–48.

Rosenthal, J.T., 'Aristocratic cultural patronage and book bequests, *History of Education Quarterly*, ix (1969), pp. 415–37.

Ross, C.D., *Edward IV*, London, 1974.

Ross, C.D., *Richard III*, London, 1981.

Rothwell, W., 'The role of French in thirteenth-century England', *BJRL*, lviii (1975–6), pp. 445–66.

Rothwell, W., 'The teaching of French in medieval England', *Modern Language Review*, lxiii (1968), pp. 37–46.

Rotuli Parliamentorum, ed. Strachey, J., 6 vols, London, 1767–77; index vol, London, 1832.

Rowland, Beryl, 'Classical and medieval ideas on the "Ages of Man"', *Poetica*, iii (1975), pp. 17–29.

Royal Commission on Historical Manuscripts, Reports, London, 1874–, in progress.

Ruhräh, J., *Pediatrics of the Past*, New York, 1925.

Rymer, T., *Foedera, Conventiones, Litterae*, 2nd edn, 20 vols, London, 1704–32.

Salter, F.M., 'Skelton's *Speculum Principis*', *Speculum*, ix (1934), pp. 25–37.

Sammut, A., *Unfredo duca di Gloucester e gli umanisti italiani*, Padua, Medioevo e umanesimo, xli (1981).

Scarisbrick, J.J., *Henry VIII*, London, 1968.

Secretum Secretorum: Nine English Versions, ed. Manzaloui, M.A., vol i, EETS, os, cclxxvi (1977).

Simon, Joan, *Education and Society in Tudor England*, Cambridge, 1967.

Simpson, A.W.B., 'The early constitution of the inns of court', *Cambridge Law Journal*, xxviii part ii (1970), pp. 241–56.

Sir Gawain and the Green Knight, ed. Tolkien, J.R.R., Gordon, E.V., and Davis, N., 2nd edn, Oxford, 1967.

Sir Tristrem, ed. McNeill, G.P., Edinburgh and London, Scottish Text Soc., viii (1886).

Smalley, Beryl, *English Friars and Antiquity in the Early Fourteenth Century*, Oxford, 1960.

De Speculo Regis Edwardi III, ed. Moisant, J., Paris, 1891.

Statutes of the Colleges of Oxford, 3 vols, London and Oxford, 1853.

The Statutes of the Realm, from Magna Carta to the end of the reign of Queen Anne, 10 vols, London, Record Commission, 1810–24.

Stevens, J., *Music at the Court of Henry VIII*, London, *Musica Britannica*, xviii (1962).

The Tain, trans. Kinsella, T., London, 1970.

Testamenta Eboracensia, ed. Raine, J. and J., and Clay, J.W., 6 vols, London and Durham, Surtees Soc., iv, xxx, xlv, liii, lxxv, cvi (1836–1902).

Testamenta Vetusta, ed. Nicolas, N.H., 2 vols, London, 1826.

Thomas, *Le Roman de Tristan par Thomas*, ed. Bédier, J., 2 vols, Paris, Société des anciens Textes français, 1902–5.

Thompson, J.W., *The Literacy of the Laity in the Middle Ages*, Berkeley, Calif., University of California Publications in Education, ix (1939).

Thomson, D., *A Descriptive Catalogue of Middle English Grammatical Texts*, New York and London, 1979.

Thorpe, L., 'Mastre Richard, a thirteenth-century translator of the "De Re Militari" of Vegetius', *Scriptorium*, vi (1952), pp. 39–50.

Tobin, Rosemary B., 'Vincent of Beauvais on the education of women', *Journal of the History of Ideas*, xxxv (1974), pp. 485–9.

Tout, T.F., *Chapters in the Administrative History of Mediaeval England*, 6 vols, Manchester and London, 1920–33.

Trefusis, Mary, *Songs, Ballads and Instrumental Pieces composed by King Henry the Eighth*, London, Roxburghe Club, 1912.

Le Roman de Tristan en Prose, ed. Curtis, R.L., 2 vols, Munich, 1963; Leiden, 1976.

Turner, R.V., 'The *Miles Literatus* in twelfth- and thirteenth-century England: how rare a phenomenon', *American Historical Review*, lxxxiii (1978), pp. 928–45.

Twiti, William, *The Art of Hunting*, ed. Danielsson, B., Stockholm Studies in English, xxxvii (1977).

Twiti, William, *La Vénerie de Twiti* [French and English versions], ed. Tilander, G., *Cynegetica*, vol ii, Uppsala, 1956.

Vegetius Renatus, Flavius, *Epitoma Rei Militaris*, ed. Lang, C., 2nd edn, Leipzig, 1885.

Vegetius Renatus, Flavius, *L'Art de Chevalerie*, trans. Meun, Jean de, ed. Robert, U., Paris, Société des anciens Textes français, 1897.

Vegetius Renatus, Flavius, *Knyghthode and Bataile*, ed. Dyboski, R., and Arend, Z.M., EETS, os, cci (1935).

The Victoria History of the Counties of England, ed. Page, W., and others, London, 1900–, in progress.

Vincent of Beauvais, *De Eruditione Filiorum Nobilium*, ed. Steiner, A., Cambridge, Mass., Medieval Academy of America, Publications, xxxii (1938).

Vincent of Beauvais, *Speculum Majus*, 4 vols, Venice, 1591; Douai, 1624.

The Vulgate Version of the Arthurian Romances, ed. Sommer, H.O., 8 vols, Washington, DC, 1909–16.

Walker, Sue S., 'Proof of age of feudal heirs in medieval England', *Mediaeval Studies*, xxxv (1973), pp. 306–23.

Walter of Henley, *Walter of Henley and other Treatises on Estate Management and Accounting*, ed. Oschinsky, Dorothea, Oxford, 1971.

Walter de Milemete, *The Treatise of Walter de Milemete De Nobilitatibus, Sapientiis et Prudentiis Regnum*, ed. James, M.R., Roxburghe Club, 1913.

Warner, G.F., and Gilson, J.P., *British Museum; Catalogue of Western MSS in the Old Royal and King's Collections*, 4 vols, London, 1921.

Warren, W.L., *Henry II*, London, 1973.

Warren, W.L., *King John*, revised edn, London, 1964.

Watson, F., *Vives and the Renascence Education of Women*, London, 1912.

West, C.B., *Courtoisie in Anglo-Norman Literature*, Oxford, 1938.

William of Malmesbury, *Gesta Regum Anglorum*, ed. Stubbs, W., 2 vols, London, RS, 1887–9.

Wisman, J.-A., 'L'Epitoma rei militaris de Végèce et sa fortune au Moyen Age', *Le Moyen Age*, lxxxv (1979), pp. 12–31.

Wolffe, B.P., *Henry VI*, London, 1981.

[Worcester, William.] *The Boke of Noblesse*, ed. Nichols, J.G., London, Roxburghe Club, 1860.

Wormald, C.P., 'The uses of literacy in Anglo-Saxon England and its neighbours', *TRHS*, 5th series, xxvii (1977), pp. 95–114.

Wydeville, Anthony, *The Dictes or Sayengis of the Philosophhres*, Westminster, 1477.

Wylie, J.H., *History of England under Henry the Fourth*, 4 vols, London, 1884–98.

Index